D0992359

Edna Young Johnson
798 Talbot St.

LIONS IN THE WAY

LIONS IN THE WAY

A Discursive History of the Oslers

By ANNE WILKINSON

> "There are often 'Lions in the Way' when I write a note—but neither lions nor dim sight hinder loving thoughts towards those who are absent. . . ."
>
> *Ellen Osler to her son William*
> *December 8, 1899*

1956
The Macmillan Company of Canada Limited
TORONTO

Copyright, Canada, 1956
BY ANNE WILKINSON

All rights reserved—no part of this book
may be reproduced in any form without
permission in writing from the publisher,
except by a reviewer who wishes to quote
brief passages in connection with a review
written for inclusion in a magazine
or newspaper.

PRINTED IN ENGLAND BY
HAZELL WATSON AND VINEY LTD
AYLESBURY AND LONDON

Foreword

THIS book calls for and should include an intelligent survey, sociological and historical, of Upper Canada during the nineteenth century. The fact that nothing of the sort will be found is due to deficiencies in the editor's education.

The form, if the book can be said to have one, is documentary and dictated by the available material. Wherever possible the characters speak for themselves, and more vividly than I can speak for them. The reader may regret that there is so much about one and so little about another equally interesting personality but the source material, though abundant, may be meagre regarding a particular person or period.

The journals and a good proportion of the letters included here were collected by William Osler and later given to Trinity College, Toronto. I wish to give special thanks to the late Mrs. Edmund Boyd, Mrs. W. L. Matthews, Mrs. Britton Osler, Mr. Kenneth Andras and Dr. William Francis, librarian of the Osler Library at McGill University—members of the family who have unearthed and generously lent quantities of letters, newspaper clippings, etc. I am indebted also to Harvey Cushing's *The Life of Sir William Osler*, Hector Charlesworth's *Candid Chronicles* and many articles, medical and otherwise, on William Osler.

A. W.

TO

J., HEATHER, AND ALAN

AND TO

THE MEMORY OF MY MOTHER

MARY OSLER BOYD

Contents

Illustrations

LIONS IN THE WAY

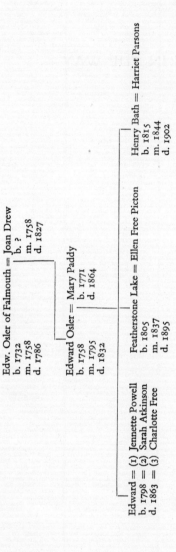

Edw. Osler of Falmouth = Joan Drew
b. 1732   b. ?
m. 1758   m. 1758
d. 1786   d. 1827

Edward Osler = Mary Paddy
b. 1758   b. 1771
m. 1795   d. 1864
d. 1832

Featherstone Lake = Ellen Free Picton
b. 1805
m. 1837
d. 1895

Henry Bath = Harriet Parsons
b. 1815
m. 1844
d. 1902

Edward = (1) Jennette Powell
b. 1798 = (2) Sarah Atkinson
d. 1863 = (3) Charlotte Free

Other children of Edward and Mary Paddy

Samuel   Samuel and Richard came between Edward and
Mary   Featherstone, but the order of the
Elizabeth   others is not known.
Richard
Emma
Henrietta

CHAPTER ONE

Cornish Beginnings

CORNWALL is a windy place and nowhere far from the sea. It includes England's most southerly as well as its most westerly point yet there is nothing soft in its landscape or its people. For the most part the soil of this rough peninsula is poor and successive generations have dragged a living from under the ground and under the sea, harvesting tin and copper and fish. Here smuggling was once a profitable concern, the long coast-line with its innumerable bays and coves being admirably suited to secret landings and departures. Though not a romantic race, Cornishmen are quick to recognize a ghost when they see one and share with the Scots, Irish and Welsh a Celtic origin. True, the rest of England has its spectres but they are upper-class spirits who glide through the halls of country houses attired in Tudor dress. In Cornwall ghosts may walk in the guise of animals or even of ungentlemanly men.

Falmouth looks out over its own fine harbour and the English Channel beyond. It was here that Edward Osler, a native of this town, married Joan Drew in 1758. Joan was an aunt or sister of Samuel Drew* whose writings earned him the title 'Cornish Metaphysician'. Of Edward's means of livelihood there is no record but his grandson Featherstone wrote without further comment, 'He died of wounds in the West Indies'.

* See Appendix I.

He may have been in the merchant service, or a pirate. Nobody knows. His wife lived to a great age and is mentioned with affection in the letters of her descendants.

To Falmouth men the sea was the source of life and often the cause of their death. The Osler record is typical of both time and place. A son of the Edward who 'died of wounds in the West Indies' was killed in action against a French privateer, another drowned, less dramatically, in Swan Pool near Falmouth. A third son, Edward (2), prudently kept his person on shore and sent only his money to sea, investing in ships and their cargoes. His son, Featherstone Lake, described him as a Falmouth merchant and shipowner but when Edward married Mary Paddy in 1795 they started life humbly enough in quarters above their shop.

The nineteenth century opened with a surge of energy generated by steam and in every English village a young man stirred to the possibility of not following in his father's footsteps. Falmouth, port of the Foreign Packet (mail), home of sailors and smugglers, was no exception. Edward (2) and Mary Osler prospered and their tribe increased until they had five sons and four daughters. The eldest, Edward (3), as potent a personality as the family produced, left the sea and the shop of his forefathers to study medicine. He was educated by a dissenting minister and after an apprenticeship with a local surgeon completed his training at Guy's Hospital, London, an expense his parents could ill afford. His letters* (1816–18) reveal the still brutal hospitals, something of Regency London, and the young man himself. After graduating he practised surgery in Swansea, Wales, where he met his future wife,

* See Appendix II.

Jennette Powell, of whom he wrote, 'It is no exaggeration to say that she is adorned with every quality that can make her Respectable in Youth, Dignified in Age and Happy in Eternity.'

At first all went well. Edward married Jennette and earned a small but growing reputation in his specialty, the surgery of the eye, but after five or six happy domestic years and success-ful professional ones Jennette died and Edward fled from Swansea to join the navy as a medical officer. While cruising in the West Indies he wrote an epic poem, 'The Voyage'; its dedication reads 'To my loved and lost Jennette'. This, as well as 'Notes on the Natural History of the Islands', were published under one cover in 1830.

Edward tired of the navy and returned to Falmouth where he lived for a time with his parents, his only occupation being prescribing treatment for his father's several ailments. When he at last left Cornwall for London, the pen, not the knife, was the tool with which he rehabilitated himself. He wrote the biography of a Cornish admiral, *Life of Lord Exmouth*, contributed two papers on marine biology to the *Philosophical Transactions*, and on the strength of these was elected to the Linnean Society. His religious works include *Church and King*, *Church and Dissent*, and several hymns, one of which, 'O God unseen but ever near', is still included in most hymn books. He married a second and then a third time but never forgot Jennette for whom he named his first daughter by his second wife. From 1841 until his death in 1863 he lived in Truro, and edited the *Royal Cornwall Gazette*. His nephew, Sir William Osler, when Regius Professor at Oxford, accepted an invitation to unveil a memorial to Edward in the Swansea

General Hospital, a pleasant duty for the man whose successive interests, church, biology and medicine, had been aroused by reading his uncle's books in a Canadian parsonage.

Of two younger brothers, Samuel and Richard, there is little to say except that they appear to have been in chronic disgrace for one misdeed or another. Edward (3) referred to Samuel when he wrote, 'keep him away from girls . . . he [is] always such a tindery chap there is no trusting him . . . When children of eighteen go courting the best cure for them is the whip . . .', and his father wrote of Richard and Richard's family, 'your prolific brother's wife has again blessed him with a son, poor headstrong unfortunate . . .'. The youngest son Henry is not mentioned in early letters.

Seven years younger than Edward, Featherstone Lake Osler, a fair, sturdy blue-eyed boy, later described himself as 'always reckless and daring'. He was born on December 14, 1805, and from early childhood determined to go to sea. But his father had other ideas and sent him to boarding-school inland 'lest [he] should be drowned'. Soon after his sixteenth birthday his brother Edward, then in Swansea, wrote to their father on his behalf. '. . . I have spoken to my intended brother-in-law, Captain Powell, who is perfectly willing to take [Featherstone] on board his ship. Could we choose through the whole merchant service I feel persuaded we could not do better. . . . Captain Powell is a perfect gentleman and will . . . treat him with the kindness of a brother. He is, at the same time, a strict disciplinarian and will not only keep an eye on Fed to do his duty but will prevent him from familiarizing with his inferiors. . . . He would not be as most lads are when they go to sea, a menial servant. I remember . . . before Edward Bath [a cousin] left Swansea hearing Aunt observe that he would have to get the Captain's breakfast. I felt astonished and almost indignant at his being thus made the servant of a man who would only be *tolerated* at his father's table. . . .'

With his family's reluctant consent Featherstone sailed in the *Sappho*, bound for Constantinople. His Captain (Powell) described him as 'a fine spirited lad and [one who will] no doubt fight his way through this rascally world as well as any person I know . . . '. The voyage was a succession of tremendous gales. It was during one of these that sea-sickness saved his life. 'I had been ill,' he wrote, 'lying on a carpenter's chest near the foremast. I moved from there to the side of the ship but before I could return to the seat where I had been lying the masts snapped off . . . and the whole wreck came down, smashing to atoms, the chest and everything near it . . . For several weeks we drifted upon the ocean and to add to our miseries the water-casks . . . had been imperfectly burned in the inside and consequently the water was scarcely usable and we were . . . famished with thirst. At length we reached Malta, refitted and returned to England. . . .'

Presumably Featherstone spent the next four years in the merchant service though no letters or journal of that period survive. By 1826 he was an officer, though a lowly one, in the Royal Navy. This promotion in respectability may have been brought about by his godfather, Edward Lake, whose influence largely determined the course of his next ten years.

The Rev. Mr. Lake lived at Worcester, a minister to the Countess of Huntingdon's Mission Church. Though the gentry considered Methodism a socially inferior state of grace, certain sections of the aristocracy, usually whig, furthered the cause of a growing evangelical movement within the Established Church. To this group Edward Lake belonged. The subject matter of his letters was divided between Christ Crucified and his illustrious friends. Through one of the latter, Lady Northesk, who in turn had intimates in the Admiralty, he furthered Featherstone's 'temporal welfare' in the navy. But he never forgot 'the eternal welfare' of his godson's soul. His letters followed Featherstone round the world: in every mail a tract to rouse the young man's still sleeping sense of sin.

But in 1826, a new boy in the navy and conscious of his sudden elevation, Featherstone was not asking, 'What shall I do to be saved?', but looking for the wherewithal to buy a sword and a cocked hat. He wrote to his father from Devonport: '. . .When I left home I expected that I should not want a sword till I could afford to buy it myself but it is here absolutely necessary. I went on board the Britannia today . . . and had scarcely deliver'd my orders when he (the Commander) called me aside and asked . . . why I came on board the Admiral ship not dress'd. I said I thought I was. His reply . . . "Where's your sword?" I could say nothing. I was ashamed to say I had none. If you will advance me £4, directly I have it in my power, I will repay it. . . .'

Edward and Mary Osler did not always understand the necessities of their son's new life and Featherstone wrote again, this time to his brother Richard, '. . . I was truly disappointed to find you were unable to pay me a visit. I wanted to see you . . . very particularly about some things which at Falmouth are thought nothing of but which here and abroad can scarcely be done without. What I allude to principally is a cocked hat. A cap is the undress and it is very rare . . . to see any officers, even little boys of thirteen or fourteen years of age, ashore without a cocked hat. The expense . . . is about £2 . 5. . . .'

His father sent the funds and they were 'immediately expended in purchasing a sword and the necessary appendages . . .'.

After many delays Featherstone's ship, the *Cynthia*, sailed for Barbadoes. A few months later he was shipwrecked for the second time. From Austin Town, on June 12, 1827, he wrote to his father:

'It is with heart felt pain I have to inform you of our misfortune which is the total wreck of the Cynthia on a ledge of rocks off the south end of Barbadoes which is not laid down in the charts. Happily no lives were lost though we have lost the greatest part of our clothes.

'I intend sending this by the sly as the Captain wishes no accounts to reach home before the official accounts are sent to the Admiralty. . . .'

Then followed an outbreak of yellow fever and for months they cruised the seas as a pest ship before returning to England for the inevitable court martial. They were honourably acquitted, 'and,' wrote Featherstone, 'glad to hear the president say, "Gentlemen, take your swords."' As officer of the watch when the ship struck, he bore the brunt of the examination. '. . . It was considered that I had acted exceptionally well [and] the court martial procured for me several valuable and influential friends so that I was immediately placed on the books of H.M.S. Britannia and then for a short time on the Victory, Nelson's old ship. . . .'

While in England he wrote and passed a naval examination and was subsequently appointed to the rank of sub-lieutenant.

To be an officer and a gentleman was a fine but an expensive way of life. When news reached him of the death of his grandmother, Joan Drew Osler, he wrote to his father from an English port:

Jan. 3, 1828.

'. . . I have been here a month, at the end of which time it is a rule for every member to pay the expense for his mess. . . . [The] crepe which I was obliged to get to attend the Captain's . . . funeral and . . . the mourning which I have got now will be about £2 . 15. It is painful to speak of such things at such a time . . . but being in a public situation I am obliged in outward appearance to make private feeling subservient to public duty. . . . Richard did not say when my *dear* grandmother was to be consigned to the grave. . . .'

The same month Featherstone complained to his brother Edward of the contents of a parcel from home: '. . . I did not expect to find two of Father's old flannel waistcoats, patched and cobbled and three pairs of my old canvas trousers only fit to wear on board a collier. . . .'

The *Tribune* sailed in June, 1828, some weeks after the scheduled date. The Captain 'did not wish to leave England until he had an increase of his family . . .'. When a boy was born sails were hoisted. Santa Cruz was the first port of call; then Bermuda, which Featherstone described as '. . . of all places in the world . . . the worst in every respect, nothing to be got without paying an exhorbitant price . . . and mosquitoes . . . almost as thick as bees in a hive . . .'.

Dinner for four, at the Colonial Hotel, consisting of a

'starved fowl and a little ham and eggs, . . . exclusive of wine . . .' cost £2 . 2s.

Britannia not only ruled the waves but rode the billows of prosperity and prestige. Featherstone shared with every Englishman of his time the stature gained by simply being English.

Featherstone wrote to his father, Rio de Janeiro, Oct. 29, 1828: '. . . Peace is concluded between Buenos Aires and the Brazils. One article is that neither power is to make war without the consent of Great Britain. This makes the representatives of other nations very jealous. . . .'

From Montevideo he wrote the same year, '. . . The Brazilians . . . detained an English merchant vessel against all laws. . . . This was not to be endured. . . . We received orders from the Admiral to retake the brig, by force if necessary. . . . About six miles from the harbour we cleared for action, double shotted the guns, ran alongside the Brazilian frigate . . . and asked if they would deliver the brig up quietly. . . .' The Captain's young bride was on board and so when he saw 'the guns primed and the men at quarters . . . [he] said he would not attempt to engage. . . . We then hoisted English colours on her . . . about a quarter of a mile from the whole Brazilian squadron. They were much mortified and talked large but could do nothing. The English merchants and residents were very proud. . . .'

Of the local navy he wrote, 'The Brazilians are very quiet now and civil. It is not surprising that they should be cowards when their Admiral, before he took command, made a contract with the Emperor that he would take charge of the ships but would not *fight*. . . .'

A lucky voyage still brought loot beyond the measure of naval pay.

Sept. 1828.

'On the morning of the 18th, a very suspicious looking brig . . . was observed . . . about five miles off. All sail was immediately set in chase, which she soon perceived and crowded all sail to get away.' After twenty-four hours 'a smart squall, of which we had the first benefit brought her within range of our two forward guns. They were instantly opened and a couple of shots close to her quarter showed it was of no use running farther, so she shortened sail and hove to.

'We ran alongside and sent a boat on board. Curiosity was now raised to the highest pitch. Who is she? What is she? Is she a rogue? Will she be any good to us? i.e. will she give us any prize money?

'To our great disappointment we found it was the Buenos Airean privateer, Bolivaro. We searched strictly but found nothing to condemn her, she having had plenty of time . . . to throw all suspicious articles overboard. . . .'

When the *Tribune* docked at Rio they learned that 'the Bolivaro had committed several piracies and . . . had taken an English ship which had not since been heard of. . . . Our Chagrin and disappointment may better be imagined than described . . . having had the rascal in our possession and then to lose her. . . .'

Featherstone found nothing to recommend Rio except its harbour and scenery. '. . . Some English gentlemen,' he wrote, 'have married natives and it would be a good thing for the Brazilians if more would do so. 'Twould improve the breed,

which is sadly wanted, for in no part of the world—and I
have visited the four quarters—have I seen any to compare
with the Brazilian females, they are so abominably ugly . . .'

From Buenos Aires, his favourite station, he wrote to a
sister, '. . . Soon after our arrival two large balls were given. . . .
I think I never before saw such an assemblage of beauty. . . . A
person may spend his time here very pleasantly, especially if
he knows the language, but in that case, the Spanish ladies are
such fascinating creatures, you are put in danger of falling in
love. They marry young—thirteen or fourteen—the usual
age for females—[in] consequence . . . they appear old women
when an English lady is in her prime. Before marriage the
mothers look very sharply after their daughters . . . Music
and dancing they are passionately fond of [and] . . . though I
know little Spanish I often visit them to hear a song or tune.

'Public opinion is much in favour of the Englishman.
Twenty years ago [he] was looked on as worse than a dog.
Now the height of ambition among the ladies is to get an
English husband. . . . Though not a marrying man, I am
strangely taken up with these seducers of mankind, and when
ashore never feel so happy as in their society. . . .'

He described with the eye of a connoisseur a certain Ruperta
as 'one of the prettiest girls I ever saw. . . . Her long hair
arranged so simply but so tastefully with a few white flowers
round the head; a good shape, though it is more than likely
she never had stays on in her life, and a pretty hand and foot
. . . in fact . . . a perfect Hebe. . . .'

Featherstone enjoyed life. Carnivals, horse racing and
dances or a four months' cruise along the coast of Patagonia,
all are mentioned with relish in his letters to Falmouth. He

reports too on the political unrest, the continual acts of violence: '. . . It is a common question to ask,' he wrote, '. . . Have you heard how many were murdered last night ?'

He walked through graveyards in which no corpse could be buried until an older one was disinterred; counted a thousand skulls in a small area lying among their decaying graveclothes. He sent home tiger skins, a Spanish hammock and Indian bows and arrows. Only occasionally is there a hint that Mr. Lake, by remote control, directed his godson's thoughts. In 1829 he wrote to his sister while at sea, off Cape Frio:

'. . . Since [knowing] Mr. Lake I have sometimes thought differently to what I did before, and would freely give up all my prospects to be like him. Should I ever be religious I think I should not be lukewarm. . . .' But his real conversion came later when all hope of further advancement in the navy was lost.

By 1830 Featherstone had been promoted to the *Algerine*, a sloop-of-war, in which he cruised around the Cape of Good Hope and the Indian Ocean. In letters to his father, written at this period, he told of useful friends and how to keep them. His comments sound strange to modern ears but to the ears of his contemporaries it was a familiar tune.

'. . . Should we go to Bahia soon . . . I intend getting a few trifles to send Lady Northesk. . . . It was her influence with Admiral Baker got me my present situation and I may be glad to use her influence again. The Earl being one of the Peers of Scotland gives him great influence and I believe the Countess is commander in chief. At any rate when I have good friends I like to keep them. . . .'

A few months later he wrote, again to his father, '. . . The Earl of Northesk's death is a loss to me. I should have had his interest which would [have been] of consequence. But thro' Lady Northesk I hope to get the present Earl's. . . . In these hard times it is necessary to make as many friends as possible. . . .' He then gives a list of the presents he plans to send his patroness. Whether they travelled on the *Swallow*, *Cygnet*, *Lapwing* or *Goldfinch* he does not mention but such were the flying names of current packets.

In letters to his parents Featherstone always signed himself 'your affectionate and dutiful son' and there is no doubt he wrote the truth.

F. Osler to Edward Sr.:

'. . . [I] look back with gratitude to my dear parents for the care and manner I have been brought up, to which I attribute my prosperity and comfort and which, while I live, I cannot forget. . . .

'My present pay I consider enough for my expenses. The rest I wish to place in your hands . . . [and] I trust you will consider it . . . as entirely at your disposal. . . .

'I am in no hurry to get married and if my present ideas and feelings continue I don't expect [to do so] . . . unless to one who can afford her own mess. . . .'

Edward Sr. replied, in a fine example of the eighteenth-century manner, the century to which despite the calendar he continued to belong:

'. . . I will now, my dear Featherstone, as you have lately been talking about it being your intention never to get married, make some few observations for the purpose of strengthening your prudent resolves.

'In situations similar to that in which you are now placed, separate from three to five years from the endearments of home, and dividing wives into three classes of Bad, Indifferent and Good . . ., on dispassionate reasonings it seems to me difficult to find sufficient sweets to make the acids palatable. . . .

'After a little holiday amongst your friends you have another three years foreign station . . . and a wife to spend all you can get and perhaps run you in debt.

'As example is allow'd to be stronger than precept I will give you the case of two Masters of the Navy, highly respectable men.

'The first, Mr. Jelliffe, who, after being knock'd about in the early part of the last war, about the meridian of life, fancied a showey girl, Kitty Bond. He had just stamina enough to get three children but after a little while, crush'd and coughing, he died and his gay widow supplied herself with another.

'The other I allude to is poor Burney. [His] genteel, pleasing, . . . improvident wife . . . has run him in debt wherever she can obtain credit. He was not seen ashore by daylight last voyage. His constitution is not strong and I should . . . think it likely eventually to crush him. . . .

'At some future period you may meet one with a Mind and a Pocket. They must not be separated, bearing in mind that a mistake in taking a wife is something like the mistake the Master of the Thetis made, both are irremediable.

'And now, should you laugh at me for those uncall'd for observations, I should . . . could I but see you, laugh also. . . .'

The family had long since moved from their quarters above the shop to a comfortable house in a 'genteel' neighbourhood.

Edward (2) suffered from gout and costive bowels. During these bouts his letters filled with woe. In one to Featherstone he regrets that 'any observations made by me during seasons of weak spirits or chagrin should have made you uneasy on account of my pecuniary resources. Although I have done much more for Edward & Sam (and been bitterly disappointed) than I could do again for their younger brothers, I have not left myself destitute. . . . It is little I require for myself but I feel anxious to sustain . . . that respectability of station & character I have enjoyed for the past forty years. . . .'

To ease the gout he recommended a diet 'generous and strengthening, neither heating nor irritating. . . . After many experiments I have come to the conclusion that the medicine best adapted to my constitution is beef and good Port Wine, without which I do really believe I could not live six months let what may be substituted. . . . It is rather expensive but cannot be avoided. . . .'

The *Algerine*, after cruising around the Cape of Good Hope and the Indian Ocean, was again stationed at Rio. From there, in 1832, Featherstone obtained leave to return to England in order to write the naval examinations necessary before his rank could be confirmed. His father's uneasy health had deteriorated and if they were to meet again it must be soon.

A few hours before his vessel was due to sail for England the Captain of a frigate on special service and bound for the East Indies asked him to replace the officer in charge of the scientific department. Sir Thomas Baker had suggested his appointment. Featherstone was tempted but refused on the grounds of his father's ill health. The frigate was the *Beagle* and had he accepted the offer it is unlikely that the Osler story would have moved to Canada. Darwin instead of Edward Lake might have become the leading influence in his life.

Featherstone returned to an England plagued by two epidemics: cholera and riots. The Established Church had reached a new peak of unpopularity when, in 1831, the Spiritual Peers in the House of Lords voted twenty-one to two against the Reform Bill.

But Featherstone's business was with the navy and at first, he did not see the lions in his way. After visiting his family in Falmouth he went to London where he passed his naval examinations 'with credit'. Though his hand was still on his sword he now desired to be a Christian as well as an officer. From London he wrote to his godfather:

'. . . I do . . . hope to know what true religion is before I again leave England, that I may be converted to the saving of my soul. My heart is hard and proud but He can soften and humble it. . . . I will endeavour to hear Mr. Hicks on Sunday morning and evening and Mr. Wilkinson in the afternoon. . . . The cholera morbis is not decreasing. . . . It seems God's judgement on earth and well we deserve it. . . .'

He stayed for some time with Mr. Lake in Worcester and though obviously affected by his godfather's efforts on behalf of his immortal soul he still felt uncertain of ultimate salvation. '. . . I endeavour to follow your directions and pray for the leadership of the Holy Spirit. I certainly do hope, tho' very faintly, that God has begun a good work in me and will carry on. . . . You will laugh at me for I cannot feel I want to love Jesus and hate my sins, and I hardly do one or the other. . . .'

The happy sailor had been displaced by a troubled soul. '. . . Could I but love Him. 'Tis that I want . . .' he wrote to a

friend, and to his sister, '. . . we try to deserve something good
from God but He will teach us that we deserve nothing but
His wrath. . . .'

A change of government and the subsequent reshuffling
at the Admiralty caused Featherstone moments of uneasiness.
but his confidence in his naval future was not yet shaken,
And he had another, more disturbing, problem to deal with.
He wrote to Captain Powell, the man with whom he had
first gone to sea:

My dear Sir,
. . . I want your advice and assistance on a very delicate
subject which distresses me. . . . It relates to Caroline. I wish
to do that which is right and will state all the circumstances
of the case. . . . By your decision I pledge my word and honour
to abide.

You are, I dare say, aware . . . that Caroline and myself
used to be joked about . . . when mere children. But on my
visiting Swansea four years after, I became much attached
to her, more so than I ever shall be again to anyone. I spoke to
her about it and her answer was "Why Featherstone, you are
but a youth" . . . said, as I thought, *very* carelessly. Soon after
there was a picnic into Caswell Bay. You were there.

I was anxious to pay every attention to Caroline and she . . .
was equally anxious to avoid me. . . . I persevered for my
affections were too deeply engaged to be easily put off. Yet
up to the last day she appeared to shrink from me. . . . A
misunderstanding at parting when I put into her hands a note
written under a great deal of excitement convinced me that
I must give up all hope. . . .

Featherstone and Caroline had neither met nor corresponded
for six years when he revisited Swansea on his return from

South America. His chagrin on discovering that he was expected to resume a childhood courtship was not surprising and he showed courage beyond the call of duty when he left the decision to Captain Powell:

'. . . I esteem Caroline very highly but do not love her. I am not engaged or matched to anyone else. If you think I ought to consider myself engaged or if I have acted wrong and can remedy it, tell me and I will cheerfully do it. . . .'

Captain Powell must have settled the 'delicate matter' to Featherstone's satisfaction for no further mention is made of Caroline.

By the autumn of 1832 Featherstone was forced to admit that his prospects in the navy looked decidedly thin. In later recollections he wrote, '. . . All my naval friends, on whose help I depended, were out of power, throwing me thereby completely on the shelf.'

Mr. Lake had been pushing the Cloth under his nose for some months but to Featherstone it had a musty smell compared to the salt sea air. Practical considerations in the end persuaded him to study for holy orders but he did not give in unconditionally. He agreed to study with the Rev. Mr. Atkinson in Falmouth preparatory to entering Cambridge but stated his determination to return to the navy should an opening appear.

In a last attempt at escape he tried to beg off on account of his weak voice, a disability that plagued him during all his years in the pulpit. 'What you write of your voice is nonsense,' brother Edward replied, 'it is nothing more than the weakness of inaction, & if you wish to overcome it, read aloud every day until you are tired, and you will quickly find nothing to

complain of. . . . Although all disappointments [he refers to
Featherstone's loss of a naval career] are very unpleasant when
they occur . . . yet no man was ever worth anything who had
not been disciplined by a few. They are the very winter of
the mind, cold & cheerless enough but concentrating [their]
powers for a burst in the Spring. . . .'

Wherever he turned, a finger pointed to the church. After
ten years at sea the sailor sadly put away his sword, took
off his cocked hat and prepared himself for a more sober
uniform.

His spirits were further dampened by his father's death
which occurred soon after he left Falmouth to study with the
Rev. Mr. Williams, rector of Woodchester. The confident,
extroverted sailor of earlier days is barely recognizable in his
letters of this period.

Having seen, however reluctantly, the Light, he was now
determined to convert his chapel-going family. From Woodchester Rectory he wrote: '. . . I wish, my dear Mother you
knew the *true* Church. You would love it as I do . . .;' and
more sternly to a sister: '. . . I could wish we knelt at the same
altar and worshipped GOD in the same Sanctuary. But considering the way you have been brought up, constantly attending the Chapel, and the imperfect means you have had of
obtaining true information concerning the Church of England,
most of which you have heard from her bitterest enemies
[Baptists] . . . I cannot wonder at the choice . . . which you have
made. . . .'

Though he must have been more than an adequate student
to prepare for Cambridge in less than a year, the confined life
irked him and his mind wandered continually from books to

the sea. He was only twenty-eight when he wrote to his
mother: '. . . My spirits are not what they used to be; age and
affliction as well as study may cause that. In truth I expect to
be obliged to wear a wig again, the little hair I have is falling
off so fast that if it continues . . . six months [hence] the greater
part of my head will be bald. If I do wear a wig again it will
be for the sake of its warmth, not appearance. . . .'

In October, 1833, he entered St. Catherine's Hall, Cambridge, where he remained for three years. He was elected
Mathematical Scholar of the College and 'worked very hard
and looked forward to the prospect of obtaining a high degree
and settling down in England in a quiet parish'.

Featherstone was a conscientious man. Once he put the navy
behind him he devoted himself, less cheerfully but with equal
ardour, to the Church. Patrons remained useful in the new life
as in the old, or so he hoped.

'My prospects of advancement were very good as I had
friends of high power in the Church, especially the Marquess
of Cholmondeley, who was an intimate . . . of my godfather.
. . . The Marquess being head of the Evangelical party, everything seemed to point to my remaining in England. . . .'

As it turned out these same friends were responsible for
sending Featherstone to Canada.

In 1836 Bishop Stewart of Quebec wrote to his nephew,
the Earl of Galloway, begging for spiritual aid in the form
of young clergymen. The Earl of Galloway, the Marquess
of Cholmondeley and Sir Walter Farquar had married
daughters of the Duke of Beaufort, three influential evangelicals. They formed and sponsored the Upper Canada
Clergy Society. Featherstone Osler they considered the very

Featherstone Lake Osler, from a portrait taken
in about his eighteenth year (born 1805)

man for their purpose—a sailor, used to hardships, accustomed to being abroad—the right man for the Canadian bush, said the lords and ladies, which was indeed the truth.

Featherstone's choice of a mate was undoubtedly the most brilliant decision of his life. A privately printed book, *Records of the Lives of Ellen F. Pickton & Featherstone L. Osler*, is the only source of information regarding the early days of the woman who became his wife. It is limited to twenty pages of notes 'jotted down by her niece Jennette Osler [Edward's daughter].' 'Ellen Free Pickton was born December 14, 1806, in Hellingdon, Kent, a few miles out of London. Her parents were Thomas Pickton, one of a company of wholesale merchants, and Mary Wigmore, a relative of Abraham Newland, Cashier of the Bank of England, of whom an old song said: "I have heard people say, sham Abraham you may, but you must not sham Abraham Newland". . . .'

She saw little of her mother, a chronic invalid who 'was sent to the country for her health and ordered to sit in the farmyard while the cows were being milked to breathe their breath which is wholesome for sick people'. Indeed she saw little of brothers and sisters and father, for when she was five years old she was adopted by Captain and Mrs. Britton and travelled with them by coach to Falmouth. Mrs. Britton, a sister of her mother, and childless, brought up Ellen and another niece, Charlotte Free.

Ellen remembered staring at 'the bodies of criminals hanging in chains near the scene of their crimes', and 'the sailor Prince William when his ship was in Falmouth Harbour'. For 'the great . . . rejoicing after the battle of Waterloo', she wore 'a white satin sash with Peace and Plenty in gold letters upon it.

Every house was illuminated; the windows . . . open and the rooms . . . a blaze of light. Flags were flying, drums beating, cheering processions filled the streets. . . .'

The November packets to Halifax were proverbially ill-fated. In six successive years six set sail and five were never heard of again; not even news of their wreckage drifted home. The sixth, almost despaired of, was first sighted by Captain Britton. 'Ellen, then in her teens, stole out of the house on Stratton Place at two o'clock in the morning and went alone to Fish Hill, the resort of half-drunken sailors, to take the news to a mother who had given up her boy for lost. . . .'

Old friends described her as 'a pretty girl, clever, witty and lively, with a power of quick repartee, wilful but good-tempered, not easily influenced, faithful in her friendships and of strong religious principles . . .'.

Her physical characteristics were those of a Latin: a body short, slim and small boned; black hair and eyes and a skin dark enough to give her a 'foreign look'. Perhaps she resembled the 'Spanish Ladies' Featherstone had loved in earlier days.

One morning Richard Osler, meeting Ellen on the street, stopped her and said, ' "I saw you walking with a young officer yesterday. I wish you would reserve yourself for my brother who is coming home next week." It was said jokingly but she was offended and determined not to see him . . . if she could help it.

'Shortly afterwards she was spending the evening with friends and they said, as she rose to go, "O, stay a little longer. Featherstone Osler will be here and he will see you home." At this she was the more bent on going at once and departed forthwith. She had not gone far when she heard a voice saying, "O Miss Picton, won't you allow me to see you home?" . . . She consented and after that "I seemed to meet him wherever I went. I think he watched for me. . . ."'

They became engaged six months before he went to Cambridge and were married three and a half years later on Feb. 6, 1837, in Budock Church, Falmouth.

Ellen shared with her husband the virtues of courage and endurance, adding to the Osler strain her own particular qualities of forbearance, gaiety and even a gentle wit. Unlike Featherstone, she possessed an inborn piety. The dogmas of her age at times dictated the verbal expression of her faith but left untouched her charity of heart.

'The request that he should go to Canada was a blow to them both' and to their family and friends. But Featherstone translated his duty into naval terms and said, 'If I was still in the navy and ordered east, west, north or south in the service of my king, I could not refuse . . . and shall I be less obedient to the call to go abroad and serve my heavenly King?'

They sailed from Falmouth on April 6, 1837, and arrived at their destination, Bond Head, 40 miles north of Toronto, on June 20, the day Victoria became Queen of England.

CHAPTER TWO

The Voyage

'THE BLUE PETER, the sailing flag was up,' so reminisced
Ellen from another century, 'and we were just weighing
anchor in Falmouth Harbour when we saw a boat push off
from the Market Strand and row hurriedly towards the ship.
When it came near someone shouted "We've got your pillow!"
and my own special down pillow was handed up the side. I
have that pillow now; it has had a new case but the feathers
are the same. My head has rested on [it] for nearly seventy
years. . . . A friend, at parting, gave me a text, "As Thy Days
So Shall Thy Strength Be".'

. . .

Besides the Oslers the only passengers on the *Bragila* were
Henry Scadding (author of *Toronto of Old*); another Cambridge
graduate on his way to Canada to be ordained; Tincombe,
a fifteen-year-old boy; and Alice Trupp, a domestic headed for
a clergyman's house in Quebec.

Featherstone wrote a day-by-day account of the seven weeks'
voyage to Francis Proctor, a fellow-clergyman and probably a
friend of his Cambridge days. On board the *Bragila* he enjoyed
the dual role of sailor and parson. '. . . On the Saturday after
we left, the William Hamilton, Barque, from Demerara, bound
to Liverpool, out 57 days, boarded us, she being in want of
provisions, and we supplied her with bread and, what to them

was indeed a treat, some fresh beef. On Sunday we had a
very interesting service; the cabin was full, and after prayers
I addressed [an] attentive congregation of "blue jackets" from
that passage in the 107th Ps. "They that go down to the sea"
&c, ... I hope . . . to have Morning Service for ourselves
and those of the crew who choose to attend . . . and Afternoon
Service for all hands. . . . Several sail have been in company
with us . . . since we left England, many of them apparently
bound for the same part of the world. . . .' Later in the letter
he gives a 'Bulletin of health: Alice very sick in bed, Scadding
not . . . well . . ., Tincombe, Mrs. O. and self very well indeed.
My wife is so good a sailor that she is now sitting by my side
on a low stool, with her back against the bulkhead and feet
against the end of the tables, at one moment supporting herself
with her hand to prevent being sent to leeward and the next
stitching the collar of a shirt. . . .'

After forty-one days at sea they sighted land, 'the high,
ironbound coast of Newfoundland', and shortly afterward
Featherstone was called to action as a sailor.

'After leaving Cape Ray the weather became hazy, which
prevented our seeing, as we had anticipated, the Bird Islands,
a small group which lies almost directly in the track of vessels
going up or down the Gulf.

'During the greater part of Friday the weather continued
thick and foggy, and that night, although we must have
passed . . . close to Anticosti, we saw nothing of it. On Saturday, 20th, the wind blew strong from ENE., sea running high
and the weather so thick that little more than a ship's length
could be seen ahead. At noon there was no observation, and
sail was shortened to double-reef'd topsails and foresails, under

which sails we were running at the rate of $7\frac{1}{2}$ or 8 knots an hour, considering ourselves about sixty miles from that part of the land for which our course was shaped. At 3 p.m. the mate, whose watch it was, observing the water to be much discoloured, was just preparing to have the lead hove when, looking earnestly through the fog, he saw breakers close at hand. Providentially he had presence of mind enough to order the helm immediately to be put hard a-port and hauled the ship to the wind. I was below in my cabin, and, hearing an unexpected bustle, ran on deck and soon perceived the cause of it. Directly under our lee the sea was breaking over a sunken reef like a boiling cauldron, and, the fog having cleared off a little, an island showed itself about a quarter of a mile within the reef, the side of which to a great height was continually white with breakers. Our situation was indeed most critical. I jumped down the companion ladder and begged my wife not to be alarmed, for it was soon known what was the matter, and I must say she behaved nobly; not an expression of fear or alarm escaped her lips, nor was any such feeling depicted on her countenance. I remained with her about a minute and then returned again to the deck, once more put on the sailor, and gave with hands and head what assistance I could. With no small anxiety I watched the reef to which we were so close until it was brought abaft the beam, when again land was seen on the lee bow. The sea was too high to allow us to hope for the vessel "staying", and though there was scarce distance between us and the reef to allow of it, yet our only chance of safety seemed, to attempt to wear. At this critical moment, whilst hesitating what to do, the land on the lee bow was perceived to be an extreme point and apparently bold. The wind at this juncture moderated considerably. We made sail, and in about a quarter of an hour could perceive ourselves, as far as the land and reef [were] concerned, out of danger. A narrower escape I never before experienced. . . . In the evening I read and commented upon the 103rd Psalm; endeavoured to refer our providential escape to the mercy of God and point out the danger of slighting so solemn a warning.'

From the Albion Hotel, Quebec, Featherstone added a postscript:

June 5th, 1837.

'You will be glad to hear . . . that we arrived here safely a week since. . . . Our passage up the River was long, having had calms nearly the whole way, and so were obliged to tide it, i.e. weigh anchor with the flood tide and let go again with the ebb. We were all heartily glad to step on shore in this place, which, with the exception of the tin roof'd churches and house[s], has a more Anglified appearance than I had expected. . . . Certainly I did not even hope to find such an Hotel as the one at which we are staying. Everything is conducted as far as possible in the English style; fare good, waiters civil, and we have our own private room. The most trouble I have had has been in transporting my luggage from the ship to the steamboat wharf, first in obtaining a permit from the Customs House, and then in the actual transportation, as there are no regular boats for letting out here.

'Passing through the streets, what we imagined to be young trees growing on every side of us called forth our warmest admiration of the good taste of the people. But on inquiry we found that they were merely stuck in for the occasion, to give additional effect to a grand procession . . . , the Fete Dieu—

in honour of Transubstantiation. We had not been long at the
hotel before the sound of music announced the approach of
the train of priests, etc., with all their mummery. . . . Curiosity
prompted us to go on the top of the house to witness the
spectacle.

'The Bishop [G. J. Mountain, 1789–1863, appointed Bishop
of Quebec, 1837] had been anxiously expecting us, and has
behaved . . . with the greatest attention and kindness. Thinking
it would be best to go to my charge . . . in full orders I proposed
it to the Bishop. He assented . . . , so on Thursday and Saturday
I was examined for Priest's Orders and Scadding for Deacon's,
and yesterday we were ordained in the Cathedral. . . . At the
Bishop's request I last evening preached a charity sermon at a
Free Chapel of Ease in the suburbs. It was literally thronged.
. . . Most unexpectedly the singers commenced . . . a kind of
anthem . . . "How beautiful upon the mountains are the feet
of him that bringeth glad tidings". My blood thrilled and my
heart rejoiced at receiving what seemed like [a] welcome . . . to
the land. . . . This evening or to-morrow morning, D.V., we
leave for Montreal per steamboat. . . . Write to me via New
York (put that on the letter); it will reach me in half the
time and the postage is also half . . . what it is by the Halifax
route. . . .'

Featherstone's naval background and many years abroad
had prepared him to face danger and endure discomfort. The
voyage was nothing more than the routine he loved. To Ellen,
coming from a sheltered middle-class home, the journey gave
a taste of the pioneer life that lay ahead of them. Her reaction
to seven weeks at sea revealed her equanimity; faced with
probable shipwreck, 'not an expression of fear or alarm escaped

her lips'; it revealed her industry (she stitched the collar of a shirt regardless of the pitching boat), and a good constitution; though pregnant she proved 'a capital sailor'. Of this coming event Featherstone wrote to his sister from Quebec, '. . . I trust that should it please the Lord to send us children, we may not through misplaced . . . affection spoil them but . . . bring them up in the way they should go. I shall be glad to have a little son or daughter of my Ellen's though I can scarcely fancy her a Mother or myself a Father. . . .' Ellen added, '. . . I find [Featherstone] has already mentioned the probability of my adding another to the family. . . . We neither of us felt over-anxious about the matter, though I believe I hoped I might not have children. Yet now I feel no uneasiness of mind and trust all will be well with me. . . .'

Ellen did not share her husband's enthusiasm for the Albion Hotel. On their arrival he 'had to leave her and go and see Bishop Mountain. She went upstairs to rest, for she was very tired. The pillow on her bed was dirty and the sheets had been slept in, so she sat on the floor and laid her head in her arms . . . and had a "thorough good cry, the first and the last, my dear, and I was very glad to get it well over before your uncle got back, as nothing would have distressed him more. After my cry I roused up and said to myself, 'Come, this will never do,' so I washed my face and was all right by the time your uncle came back. We dined at Bishop Mountain's that evening and stayed there for the night. Our bedroom was about 12 × 12 and the water-jug had a broken handle, mended with a piece of tin. I looked out of the window in the morning and my heart sank; there was the yard with chips and bits of wood scattered all over it and piles of wood for burning. I should think it fairly tidy now, but just coming from England it all looked very rough and unfinished. . . .'''

There is no mention of homesickness or discomforts in a cheerful letter she wrote from Quebec to her sister-in-law, Elizabeth Osler. Only in the last lines is there a hint of present loneliness, of apprehension for the future. '. . . Beseech the Lord for me, my dear Lizzy, that I may be fitted for all there is before me to do and bear. He has said "My grace is sufficient for thee" but my faith is weak. . . .'

The ocean had been safely crossed but Bond Head was still many days away.

Featherstone Osler to F. Proctor:

Tecumseth, July 12th, 1837.

'As I know you like a regular account of matters I will commence from where I concluded your last letter, i.e. Quebec. On Sunday . . . [we] embarked with our luggage in a large steamer called the British American. She took us to Montreal, a dist. of 170 miles. As I had at that time not seen so much forest as I have done since, I called the scenery fine, for with few exceptions the trees grow close to the water's edge and the St. Lawrence is indeed a noble river—it is deep and above Quebec not broader than the Thames between Graves-end and Woolwich—Most of the steamers on the river are splendidly fitted up and are differently constructed from those at home, having their engines separate and a good part of the machinery above deck so that the main cabin runs the whole length of the vessel—it is the custom also to have your living included in the fare whether you eat or not. . . .

'At Montreal we remained one day, the greater part of which

I was busily employed superintending the moving and stowing of luggage in a barge to go by the Rideau Canal, the route we thought preferable. In the evening we walked about the city and suburbs. A great number of the houses are built with stone, the rest with wood and altogether the city presents a very respectable appearance. In the suburbs there are some good gentlemens' houses & grounds.

'We left Montreal early and went to Lachine . . . in a stage coach carrying nine inside passengers [and] drawn by six cream coloured horses—driven by a Yankee coachman, six in hand, in as good style as the roughness of the roads would allow. At Lachine we embarked on the steamer which towed the barge with goods and luggage up the River Ottawa, passing close by the Rapids of St. Ann (alluded to in the Canadian Boat Song). In the evening we left her and went on board a Packet which was towed by horses up a Canal for 12 miles—passing the night in the best manner we could on the deck and benches. . . . In the morning another steamer received us and took us to By Town [Ottawa] where the Rideau Canal commences. Here we embarked in another steamer which took us to Kingston. . . .

'I have heard, when in the Navy, sailors' yarns of going up the Straits of Babelmandele where they could not haul the Yards round for Monkeys' tails getting in the blocks, as a kind of technical way of describing its narrowness—but really, a square rigged vessel would scarcely go by the Rideau route without her Yards being locked in the trees. In many parts 'tis like a stream through a mighty forest and so narrow that the small steamer was obliged to have the two barges dropped entire—there not being width for her to pass with them lashed alongside. The trees were in some places almost over our heads. The mosquitoes were our greatest annoyance— they revelled in our blood, fresh from the Old Country. . . .

'We were 4½ days going from Montreal to Kingston. At the latter place we were hospitably entertained by Mr. Cartwright, the clergyman of the place to whom I had letters of introduc- tion. . . . Kingston is not so large as Montreal . . . and more of a Military Station. Montreal is quite a mercantile place— Toronto, where we arrived safely on Thursday afternoon, is really a nice Town or rather City. There we remained at the Rectory with Grassett, the Curate, a Cambridge man, until Monday. *The Archdeacon* is a dry morality preacher and as he said *at* Grassett and myself, he did not like the bad Cambridge doctrine. . . .'

The Archdeacon was no other than John Strachan who two years later became the first Bishop of Toronto. Featherstone's initial impression was prophetic of their future relationship. The pawky Aberdonian and the independent Cornishman failed then and later to see eye to eye.

'A regular stage coach took us on Monday from Toronto to Holland Landing which is on the borders of West Gwillimbury. There we remained until Wednesday, making the acquaintance of the people . . . [before starting] in a light wagon for Tecum- seth. A finished house was not to be had, so for the summer we must be content with a sitting room and bedroom with the use of a kitchen, in a new brick farm house. The farmer and his wife (without family) occupy the remainder. Where we shall pass the winter, should we be spared so long, is not yet decided. . . .'

CHAPTER THREE

Winter—The Mackenzie Rebellion

IF ELLEN found Quebec 'rough and unfinished', Tecumseth
Township with its little village of Bond Head must have
looked desolate indeed. The forest still dominated the horizon;
only a clearing here and there in a land where neighbour
was cut off from neighbour by distance and bad roads.

The farmer and his wife were unwilling to house the young
couple for long and in September, three months after their
arrival, they were forced to look for other shelter.

'Mr. Carter,' Featherstone wrote in his journal, 'offered
us the use of his old log house [and] though situated in a very
lonely, inconvenient place, [I] determined on accepting it.
The masons have volunteered to fill up the crevices between
the logs. [On] Thursday had our luggage conveyed there, and
on Friday, sick and tired of having no home or habitation of
our own, [we] removed to the house or rather hut, which for
the great part of the winter, if life . . . is spared to us, it is
proposed we shall occupy.' Ellen described it as 'a shed . . . in
a clearing in the wood, one room upstairs and one down, in
which the cattle had been wont to shelter. . . . The horses used
to come and look in at the window as much as to say, "Why
have you taken our stable and shut us out?"' Featherstone

grumbled, and with reason, 'I believe we both feel heartily sick of our present abode. . . . It is scarcely possible to move a step without being over shoes in dung and dirt. Nothing has tended so much to dishearten me. Fatigue I do not mind, but to be all together [Ellen, Featherstone, servant girl] in one room, no place to write or study . . . and surrounded with filth, I find difficulty in being reconciled to.'

But Featherstone rode off every Tuesday, not to return until the end of the week. Ellen, waiting the birth of her first child, with no company except a backwoods servant girl, endured the isolation and the filth with 'never a repining look'. 'On Friday afternoon in the dusk [she] would kneel on a box in the window, her face pressed against the pane, watching for his return.'

'And now I will give you some account of my charge,' wrote Featherstone to his friend Proctor, July 12, 1837.

Each of the Townships of Tecumseth and West Gwillimbury contain 120 sq. miles so that I have 240 sq. miles of country under my direct superintendence and as there is not a clergyman within 30 miles of me in any direction—and the nearest— Rev. M. Mortimer, being in a very delicate state of health, whenever I can steal a day or two I shall feel it my duty to visit the neighbouring Township.

There is a Church in each of my two Townships but in a very unfinished state—that of Tecumseth is partly glazed but neither lathed or plastered and the only seats are a few rough planks. There I perform services amidst the snarling of dogs, the chattering of swallows and the screaming of children. . . . The Church of West Gwillimbury is not even . . . enclosed nor is the floor laid. For the present I perform service in a large log barn. A winnowing machine serves me for a pulpit. The churches are about 7 miles apart and I am residing near 8 miles from each of them. On my first Sunday I preached in both and rode 24 miles on horseback but that is more than I purpose undertaking again. . . . I have passed through mud holes where the mud was nearly up to the horse's belly and across swamps where the horse had to pick his way, stepping from one log to another and some of these logs [were] floating in . . . mud & water—indeed I have had more intricate navigation here than . . . ever . . . in my life before. . . .

I have been trying to get . . . money to finish the churches. Hitherto it has been everybody's business and consequently no one took it in hand. . . . But to collect £160 is no easy matter. I am promised £50 towards it and shall have hard riding and hard talking to raise the remainder. . . . The people in these Townships are far from wealthy [and] nearly all Irish. . . . [They] came here when the land was to be had for a mere trifle and by hard industry and frugality have cleared farms. They have abundance of the necessaries of life but very little money. For many years they have been anxious for a Clergyman but I am the first who has settled amongst them. The Devil, I grieve to say, almost reigns triumphant. Drunkenness, blaspheming and any species of vice is common, yet there are some exceptions. . . . All bid me welcome and a common addition is "we are a wild people here, Sir". . . . Wicked as the people are they listen most attentively. . . .

As to writing sermons, at present I have not time and must study them chiefly on horseback. . . . The plan I adopt . . . is to have service at Tecumseth and West Gwillimbury on alternate Sunday mornings and in the afternoon in some large barn or stable. . . . Many of the adults cannot read, and I have been told numbers of the females cannot sew. Last Sunday I gave notice that Mrs. Osler would instruct any females in needle work who chose to come to her on Tuesday and Friday afternoon.

A few days since I [was] invited [to see] a young man who had received a hurt. He could not read and was ignorant of God and of Christ. At times he was deranged but in his sane moments he was anxious for instruction. Of Xt. he knew nothing except perhaps to swear by him. . . . When asked . . . what that man was like who lived without thanking God for his mercies, who opened his mouth only to drink or blaspheme, he seemed to feel it deeply as having been his own case—and shaking his head faintly said—"like a filthy brute". . . .

One day last week as I was riding, two women stood before my horse's head and begged to speak a few words with me—it was to entreat me to visit Innisfield, a place 8 miles dist. I promised them DV that I would do so and yesterday fulfilled my promise. Never before did I pass over such a road; two miles of it is through a cedar swamp which is made passable by large trunks of trees being first laid lengthways and then other trunks laid across them, quite in the rough, their branches only being lopped off. I would not venture to ride over it so dismounted and led my horse through this chosen haunt of deer, wolves & bears. . . . Several times did I say to myself—Good people, you will not often see me across this [way]. But my tale altered after being there. An old log school house was fitted up for service. The wind blew through it but . . . the weather was warm. . . . About 50 assembled to hear the word of God. I addressed them, after prayers and baptizing five children, from Ezek xxxiii. . . . It was hearing the service they had been accustomed to at home and once more seeing a Clergyman which affected them so much, for some could not suppress their sobs. They looked upon me almost as an angel of light and did not know what to do to express their gratitude. I was obliged to eat two dinners and had some difficulty in getting off without being forced to take tea. . . . I made arrangements for a Sunday School . . . and purpose DV visiting them, when the roads are passable, once a fortnight. I have also made similar arrange-

Ellen Free Picton in 1828 or 1829, before
her marriage to Featherstone Lake Osler

ments for Holland Landing, a village 11 miles from this. . . .
The kind supply of books from my various friends . . . enables
me to do more than I could else have attempted. . . .

I have got all my luggage, books &c safe—and am quite
satisfied with my situation. . . . Véry thankful am I that I
married before I came out. I should have been very lonely
otherwise. . . .

Trusting that the Lord is blessing your labours and defending
you from all evils, believe me to be, my very dear friend,
most faithfully yours,
F. L. Osler.

Featherstone was now quite at home in the woods. 'I have
lost myself but once,' he wrote (Aug. 1837) to his brother
Henry, 'and though there are plenty of bears and wolves
here, I have seen nothing wild but deer and squirrels. In the
course of a few years the country . . . will appear beautiful.
The face of it gently undulates and the soil is rich. The people
are very kind but not very clean, either in their houses or
persons. . . . I have been told that the Presbyterian minister
who resides not far distant considers them too bad to be
meddled with. These poor creatures have immortal souls and
are in my charge. May the Lord enable me to do my duty
towards them and bless the means used. Already it has been
observed that a great change has been wrought in the outward conduct of many. The presence of a clergyman has not
a little effect and the preached Gospel . . . I trust, has had more.
I don't know whether, when I last wrote, I had any Sunday
Schools established. Now I have five . . . with about 180
scholars, which I could soon . . . double or treble. . . . My
greatest difficulty is in procuring suitable persons as teachers.
. . . The only assistance I have in procuring books, is a grant

L.W.—4

of 8 dollars from the Toronto Sunday School Society [and]
with the exception of this I have to pay for all. . . . Dear
Uncle's allowance comes in here most serviceable. . . .

'. . . I have just established a kind of lending library. . . .
Tis very popular and I expect there will be about 80 or
100 members. I have named the annual payment one dollar
that none might be excluded by poverty.

'. . . Some payment was necessary, not only to augment the
number of books but people value more what they pay for.
. . . As a commencement I have given 50 volumes.

'So soon as the bustle of harvest is over, I have given notice
that I shall be glad to see any young men, every Monday
evening, to give them what instruction they need. My Ellen
for some time past has been teaching . . . young females . . .
needlework . . . and reading. . . . The people are very partial
to her and think a great deal of her teaching the girls. I have
said nothing about an Abstinence Society yet though I have it in
my mind for it is much needed. . . . But two of my strongest
supporters partly gain their livelihood by selling spirits. Under
these circumstances, caution and prudence are necessary.

'The plan I am pursuing is to win their affections by proving
myself their friend, endeavouring to give those who can read
a taste for reading, and by devizing means for teaching those
who cannot, and by steadily refusing to drink anything
stronger than milk. . . . My purpose, as soon as I am a little
settled, [is] to give a lecture every week or fortnight on general
subjects such as geography, the manners &c of different
countries . . . and by so doing, I hope with God's blessing, to
expand their minds. . . . Given employment for their thoughts,
they will not as heretofore be driven to drink. . . .'

'In this country there are thousands who [have] never heard
of A Saviour, even by name, and the Sabbath is known from
being the day chiefly devoted to sporting. . . . Wherever I go
I distribute tracts . . . and give the people handbills to paste
on the walls of their cottages. They have quite superseded the
old songs and ballads. . . .'

(There is no way of knowing what songs and ballads were
ripped from cabin walls to make way for 'Sinners Repent'.
Featherstone in his zeal may have destroyed a source of
folklore.)

Featherstone's flock was reluctant to give up either blas-
phemy or whisky. 'Unless pushed very hard their professions
all end in talk,' wrote their spiritual adviser. But a few months
later he felt justified in a temperate optimism.

'It gratifies me to observe the people . . . more attentive than
they were at first. Many more join in the responses and kneel
during prayers. Less dogs come to Church and the children are
more orderly. . . .' Inevitably there were setbacks. '. . . In the
afternoon preached at Bond Head to a large congregation, but
to my great annoyance a calf was tied up in the stall, at the front
of which, on a barrel, I was standing and by frequent bleatings
[it] would drown my voice. These things at first used almost to
distress me, but now I am accustomed to them.'

In this rough community the Oslers stood for the gentry.
Among the wolves and the Irish, Featherstone was top
man.

Witches still rode their broomsticks and on a parish visit
to Mrs. Willoughby he found her '. . . in great trouble from the
accusation of a foolish woman who had accused her of be-
witching a horse and causing its death.' Featherstone, rejecting

this particular superstition, 'reasoned her out of what she really felt an affliction . . .'.

His responsibilities did not end with the souls of his parishioners.

F. Osler to Proctor:

Oct. 26, 1837.

'Picture to yourself, my people scattered over a surface of 240 sq. miles—two churches not half finished, depending on me as architect, overlooker of the workmen and what is more difficult, paymaster—having to labour hard to get the money. . . .

'I was riding out not long since when a poor woman stopped me to say that she had a sick infant in her arms which she wished me to see and prescribe for . . . another woman came to me with a bad leg, another with his arm, two women came to have their teeth drawn &c—'tis of no use for me to plead ignorance—they shake their heads and say "Oh you know very well, Sir", so that I am obliged to think of something, always taking care to give nothing but what I am sure will do no hurt, should it do no good. . . .

'The people have no idea of comfort . . . and they live, now that they have an abundance of the necessaries of life, in dirt and wasteful extravagance—ignorant almost as the brutes. . . . They are warm hearted and, I believe, idolize both my wife and myself, but they have no stability. O how thankful I am that I married before coming out. I should be in every sense of the word, so far as human friends are concerned, alone but for my beloved wife. . . . With her I do not feel the want of other society and I can truly say happiness is the inmate of our humble shed. . . .

'With respect to my preaching—I have been compelled, contrary to my wishes . . . to adopt what is termed extempore. I found when I came here a strong prejudice against the Church of England, especially her ministers, which the Methodists had excited—they had propagated the most unfounded calumnies— [saying that] whilst they, the Methodists, like the Apostles, prayed and preached by the spirit, the Ch. of Eng. ministers were mere book parson &c. As soon as I found this I adopted a style of preaching which I find profitable both to myself and my hearers—I study my sermons well beforehand [and] illustrate as much as possible. . . . I also visit the people in their homes for they had been led to believe by the Methodist ministers that a Clergyman of the Ch. of Eng. would not deign to enter their doors.

'You could not have sent your letter in a better way (New York). I received it within 6 weeks and 2 days after date, whilst another letter from home sent via Halifax by the Packet was 11 weeks & 2 days before reaching me.

'During last winter and this spring, many and great were the hardships of the back settlers, several, I have been told, were absolutely starved to death. People at home have . . . a very mistaken idea of Canada. They think there is nothing to do but sow the seed and soon after gather in the crops, whereas those who would thrive here must labour . . . and for some years be content to endure many privations. . . .

'The system of barter is very general . . . but this I do not intend to adopt. I pay ready money for everything . . . and expect to be paid in the same way. . . . In the back Townships this would be scarcely possible. . . .

'Situated as we are at present we have to lay in a complete

stock of provisions—my good wife and servant between them have just salted in a hundred weight of beef. A pig is to be bought for the same purpose . . . so that we are not likely to starve. . . .

'May the Lord provide for you, my very dear friends, such a wife as He has given me, a help meet in every sense of the word. Everyone who knows her loves her. . . .

'P.S. The country is in a very disturbed state within 10 miles of my residence. A party of men are exercising with the avowed purpose of joining any rebels—but this troubles me not—the Lord God Omnipotent reigneth. . . .'

Winter came and proved past hardships light compared with those they must yet endure. Ellen's letters of this period have not survived. We catch a glimpse of her environment only through Featherstone's words. 'The snow continues to fall without intermission. At first half the kitchen floor was completely covered with snow which was blown in through the chinks. These we filled with snow hardened from the inside, which, though a large fire was constantly burning within a short distance, continued unmelted; . . . the milk kept in a cupboard within a yard of the fire was frozen so hard as to require a knife to cut it out. . . . The hut is swarming with vermin. . . .' Here they lived until, early in December, Ellen left for Newmarket, a village twelve miles east of Bond Head. She stayed with Colonel and Mrs. Hill, meaning in a few days to move into the lodgings engaged for her confinement. But 'the times became disturbed and they would not let her leave . . .'.

F.O. to his mother:

Tecumseth, Jan. 1838.

My much loved Mother,

Let me begin . . . by telling you that you have another little Grandson who was born on the 4th of this month and who, with his Mother (fancy Ellen a Mother and me a Father) is doing well, though the poor little fellow had a very narrow escape. 24 hours after he was born it was discovered that there was an obstruction in the lower gut. . . . The doctor gave us no hope but when he came to operate he found it not near so bad as he expected. . . . I baptized him Featherstone, thinking the first born should always bear the Parent's name, and having thus committed him to GOD and brought him within the pale of Xt's visible church, left him with the doctor, hardly hoping to see him again alive. But GOD was better to us than our fear and indeed throughout . . . the Lord has been with us.

Whilst my E. is away I am keeping . . . bachelor's hall, having not a soul in the house with me. Half the week . . . I am here, the other half travelling backwards and forwards or at Newmarket. . . .

Last night when I reached my solitary home at dark, after making my horse comfortable for the night, kindling my fire and getting some tea, I felt quite exhausted and was glad to lie down. Today I am all right again. . . . I find the benefit of having been a Sailor and my health appears to be just as it used to be when I was at sea. The tools you so kindly gave me are invaluable. . . . I find it such an amusement to make any little thing. Our sofa is really smart and . . . comfortable. My next leisure [is] to be given for a kitchen table, a clothes horse and side board for the bed to prevent the little master from tumbling out. . . .

Ellen added, 'My dearest Fed has left me this side of his letter. Here, [with Col. & Mrs. Hill in Newmarket] for *seven weeks* I have been as welcome as a sister's kindness could have made me. . . . Up to the very day of my trial my health continued firm, nor was I in the least nervous. "I cast my care on the Lord knowing that he would care for me" and he did deal very graciously with me. . . .

'Everyone says our baby is like its papa. Heny [sister of Featherstone] will say, "I wonder if he has a large mouth". No, Heny, my dear, he has not. . . .'

In 1837 the political machinery of Upper Canada (now the province of Ontario) consisted of a Lieutenant-Governor appointed by the Colonial Office assisted by an Executive Council which he himself appointed, and an elected Assembly. There was also a Legislative Council of outstanding citizens appointed from London and acting as an upper chamber with the power of veto over the decisions of the elected Assembly. The Colonial Office view of Canadian affairs came officially from the Lieutenant-Governor, and unofficially in times of unrest from various protests and petitions which found their way across the ocean.

In the circumscribed backwoods society of Upper Canada there was a limited number of qualified people to fill the various official posts; the same small group formed the core of élite society based on Government House. Some of these men and their wives were people of genuine distinction and, as original Loyalist settlers, of substantial claims. But the core gathered less worthy peripheral elements and being answerable directly to no one but the Lieutenant-Governor tended to increase their holdings and share the opportunities among themselves. Some interlocking of families gave colour to their nickname of The Family Compact which by 1837 had become synonymous with unwarranted social privilege and unchecked political plundering.

There had been minor smoulderings of discontent in Upper Canada for many years which the liberal winds from Europe fanned to a steady fire. The Family Compact had a way of granting the Crown Lands to its friends, who, holding them for profitable sale, left them undeveloped and an impediment to the opening of the country. To some people the most irritating of all were the privileges granted the Church of England— the Established Church—whose blocks of reserved land similarly frustrated progress.

William Lyon Mackenzie, a fiery Scot, led a mixed bag of Reformers—members of the unestablished churches, thoughtful liberal-minded men as well as professional opportunists and agitators. But as events moved toward armed revolt all but the few most ardent or most confused fell away. The rabble which Mackenzie led down Yonge St. toward Toronto in December, 1837, was a pitiful remnant trailing pikes, muskets or pitchforks with surliness but without conviction. One drawn battle in which both sides ran away was followed by a total defeat of the rebels at Montgomery's Tavern north of the city. Faced suddenly with the full understanding of their treason they fled into the back country east and west of Yonge St., or joined the bands marching into Toronto with chests expanded by a sudden loyalty. Overnight, as far as the eye could see, a restless population had become loyal to a man.

Featherstone, well-meaning, pig-headed, a former officer of the King and a member of the Established Church, could hold only one view of these events. It is hardly surprising that he remained unaware that there was another tenable view. And pitiful—almost comic opera—as the uprising proved, he was right to consider that it might have turned out more seriously.

York County was a focus of disaffection and the ex-sailor must have felt that he was living in the eye of a hurricane.

F. Osler to Proctor:

March 29, 1838.

'The standard of rebellion has been unfurled, but through the special intervention of God the rebels were prevented from doing much mischief. When the news first arrived of a large body of men having gone to attack Toronto, I was at Newmarket with my wife. . . . We were at the house of Col. Hill [and] could scarcely credit the report, but it was soon found to be . . . true. It was an anxious time. I took despatches out to this neighbourhood and though I might not fight myself, felt it my duty to stir up others. Night and day I was riding about. In an ordinary war this would have been out of my sphere, but we all stood for our lives, it having been discovered that the rebels had sworn to spare none who were opposed to them, not even women or children. The Clergy of the Ch. of Eng. were among the first to be sacrificed. . . .

'On Wednesday night I again went to Newmarket. The ladies had assembled at the house of Col. Hill, which is about half a mile out of the village, for mutual encouragement, the gentlemen being away with a body of Loyalists. . . . About midnight Col. Carthew [came in] to say that there was every reason to expect the rebels intended to attack the house that night. Much against their will he prevailed on the ladies to retire to their rooms with the children. Col. C., two boys and myself kept watch. At one o'clock a despatch from the governor . . . obliged Col. C. to leave. I then assumed command of the Garrison—having with me two boys, three dogs and five guns. The house stood by itself and the noble dogs, as if aware that watchfulness was necessary, kept patrolling round the house and grounds. . . . I had great reason to be thankful that my dear wife, who every day expected to be confined, felt no alarm whilst the other ladies were in the greatest consternation. . . . The storm passed over. . . . The unhappy men are now being tried. Two of the ringleaders [Lount & Matthews], are sentenced to die in a few days—they were perfect infidels, as indeed were most of the deluded men engaged in the rebellion. The disturbances completely upset my work, every Sunday School was closed, the teachers having gone to the war. . . .'

To Featherstone the Mackenzie rebellion brought back the gusto of his naval days. True, he rode a horse in search of 'infidels' instead of riding the high seas in a man-o'-war, alert for pirates, but for a few brief weeks the submerged head of the sailor appeared above the clerical collar.

Journal, Mon. Dec. 4th:

'The people of Newmarket, being mostly a miserable, disaffected set, . . . seemed panic stricken and but few assembled for the purpose of defence. In the afternoon left Newmarket for Tecumseth. Took dispatches to Holland Landing and Bradford, to raise men and search for arms. Met many small parties . . . on the road; cheered them on and gave as much encouragement as possible, but the general cry was, "We have no arms, what can we do ?"

'At a late hour on Tuesday night I was riding, giving intelligence, stirring up the men, and quieting the women. The few valuables or rather the little specie I had I buried . . . that we might not, if our lives were spared be quite destitute. . . .'

Two days later he wrote, 'Gave my gun to Mr. Robinson, to arm one man. Met Chapman, who, in the midst of all the excitement, wished me to marry him. . . . As he had procured a licence I could not refuse. . . .

'In the afternoon started for Newmarket; overtook a party of Loyalists on horseback on the way to Bradford. At Bradford found about 200 men collected, the principal of whom begged me to stop and consult with them on the best measures to be adopted. After some discussion it was determined to march with a body of about 500 early on Friday morning, and in the meantime to collect all the arms and ammunition possible. . . .'

After the 'infidels' were routed, at least for the time being, Featherstone, back in his pulpit, wrote: 'A more bloody conspiracy was scarcely ever formed. . . . *They had even gone so far as to portion out the Loyalists' lands amongst themselves,* making quite sure of success. But the Lord was on our side and fought for us. To Him be the glory !'

The rebellion had such far-reaching effects that it even caused a choir to mutiny. On Sunday Featherstone wrote, '. . . Gave notice of Sacrament. Found to my annoyance that the family who had been my chief aid in singing had come to the resolution to give aid no longer *because they were not made officers in the Militia.* The whole blame was conceived to rest upon me simply because the Col. [Hill] was an intimate friend. . . .'

Ellen returned with the infant Featherston* to their hovel in the wood but before the end of March the Oslers were again dispossessed, 'the owner needing' their verminous shelter 'for cattle'. Another and similar hut was found.

---

* Featherston Jr. dropped the 'e' from his name while still in his teens. Here it is dropped from birth to distinguish him from his father.

Featherstone Osler to Proctor:

March 29, 1838.

'The place we at present occupy . . . is small and inconvenient [and] I have no stabling for my horse nearer than three quarters of a mile. . . . But I look forward to better times—About six weeks since I called my people together and told them that unless they [build] a Parsonage . . . I must leave them—this stirred them up. A subscription was entered into immediately. It was unanimously resolved that a house be put up forthwith. . . . For the last month workmen have been busily engaged . . . and by dint of hard pushing I hope we shall go to it DV the first week in July. This has added much to my labours [and] at times I have felt quite exhausted. My poor horse from sheer hard work is laid up. . . . I have not been so punctual in writing as I ought but picture to yourself—my wife and infant son, a servant and myself all together in one small, cold room which has to serve for kitchen, parlour, study, wash-house, in fact everything but sleeping room—is it surprising . . . I feel no heart to write ? My beloved wife has, I believe, never indulged in a repining thought. She is and has been truly a comfort to me and God [has] given us good health and our spirits are generally good amidst all our privations. We have had, since coming to Canada, as large a portion of happiness as we could ever expect this side of Eternity. . . .'

Ellen must surely have 'indulged in a repining thought' during the many days when Featherstone was away from home; that Featherstone never guessed may reveal his lack of imagination (though he often wrote that Ellen had far more to endure than he) but it proves without question that Ellen possessed an indestructible harmony of being.

CHAPTER FOUR

Early Years

FEATHERSTONE, architect, contractor, superintendent, all in one, had at last persuaded his parishioners to contribute land and the promise of labour for a parsonage.

On Friday, April 8, 1838, he wrote in his journal: 'Rode to the spot where the house is to be erected. Found that the persons who were engaged to bring the lumber had neglected to do so. The people have so little regard for their word that unless I see things done myself I cannot trust to one. With some difficulty obtained a team to take some planks from the saw-mill for the carpenters to go on with. . . .' A few days later he 'rode round to . . . different friends, desiring them to send their horses and oxen to draw the timber out of the woods. . . . Tuesday—With twenty two oxen and 8 horses an excellent day's work was done.'

A week later: 'Wednesday, Thursday, Friday—engaged from early in the morning till late at night looking after materials for the building, none having been provided. . . . The fatigue has been more than my poor horse and myself can bear. . . . I could not have imagined till taught by experience that the putting up of a small building would have cost me so much labour. In a town or even a village, most materials necessary may be had on the spot. Here, I often ride many miles to procure a very small article. Indeed, it is only by personal experience that the inconveniences of residing in the backwoods of Canada can be known.'

In late July they moved into the first weather-tight, vermin-less house that Ellen had slept in since she left Newmarket after her son was born. Featherstone described the day: 'We packed up the few things remaining in our old hut, and having obtained a wagon, removed to our new abode, which is still far from being finished. . . . After the manner in which we have been tossed about for the past thirteen months these comfortable rooms appear to us almost equal to the accom-modation of a palace. May the gracious God ever keep the house and those who dwell in it under his special care and protection! During the remainder of the week engaged seeking for lime and brick and putting our things a little to rights, some of our luggage not having been opened since they were packed up in England.'

Five weeks later Ellen was entertaining: Journal, Sept. 7, 1838. '. . . In the evening thirty young people took tea with us, twenty four of whom were Mrs. Osler's sewing scholars, twenty five young females in all having availed themselves of [her] instruction, which she gives on Tuesdays and Fridays. It was a treat to the young people such as they never had before, and I trust it will prove a stimulus to them, not only to improve their needlework but in the religious instruction which they always receive at the same time. I did hope to have given my Sunday School children, about two hundred, a treat this year, but must defer it until the Queen's birthday.'

F. Osler to Proctor, 1838:

Parsonage House, Tecumseth,

July 27th, 1838.

'At length I am enabled to write you from a settled dwelling place, the first we have had since coming to the country. A more arduous year I never passed [and I] soon hope to have a little comparative rest and . . . only from 8 to 10 miles . . . to ride on the Sundays. It seems in the anticipation almost too much of ease, only to ride to one of my Churches and back, and to walk from my own house to perform afternoon Service. . . .

'My Parsonage will be, when finished, a very pretty place. Having planned it and superintended the work entirely myself I naturally feel . . . interested in it. . . . I have to advance more money on it than I can conveniently spare, but what was to be done ? Unless a house was built I could not remain here. Once I seriously thought of removing—but I could not find it in my heart to leave my poor people—between two and three hundred children look up to me for instruction; six stations, besides occasional congregations which I have gathered, would be destitute. Most of them are very poor and their poverty pleads strongly for many sacrifices on my part. . . .

'. . . For the Parsonage house I have paid or promised upwards of £100 and Tecumseth Church, which is decaying with the weather, never having been painted outside, will not cost me far short of £20. My little Chapel I have commenced and hope to have it finished before winter. . . . When I have finished all in my neighbourhood I purpose endeavouring to get churches erected in the adjoining Townships. . . .

'. . . I may almost say I never knew fatigue till I came to Canada. And now dear and highly valued friend, once more farewell. The blessing of the Lord rest upon you and upon your ministry and whilst we look after the Souls of others let us see to it that we do not neglect our own. The longer I live the more I feel that I am an unprofitable servant. . . .'

F. Osler to Proctor:

Parsonage, Tecumseth, Feb. 8th, 1839.

'Our political horizon . . . seems brighter. The hordes of ruffians from the United States who threatened to overwhelm us . . . have learned by dear bought experience that the conquest of Canada is not quite so easy a matter as they imagined. . . .

'. . . I perfectly agree with you in thinking that the most likely method for producing lasting good is to have the ministrations of the Gospel regularly performed. . . . This is the plan I have adopted. In eight different places, at regular intervals of one, two, and four weeks, I perform Divine Service, and they all know when to expect me. But I certainly am not confined to them. What would be your reply were you accosted as I frequently am with "O Sir, will a minister never come to our part of the country, our children are growing up like heathen, our little ones have never been baptized, we have not seen a clergyman in our place for more than three years". Your answer would have been what mine was "I will, God helping me, come to you". . . .

'On Sunday morning I performed Divine Service & administered the Sacrament in Tecumseth Church, from there I proceeded to Lloyd Township which is about 9 miles from this, preached there in the evening and after service rode on about 3 miles farther to a house and there slept—early in the morning I started with two guides for the Township of Albion about 12 miles dist. This was a very severe journey in consequence of the cold and hard roads—preached there to about 40 people—on Tuesday morning I proceeded through the woods with one guide to Caledon & Mona, and it was night before I reached my stopping place—messengers were instantly despatched in all directions to say that a "Minister was come".'

Featherstone continued for the rest of the week to visit outlying settlements, baptizing the children and preaching to the people. The letter continues—'Nothing distresses me so much as to witness the feelings of the people in some of the back parts—they crowd around me, they tell of their destitution and compare it with the privileges they had at home—they load me with blessings for coming to see them, and tears run down many a rugged cheek when compelled to bid me farewell. . . .'

If the winter trips to Lloydtown, Mona, Albion, etc. proved rough going, summer hardly lessened the burden.

F. Osler to Proctor:

June 13th, 1839

'. . . I am now in the midst of my summer visits and find them rather severe. . . . After riding 20 miles (or rather passing over, for in some places twas as much as the horses could do to get along themselves without the additional weight of their riders) . . . preached and baptized some children and then . . . set off with another guide for a part of Mona 9 miles further back—reached it between 8 and 9 in the evening and after supper went to bed feeling rather fatigued. I lay down but vermin of almost every description soon forced me to rise again, and the poor people not having a bit of candle in the house I had no alternative but to sit upon a bench for the night and wish

for daylight. . . .' The next night in a different place the experience was repeated: '. . . I went to bed and endured it for
half an hour, by which time I was blistered from head to foot.
. . . I had no remedy but to sit up the second night also—however about daylight I procured a bundle of straw on which I
obtained an hour's sleep. . . . I am sorry to say that I find my
back not so strong as it used to be, and sometimes find it to be a
trial of patience to be obliged to sit up the whole night after a
severe journey. At such seasons I generally question myself as
to whether I am in the path of duty. Conscience answers in the
affirmative and then I feel easy. I know that my labours . . . are
more than I can bear for any length of time. . . . I have en-
treated for help [more clergy] but without success. . . . Lately,
on my own responsibility, I engaged an excellent young man
as Catechist. [He will] visit the most destitute places, search
out the aged, the poor and the distressed, distribute tracts and
catechisms &c and on Sundays assemble the people and read
the prayers and a sermon with which I provide him. . . . The
thought has crossed my mind as to whether my kind friends
may not feel inclined to assist me in paying his salary which is
but £30 per ann. . . .'

Letter from F. Osler to Proctor:

Feb. 8th, 1839.

'. . . My Chapel of Ease or School house (for it is to answer
both purposes) I hope will be finished the early part of summer.
I have received about £80 for it, and about £60 more would
finish it. . . . I trust soon now to be comfortably settled. . . . Tis
true that I am often exposed to wet & cold—but what of it?
tis no trouble to me—even such a day as last Sunday week. . . .
I left home to go to W. Gwillimbury Church—twas blowing a

hurricane. The sleet and drifted snow quite darkened the air—with difficulty I reached about 2 and a half miles, i.e. half way, and then the snow was so deep that my horse and myself were nearly buried. My horse commenced plunging and after some time and trouble I loosed him from the cutter (a sleigh drawn by one horse like a gig with runners instead of wheels) and let him plunge his way through the snow. I secured him to a tree and went to a house half a mile dist. for assistance. With the help of two men I extracted my sleigh, and, it being impossible to proceed, turned back. I had then the wind in my face, which was soon covered with ice, one eye was frozen up and the other nearly so. Through the mercy of God I reached home in safety, rubbed myself well to promote circulation and excepting in soreness was soon well again. I have never experienced such a day before but these things give me no concern—my greatest grief is that I do so little compared with what requires to be done. I am also sometimes annoyed by the Methodists—God knows that I strive to do good to all and offend none but the Methodists strain every nerve to thwart my plans and make the church unpopular. They are here a violent political party. . . .'

While the Church of England backed the Family Compact and the powers that be, the Methodists, or sections of them, stood for reform. Politics and religion were closely linked and this perhaps explains the open hostility between the two. They showed one another little Christian charity though each claimed to be the sole dispenser of this grace.

'My mind has been more harassed with the waywardness and pride of my people [Featherstone wrote in his journal] during the last few months than I can express, and owing to the disturbed state of things all are in a high state of excitement. One general topic is that tithes are to be established. They [the Methodists] draw a highly wrought picture of the miseries endured in Ireland, all of which they say is owing to the tithe system. Then they tell them that all this is now about to be established here, . . . that all who adhere to the Church of England help to bring these miseries upon themselves and their fellow sufferers. By this mode of proceeding they poison the minds of many, notwithstanding that there is an Act of Legislature against tithes, and every deed of Government land specifies that tithes cannot be demanded. It does grieve me to see the people thus led away.'

A few days later he wrote: '. . . My people have shown themselves to be peaceful and loyal and it has annoyed and grieved me to find the Presbyterian minister and ladies amongst the Methodists are doing all in their power to cause discontent and excite seditious feelings. . . .'

Featherstone retaliated with counter plots and counter defamation. In July, 1837, he wrote in his journal, 'I made some arrangements for establishing . . . a Sunday school [in Innisfil]. They had formerly been visited by Methodists, who left them because they did not get money enough. . . .'

A few months later his journal tells a tale difficult to credit. 'An old woman between 60 and 70 years of age and a little girl of nine left home for the purpose of going to the store for something. When they did not return at night the father of the child thought they had remained at a friend's house and went the following day to look for them. They had not been seen, and it soon became evident that the old woman and child were lost in the woods.

'The father, as one may suppose, was distracted, for the wolves are so bad there that even the large cattle are obliged to be kept near the houses.

'The Methodists were just assembled for Class Meeting. [The father] sent two messengers to entreat the men to help him search for the lost ones and when no attention was paid to them he went himself, but to his entreaties a deaf ear was turned. . . . Well might the poor man . . . exclaim "If that is your religion, I will have no more of it". . . . Some men who called themselves Church of England commenced scouring the woods, and after [a] time found the old woman and the child, safe. . . .'

Featherstone complained that the Methodists were 'very different from those I had intercourse with at home. They are . . . ignorant, imagine conversion consists in highly wrought feelings, and the calm which follows is called sanctification. A woman who lives opposite, the wife of a class-leader, wise in her own opinion . . . I overhear occasionally telling of the conversion of different people: One . . . woman lay for two hours in a trance and when she awoke she got perfect sanctification. O how many blind are there here, leaders of the blind! They agree in one thing, bitter hatred and abuse of the Church. . . .'

Newmarket was hardly more virtuous than Tecumseth. In September, 1837, Featherstone wrote, 'Called on Mr. Roe, Col. Hill, Messrs. Carthew and Scadding and Captain Cotter and stated my intention (D.V.) of visiting Newmarket on the first Wednesday in every month, and also that I should be happy to attend to any clerical duty that might be needed amongst them. For this they expressed themselves as very grateful. . . . They lamented the want of a clergyman, and spoke so feelingly of their destitution, and the wickedness of the people generally, that my soul was grieved for them. Not that there is a lack of preachers, such as they are, for in this little village no less than eight different sects hold forth on a Sunday, but it would be better if all or nearly all of them held their peace rather than set forth such absurd dogmas as they hold. . . . The people . . . are very careless about all connected with religion. On the Sabbath . . . more guns [are] heard firing than on any other day of the week.'

Featherstone was no more tolerant of the Roman Catholic faith than of the Methodist but as the former had little power in his section of the country he thought of its members as individual lost souls rather than a menace to his church. (1838, winter): '. . . Whilst riding through Bond Head I observed a poor man who wished to speak to me. I stopped. . . . He said he was a Roman Catholic and [wanted] to know my opinion of that religion. He seemed doubtful about many of its tenets, yet the prejudice of education made him unwilling to entertain these doubts. When I told him, in answer to his inquiries, that the Mass and Extreme Unction were of no avail, that the priest has not the power to convert bread and wine into the real flesh and blood of Christ, he seemed deeply affected, and more than once said, "Remember, Sir, God sees and hears us", as if entreating me to tell him the truth. I directed him to the only Mediator between God and man, and left him apparently deeply impressed with what I had said to him.'

Many years later Featherstone received a letter from a man who wished to make a marriage of convenience with the Church of England.

Reverent Sir,

I have taken the liberty to inform you that i am an eaged man liveing in your district and under many inconvenences on account of my lonly situation and there has come to me a well reared eaged Woman who ofers to me her Servatud and she is a member of your curch and I went to your Brother Mr. Osler in Loyde town and he told me that I shold com to you and draw liceings and as I was reared in the curch of room that you w'old hold it leagle accroding to the ruals of the Curch. . . . As it is my wishes and hers to do so you will feavour me to send word by the bearer what Day wold be convent to you to wed us.

Humbely Yours,
John O'Brian.

Featherstone married them but not before John O'Brian signed the following document:

I, John O'Brian, of the Township of Tecumseth, having the fear of God before my eyes and mindful of my Soul's Salvation, do hereby solemnly declare my conviction that the doctrines taught by the Church of Rome in which I was brought up are erroneous and contrary to God's Holy Word.

That in the prospect of appearing in the presence of Almighty God I declare that my only hope of Salvation to be in the blood-shedding and merits of our Saviour, Jesus Christ as revealed to us in the Holy Scriptures, and do humbly trust the blessed Saviour's command and promise, that those who Believe in His Name shall not perish but have everlasting life.

I further declare it to be my desire to be admitted as a Member of the Church of England and Ireland.

Witness my hand this Seventeenth day of January, 1855,

John O'Brian.

There is no doubt that Featherstone and Ellen brought many blessings to the backwoodsmen and their families.

Ellen played a vigorous role in the community, teaching the 'young females' needlework and morals. Her well-run parsonage set a new standard for aspiring housewives and her gay and giving spirit lightened the loneliness of the bush. Featherstone, in addition to his clerical duties, introduced books to their bookless lives, gave rough and ready medical care and settled their legal disputes.

At the sick bed he was perhaps less successful. 'Having heard that Mrs. Matchett was ill, as also a young man in an adjoining house, visited them. . . . Found Mrs. M. one of those characters most difficult for a minister to deal with; she would assent to everything and whilst I knew from her neighbours that she was not a very good character, she appeared quite satisfied that all would be well with her at the last. Endeavoured to convince her of her delusions. . . .'

At great discomfort to himself he rode interminable miles to save the souls of his flock from perdition.

'Visited a poor woman who was very ill, and in greater poverty than I have before met with here. Found her to be lamentably ignorant, expecting she should be saved. She had a good heart and I showed her how wretched such a state would prove in the hour of death and the day of judgment.'

Mrs. Green would appear to have been full of grace, but no: 'I reached her house by three o'clock in the afternoon. Found her quite ignorant of the way of salvation. . . . She felt that she was a sinner, but thought as God had been so good to her all her life He would receive her soul at death. . . . Fancying she would now die she was anxious to have the benefit of the clergy, namely, the Sacrament. Explained to her the danger of her state, and that the Sacrament could not save her.

Directed her to Jesus, prayed with her and returned home late at night.'

Featherstone's words have to be compared with the common message of his Church and time. Edward Lake preached the same brand of comfort. A similar tone is evident in contemporary letters of both laymen and clergy. A niece of Ellen's wrote approximately five thousand words describing the illness and death of a five-year-old child, a document no one could read today without sensations of nausea: 'Mother felt anxious about her spiritual welfare, for though she had had sweet evidence of her change of heart, she did not think Patty was at all aware how near her end was. . . . She felt it her duty to tell [her] . . . that she must die, but it was a duty painful to perform. . . .'

There were, in every Church, men who rose above the current dogma. Featherstone was not one of them but poverty of imagination rather than cruelty directed his words. He lacked spiritual insight, he lacked humour; the Church had been thrust upon him; he did his always literal best.

Mr. Willoughby was one of Featherstone's fluctuating souls. His state of grace depended on his state of health. It flourished on ills of the flesh and declined as the flesh grew stronger. 'Mrs. Willoughby . . . told me that before I came her husband used to be very passionate and hard upon the children, but that now he is quite another man. He often sits, covering his face with his hands, weeping for his sins, . . . saying, "No one told me I was a sinner till Mr. Osler came. . . ."
To God be the glory !' wrote Featherstone.

CHAPTER FIVE

Children and Tracts

FEATHERSTONE at the sick bed and Featherstone in the parsonage were two different men. At home he was a devoted husband, an indulgent father in an era of patriarchs. There are many references to 'Osler temper' in the early letters, so possibly he shouted now and then, though one suspects that a look from Ellen quickly reduced the volume. After almost two years in Canada the Oslers had settled in.

'. . . Many many thanks to you all, my dear friends,' Ellen wrote to her mother-in-law, 'for such kind remembrances. If my little darling boy [Featherston] is spared to see his dear relatives he too will have much to thank you for—his health is excellent. Papa has made him such a nice little wagon in which it is his delight to ride. Now that he walks I have not much trouble with him, for considering *whose boy he is he is pretty tractable*. The little stranger [B.B. Osler] expected now in about 3 weeks will add much to domestic duties. . . . I have spoken to a very nice woman to be with me as nurse. . . . I have every comfort that the Bush affords and my beloved Fed can procure, and my trust is in Him who has so graciously helped me hitherto. . . .'

Britton Bath Osler was born the following month on June 10, 1839.

F. Osler to Proctor:

Feb. 6, 1840.

'. . . You seem very anxious to hear something about our domestic concerns &c. I never thought of mentioning them, that being entirely the ladies' province. I will however make the attempt. . . . To begin then with my dearest earthly comfort—my wife. This day, three years [ago] I led to the altar a young lady named Ellen F. Pickton, rather slight, a brunette as to complexion, dark eyes and black hair, since which time she has looked rather more matronly though I see very little difference. Fearing that I should lack company [she] has made me a present of two boys—the eldest of whom is an active spirited little fellow, 2 yrs & a month old, chatters like a magpie and [is as] full of mischief as any monkey I ever saw. As to size he is neither very large or very small—his complexion is unusually fair, with light hair and blue eyes; in features everyone says he is the very image of his father, to sit in whose lap he will leave everything and everybody. His name is "Featherstone". The other, "Britton Bath", (named after two uncles) is a few months old, a stout child, just as good tempered as the other is naturally passionate. He has a dark complexion with eyes and hair like his mother's. . . .

'Next come the servants—the greatest plague of this country— . . . We have two girls or women, very indifferent servants and, as all the families here, dirty and careless. But I have a good boy of 14 years of age. I have never yet had occasion to tell him [anything] twice. Next in rank comes my horse, a strong powerful beast, but not quite fast enough for me. I purpose parting with him and purchasing a very fine one which will take me swiftly over the ground, time being

. . . a . . . precious commodity. The cow ranks next. She supplies us with milk and butter and is black as jet all over. Three white sheep, a white pig, three breeding geese, six or eight hens & a cock and two cats I believe complete the list of live stock. As to vehicles, I have at present only a cutter, a single sleigh like the body of a gig on runners instead of wheels, but I have ordered to be ready against the summer a neat strong kind of open carriage . . . to carry two or four persons—to run on four wheels. It is purposely for Mrs. Osler and the children. Hitherto they have had no means of going out in the summer. It will also be a relief for me to drive when the roads are good. I have also ordered a cart with which my boy can fetch fire wood, go to the mill &c and a wheelbarrow. . . . As to our mode of living—in that respect we do not differ much from what we should do at home.

'On our first coming here we seldom saw anything in the shape of fresh meat during the summer . . . so that we had eggs and bacon one day for dinner and bacon and eggs the next. . . . Now a butcher passes the house once a fortnight from whom we are supplied with fresh meat. When we have opportunity we lay in a large store such as one or two whole pigs, a quarter of beef &c. At present we have packed in snow—in which meat will keep frozen hard three or four months—a good part of a quarter of fresh beef, a leg of mutton, two geese and two turkeys. This, with about two hundred weight of salt pork, three hundred weight of flour and the smaller &c complete the stock of eatables. Of groceries we commonly lay in at least a six months store. You will perceive that we are in no danger of starving. I like to keep a good supply of eatables as persons are continually calling. My poor back settlement people I . . . wish to be kindly treated when they come on any account. At times too I have many men at work. Yesterday there were eighteen. . . . I think you will allow that I have been particular enough. I said that my wife was my dearest earthly comfort and I may with reason say so. Her privations have been far greater than mine yet I never saw a repining look or heard a discontented word escape her lips. And much as she is left alone never has she said "don't go". She has a strong mind and what is absolutely necessary for a Clergyman's wife, devoted Piety. She is an invaluable assistant in my central Sunday School and able to turn her hand to anything. . . .

'. . . This is the severest winter . . . for the past 8 years . . . yet I think it far more bearable than an English [one]—the cold is more intense but it is a dry cold and through the winter men work outdoors, often without their coats. . . .

'. . . Mr. P. Thomson, our Governor General, is taking open part with the radicals & rebels—the Loyalists are distracted and disgusted and look with longing to England, hoping the incubus, the Whig radical ministry, will be kicked out with disgrace. . . .'

Featherstone hoped to return to England for a few months' holiday in 1840. As well as a deep desire to go home, for so England always remained to him, he had family matters to settle. But the Society that had sent him out begged him to stay, at least until the end of five years' service. '. . . I certainly have not felt pleased with this interference with my plans,' he wrote, 'but though painful it is doubtless one of those things which shall work for my good. . . . Satan [Methodists] is striving to introduce grievous errors amongst two or three of my distant congregations and were I to leave 'tis impossible to say how many might be led away. . . .' Ellen went in his stead, taking with her the two-year-old Featherston and leaving baby Britton with his father. They sailed on the *Great Western*, 'the Captain of which,' wrote Featherstone, 'is an old friend. I accompanied her so far as New York, it being next to an impossibility for a lady to travel through that country of rogues & thieves without being robbed. . . .'

Featherstone had conceived the plan (approved by Bishop Strachan) of personally training young men for the Church as the only guarantee of eventual assistance in his labour. He wrote to Proctor (Nov. 14, 1840), 'Though Mrs. Osler is away I have no lack of company. . . . Three gents are now with me preparing for the Ministry, one of whom is married and his wife acts as housekeeper. The other two are sons of Military officers, fine gentlemanly young men and decidedly pious. 'Tis now upwards of two years since I was first promised two clergymen to assist me but the promise remains unfulfilled. Indeed the Bishop has not the men to send. . . .

'. . . The following is the plan I pursue with regards to them. At 6 A.M. they meet in my study for Scripture reading. This engages them until ½ past 7 when we breakfast. Afterwards they study . . . until evening. . . . We take an early tea after which I give them three hours to correct their exercises, hear them read &c. By this means none of my public duties [is] neglected as I attend to [the students] when my outdoor . . . work is done. . . . On Sunday I send out two of them to . . . different outposts to read prayers, superintend the Sunday Schools and visit the sick. . . . One I keep home to assist me in my central Sunday School. . . .'

Ellen's only surviving letters from England were written to Mr. and Mrs. Proctor, neither of whom she had met. The letters to Mr. Proctor deal principally with missionary matters, raising money etc. To Mrs. Proctor she wrote, '. . . The happiness I experience in being permitted to enjoy the society of beloved friends in dear England after an absence of three years and a half is not trifling, yet to be separated from one of the best husbands and a darling child is a severe trial. . . .

'During my sojourn in a strange land and shut out from all congenial society, I can truly say that the Lord hath been my helper, continually suiting his mercies to my necessities. . . . My beloved partner too is privileged to see the Lord's work prospering in his hand and that, of course, would more than recompense [for] all toil and deprivation. . . .

'The latter end of next month I expect to be confined, and as soon after . . . as I can safely travel with a young infant, I [go] to see some . . . friends in Birmingham and then prepare to cross the Atlantic in the Gt. Western the early part of June. . . . I look forward with pleasure to meeting all my little wild-irish scholars in the bush. . . .'

On March 18, 1841, Ellen Mary, her third child and first daughter, was born in Falmouth. Shortly before the event Featherstone wrote to his mother:

March 9, 1841.

'I know you will feel it much to part with . . . Ellen and my boy but . . . we may yet all return and live in England. God who led me here may think good to bring me back. . . . [Do] not strive to keep Ellen longer than is absolutely necessary. I need her with me, for indeed I have had a comfortless winter without her. I cannot help feeling anxious. . . . Before this I

The Parsonage at Tecumseth

trust her confinement is over. About the child I care nothing so that she is safe and well. . . .' Here Featherstone speaks with the urgency of love. It is no exaggeration to say that he was lost without her.

For some months Featherstone had been encouraging a younger brother to come to Canada and train with him for the ministry. Henry had no special 'call' but prospects in Falmouth looked bleak and he decided in favour of the new world.

F. Osler to his mother:

Tecumseth, April 8, 1841.

'. . . I am glad Henry has decided on accepting my offer. There is an opening for much usefulness . . . with a certain comfortable income. [And] is it not better that he should be labouring as a Minister of Xt than failing or struggling for a subsistence in business ? Your mind will be far easier when he is with me. . . . It will be no small advantage to him that my two present students are very pious gentlemanly young men. . . . Let him bring a . . . stock of good clothes with him and none of his old clothes because here he will always have to appear as a gentleman and be dressed as one. He had better bring a dressing gown which he might wear in the house and about the grounds. For my sake as well as his own he must be particular. . . .'

Where two had left for England, four would return to the Tecumseth parsonage: Ellen, Featherston, Henry and the new baby. 'The Master', his three 'young gents' (one with wife), and two servant girls would make a total of eleven inhabitants under one modest roof. Featherstone set to work.

'I am busy . . . getting materials ready for enlarging the

Parsonage and making it in every respect a . . . comfortable dwelling house as well as a tolerably commodious one. Besides the bedrooms there will be a drawing room 23 ft. long, study 16 ft. and dining room 16 ft. . . . . Adjoining our bedroom there will be a little room with a door also opening into it from the nursery in which there will be a Bath and within conveniences for the female part of the household.

'. . . I must expect a Babel sometimes with the two boys and my E's addition. . . . To guard against it in some degree I have arranged to have the nursery at one end of the house and my study at the other but I am afraid my case is hopeless as the young urchins are sure to find me out. B.B. is very persevering and will stand kicking at the door and calling Papa Papa until the door is opened and will fight lustily with anyone who attempts to take him away. He is a far more tractable child naturally than Featherston though he can show that he partakes of his father's natural temper. . . .'

The travellers returned and Featherstone relaxed, his guiding light once more restored to him. 'God graciously makes us of one mind,' he wrote to his mother. Henry, his temperament easier in every respect than that of his elder brother, became a Canadian almost overnight. In his first letter home he wrote, 'I desire to be thankful to GOD I enjoy good health and like the woods better & better. . . .' A year later he had not changed his views. 'For some things I should certainly prefer England and should like, after the course of years to visit you, but not to live continually. . . . Last week Fed bought a carriage to carry four, . . . and a nice pair of bay horses. You will begin to think we are quite high folks here—whether high or not . . . we are very comfortable. Truly the lines have fallen to us in pleasant places & we have a goodly heritage . . . for our bread is given us and our water sure. . . .'

As Edward had impressed on Featherstone the importance of not mixing with one's inferiors, so Featherstone trained his cheerful brother, for Henry wrote, '. . . there are very many in England with whom at one time I was intimate who now I should consider beneath me so far as associating with them was concerned. . . .'

Featherstone's affection for Henry was diluted by a fair portion of condescension which he made no effort to conceal in letters to his mother. 'As I get my present students ordained and stationed they will relieve me of much labour and anxiety. Henry, as I have mentioned before, I hope to station near me. He is much of Saml's disposition in very many points but . . . is doing far better than I had anticipated. . . . He is teachable and tractable and anxious to do anything to please E[llen] or myself, and in the Chapel Sunday School is very useful. . . . He is regularly inducted into the office of head gardener . . . [and] I think it likely, if spared, he will make a useful and, where I purpose placing him, a popular clergyman. The people feel indebted to me for what I have voluntarily done for them, of which Henry, as my brother, will reap the benefit. . . .'

Featherstone must be cock of the walk and his curates, though he needed their help, might end by being competitors. In another letter to his mother, written a year later, he stressed the frailties of others only to prove his own.

Aug. 8th, 1842.

'Henry is deficient in judgement—well intentioned and zealous, he needs a guiding hand. He is also too self important, especially when carrying on any of the Sunday Schools *out of my sight*, but on the whole he is greatly improved. Mr. Bourne [a new assistant] is at length arrived and I am much disappointed in him. He is very forward, self sufficient and *very* deficient. I have rarely met with one on better terms with himself. . . . The first lesson he must learn is that he is ignorant. I trust he will improve. . . .' (Mr. Bourne was hardly more popular with Henry; '. . . He is much too fine a lady to please me . . . , a *"domesticated young man"* who can hem muslin, wash the tea things etc.')

'. . . . My duties lately have been very heavy and . . . I suffer much from fatigue. Sometimes I wish I could obtain a little rest but see no prospect of it until, through the merits of our Saviour, I hope to enjoy that rest which remaineth for the people of God. . . .

'. . . I must hasten now to Lloydtown that for an hour before service I may give directions and draw out plans for the carpenters.'

Henry was equally frank when he described his nephews to their Aunt Lizzie: 'Featherston [aged almost five] is to all intents & purposes the best of the bunch. He was a tartar but there is a decided improvement. . . . I wish I could say so much for Britton Bath [aged 3]. He is a regular bouncing fellow and not the most agreeable child. I hope however he will "improve with age". . . . They are all of them *Oslers* and have their tempers as well as the rest. . . .'

In another letter he reversed his opinion. 'Little Britton is a *very* nice child worth a dozen Featherstons in *every* respect. . . .'

Lloydtown was the stronghold of the Methodists, its inhabitants supporters of William Lyon Mackenzie 'who, to further his rebellious designs, circulated very freely Tom Paine's works'. 'It appeared to me,' Featherstone wrote to Proctor, '. . . a hopeless place and yet [I] could not bear the idea that a populous village . . . should, without an effort, be resigned to the enemy. . . . Any direct attempt to benefit them would be received with suspicion and it seemed necessary to use a little wisdom of the serpent which God has certainly blessed.

'I first established a preaching station and a good Sunday School a few miles from the village. . . . This I left to silently work for some time and then established another station in another quarter of the Village . . . [it] prospered and the congregation [was] large & grateful. . . . These and many other little expedients I adopted that they might observe, rather by deeds than words, that I was anxious to do good unto all men. I permitted . . . this to work together quietly until the early part of this year. . . . I then said we must erect a church and I would call on the different families for subscriptions. . . . We obtained . . . the amount of £120 which soon increased to £200. . . .

'The church is to be 50 ft. long by 30 wide and will be a very pretty building when finished. Everything is going on well notwithstanding that the Methodists have been doing all in their power to oppose me. . . . If the Bp will give me a Clergyman to station there . . . , one who will faithfully preach Xt Crucified, that hitherto very bad part of the province will, I am persuaded, be morally revolutionized.'

The Bishop elected Henry to head the revolution.

After being ordained in 1844 Henry married Harriet Parsons and the newly-weds moved to Lloydtown, nine miles distant from the Tecumseth parsonage. The cloth never sub-

dued Henry's natural jollity and he performed his parish duties
with exceptional zeal. After thirty-two years at Lloydtown he
became Rector of York Mills, Canon of St. Alban's Cathedral,
Toronto, and Rural Dean of York. How Featherstone, who
did not become a Canon until 1881, felt when he found himself
outstripped by one 'deficient in judgement' can only be
guessed.

Hector Charlesworth wrote in *Candid Chronicles* '. . . I . . .
knew very well the late Canon Henry Bath Osler of York
Mills, who prepared me for confirmation, and who was as
devoted and indefatigable a country parson as ever lived,
driving many miles to offer consolation at sick beds and to
bury the dead,—a bright cheery little man who literally
diffused human kindness.'

Featherstone had more than a tendency to feel misunderstood. While in the navy his Falmouth parents had never fully
grasped the importance of his position. In 1842, he still had to
bring it to his mother's attention.

'. . . I don't think . . . the ideas of those at home are exactly
correct with regard to Canada. It is now very little different
from the country parts of England in so far as the people are
concerned, and as much or more regard is necessary to appearance.'

Nor did he feel that he received full justice from his Bishop
though this same Bishop had written to the Missionary Society
in 1840: 'The Rev. F. L. Osler is indeed a treasure, indefatigable in his labours and journeys, judicious in his arrangements,
frank, kind & conciliating in his manner. He has acquired a
most beneficial influence over the population of an extensive
section of the province. . . .'

F. L. Osler to Proctor:

April, 1842.

'Had I a little assistance the whole of the inhabitants of an immense district might be attached to the church but the Bishop [Strachan], I believe, seems to think I can do everything by myself. . . . And now, when I depended on his Lordship's promise that Mr. Darling, one of my students who DV will be ordained next month, should be appointed to assist me in the more backward Townships, the Bishop writes to say that he is . . . borrowing Mr. Darling for a few months to enable Mr. Grasset to proceed to Cambridge to take his Master's degree. I much wish to visit England for the same purpose . . . but so urgent is the necessity for . . . a Clergyman in the . . . backward Townships that I felt I dared not keep Mr. D back . . . on any personal consideration. You may therefore suppose how much annoyed and grieved I felt and still feel—sinking under the pressure of my duties, help long promised . . . plenty of fair speeches and professions of regard—but I like deeds not words. I wrote to the Bishop rather a strong letter . . . which seems to have greatly offended him so I must write to say that not the slightest offence or disrespect was meant. . . .

'. . . I have already during this present year expended upon my mission £100 from my private means which is . . . more than I can well afford. . . . I purpose DV remaining here until April 1843 when I hope to visit England, and certainly unless the Bishop treats me with a little more consideration . . ., 'tis not likely I will return to Canada. . . .

'. . . I am truly rejoiced to hear that so many of our English bishops have expressed themselves . . . against the Oxford

Tract. The Bishop of Toronto is rather in favour of them. . . .'
Featherstone, strongly protestant, was genuinely scandalized
by the 'Tracts for the Times' issued by members of the
Oxford Movement.

Keble, Pusey and Newman, instigators and leaders of this
renaissance of mediaeval ideas and doctrines, almost caused a
civil war within the Church.

To the evangelicals it was a popish plot but Strachan and his
prime favourite and successor, Bethune, were no evangelicals.
They relished the unexpected right to indulge in a little priestly
pomp and circumstance.

Pusey's name became a synonym for extreme forms of
ritualism, though actually it was the followers of Pusey rather
than Pusey himself who swung the censer.

Bishop Strachan sent back Mr. Darling. Featherstone was
soothed but not completely softened. 'I should do better,' he
wrote, 'if I had Bishop Mountain of Montreal to deal with
[rather] than the Bp of Toronto. The latter is *ultra* high Church
and most anxious for the respectability of the Church . . . , the
former is the Xtian Bishop one can look up to as a Father and
love. . . .'

The Sunday school 'treat' was an annual and important
event. 'It was indeed a busy time for Ellen,' Henry wrote to
his mother. 'We used . . . a barrel & half of flour & there were
full 300 rhubarb pasties made, all of which with the exception
of a single cake was used. . . . On Tuesday evening we began
to form the booth and contrived to finish, putting the stakes
and plates in. Early on Wednesday morning Thos. Duke & I
took our axes and went into the bush to cut balsams & hem-
locks to cover it. . . . The next morning . . . we hoisted the only

flag we have, together with the motto . . . "Glory to God in
the Highest, on earth peace & good will toward men". . .
After all was finished [I] dressed and having taken a hasty lunch
hastened to the chapel to see the children were in their places. . . .
The chapel was crammed inside & crowded outside. According
to Fed's account there were between 900 and 1000 persons.
After a very appropriate sermon the children were formed in a
semicircle on the lawn & examined. [They] then had tea &
after they had finished their parents or anyone who felt disposed
sat down. . . . You perhaps ask how we managed to get tea for
& wait on so many. . . . In the first place we had two or three
large iron sugar pans (such as are used for boiling the sap in the
sugar season). Into those were put so much tea. . . . Then we
got tin cans & dipped it out . . . & whenever we found a cup
empty we filled it. The young ladies from Thornhill were
valuable assistants, for they stood ready with milk & sugar. . . .
The dismissal was sung & all left looking as if nothing but
happiness filled their hearts. GOD grant that many who came
only for *pleasure* may have returned to pray !'

Featherstone adds, 'I gave rewards to . . . 50 of the children
of the central and nearer schools and 16 to the Lloydtown
schools—It was rather an expensive day. But yet it was
money well laid out.'

The plenty in their larder had increased since its contents
had been listed in a letter to Francis Proctor two years before.
One senses the feeling of security the family derived from such
a noble stock of food. 'Four large hogs have just been salted
and also a quantity of beef. There is now hanging up in the
larder 13 fowls, 3 geese, a turkey [and] some pigeons. . . . Next
week I propose having four sheep killed. Yesterday I purchased

wheat enough to make a ton of flour and am about to purchase as much more. . . .'

Ellen was no doubt dairy maid and cook as well as seamstress for her large household, the Irish girls being fit only for un-skilled labour. Featherstone's 'school for sucking parsons', as it was later referred to by his son Edmund, relieved him of a portion of his work but added a considerable load to Ellen's.

Though bountifully provided with food they were many miles from a good shopping district and the arrival of a 'box from England' created excitement equal almost to the stir of Christmas day.

'You would like doubtless to have been here,' Ellen wrote in a letter of rather dubious thanks to her mother-in-law, 'when we opened the box but . . . I will try to make the scene plain to your imagination. Dear Fed had to be away that afternoon . . . so to me half the pleasure of unpacking was lost, and but that Henry was a party largely concerned I should have reserved it till his return. . . . The boys had watched many waggons up the hill, often running in to [tell] me "Now Mama, Mr. B. is coming with the sugar plums and our books". . . . When Mr. B. actually came . . . they were almost crazy with joy . . . and could scarcely wait for the cording to be removed. I believe they fancied the box filled with *their* books and *their* sugar plums. We were not any time finding the *mixed pickle*, both the contents of which proved very nice. The little animals each had one . . . and away they ran with a paper full to distribute in the kitchen. A tooth-powder box with *Garden Seeds* written on the outside was uppermost; it was all in a syrup and tasted a *little* of ginger but *strongly* of the box—what was it? Next came my poplin dress which alas! is lamentably spotted. All smelt very strongly of damp . . . but fortunately nothing else was [spoiled] but the gloves. . . . Nevertheless, dear Hetta, I do not thank you the less for the pair . . . [though] they are so very small that even if they had been otherwise wearable they would have been useless. . . .' Fortunately there follows a long list of things that met with Ellen's approval; 'a little bag' which she would enjoy because 'we are not altogether out of the world here in the Bush'. A pair of trousers for Featherstone 'were too tight by far' but 'the mackintosh capes seem good ones, and Fed's has already proved friendly in that it saved him a drenching the Saturday after he had it. . . . I can't say I admire the plaid dress or the collars. . . . I remember saying to Charlotte I did not want *expensive* collars but I said that, knowing that you ladies are sometimes rather *ex* in those things [and] feared you might be sending *Handsome pelmines*. And I wanted only indoor collars, but however they'll do very well, and I've many thanks to send all of you for the trouble taken. . . .'

This qualified appreciation is unlike Ellen but she was pregnant again, the fourth time in her five strenuous years of married life. An undertone of sadness at the end of the letter is heightened by the half wry, half whimsical, reference to a nursery rhyme.

'. . . I assure you I am not anticipating the event with pleasure—it is a sad time of the year—and 3 young gents in the house at such a time is not over agreable. . . . I am getting quite an old woman now—the idea of *four*, at one time would have startled me, now *half a score* will not surprise me or trouble more than two—I learn a lesson from the wren and the dove: "Coo coo, says the dove, what shall I do? for I have got *two*! Twit, twit, said the wren, I have got *ten* and shall bring them up like gentlemen."'

The sun never shone on Edward. He was born on Nov. 20, 1842, 'a sad time of the year' that seemed to cling to him. But Ellen's spirits had revived when she wrote to her sister-in-law Lizzie:

Tecumseth, Dec. 1842.

'With baby on my lap I make the attempt to write one line on the envelope just to tell you how it fares with us. I have been confined 3 weeks and this morning for the first time made my appearance at the breakfast table, having like a good nurse, washed and dressed my bantling; This will tell you that I am going on very well indeed. I have much reason to be . . . thankful to the Father of all our mercies for He has dealt very graciously with me. . . .

'Time is drawing so near for dear Fed to leave that my heart quite sinks to think of it. You will soon have him with you if he is spared. Our boys are very well and so is the little English girl. [She] has quite got over her last teething attack . . . is full of spirits and on the whole a dear good child but has temper to be kept under. If anything offend My Lady her shoulders are up and she turns away in such a tiff that it is quite absurdly ridiculous. . . .

'And now dear Lizzie, good bye. My little fellow is grunting for me and the young ones in the next room are playing such a bobbery that I know not what I write.'

Featherstone was going home at last. Ellen had now to face six months' separation from 'the best of husbands' and lonely responsibility for a large household.

Featherstone left for England early in April, 1843, '. . . completely broken in health with a bad cough and an abscess in the
back, caused by continuous riding on horseback. . . .' His
parishioners gave him a fine send-off, '. . . Great was my
surprise on reaching the village of Bond Head to find the whole
place crowded with sleighs and wagons filled with people
determined to accompany me for part of the journey. In all,
there were 110 vehicles . . . forming the cavalcade. After going
as far as Holland Landing, a distance of ten miles, I insisted
upon their not going farther, and stopping at the cross-roads
each . . . bid me good-bye and good-speed. . . .'

Six years earlier the trip from Falmouth to Quebec had taken
seven weeks. On the return voyage Featherstone reached
England ten days after he left New York.

In letters to Ellen he showed his unabashed delight at the
high company in which he moved but a few paragraphs from
a later memoir give the necessary facts: '. . . My reception in
London was flattering. My old and kind friend, the Earl of
Galloway, invited some leading noblemen and clergymen to
meet me at his house, and after dinner there was a grand
reception. Fully three hundred were present to bid me welcome
home, and to hear what I had to tell them respecting Canada,
its conditions and its wants.

'The Society for Christian Knowledge voted books to the
value of £84, being at the rate of £3 worth . . . to [each] of
twenty eight Sunday schools, and several of the nobility of
London, headed by the Marquis of Cholmondeley, gave me
£500 to spend as I might deem best. Sir Robert Inglis kindly
invited me to meet at breakfast several leading members of
Parliament. Among the guests was Baron de Bunsen, Prussian

Ambassador, with whom I had a long and interesting conversation.

'As soon as my health was sufficiently established, I preached in London the annual sermon of the Society and afterwards spent six weeks in Ireland advocating its cause. The remainder of my time I spent happily at home [Falmouth] and late in the autumn, recruited in health, I returned to Canada, happy to find that during my absence everything had gone on well and prosperously. . . .'

Featherstone's letters to Ellen show the soft underside of this sturdy character.

In one he makes a wish that was not destined to be fulfilled—
'. . . Mr. R—— is a fat good humoured looking man and Mrs. R—— is rather taller than yourself and, as I do not wish to see you again, my precious E, with a very large stomach. . . .'
Featherstone was a farmer as well as a clergyman and he hopes
'. . . the garden is now put to rights and the potatoes planted— tell James to be sure to go round frequently to see that the fences are all right and about once a fortnight to turn the wheat and oats by emptying it out of the bins upon the coach house floor—also that the young apple trees are taken care of and the . . . acacias in the upper field kept weeded. . . .'

He closes with '. . . right glad I will be, my precious Ellen, again to be restored to you. . . . I have enclosed two or three pansies from Ireland. Either let the children have one each or keep them yourself, my own dear Ellen. . . .'

Another letter begins, 'My much loved Ellen, Before retiring to bed I sit down to commence a letter to you who are in my thoughts the first thing in the morning and the last at night. The longer I am separated from you the more you seem to twine round my heart. . . .' And in another, '. . . I long to have the dear boys hanging about me. Tell them Papa is continually thinking about them and hopes they are good. . . . I do trust that, as you say, we shall never again be separated till death do us part.'

Few of Ellen's letters dated before 1854, when the elder boys left home for boarding-school, survive, but two, written to Featherstone during his six months in England and Ireland, reveal the wife as well as the mother. Ellen's duties were many, her working hours long and time a precious commodity not to be wasted on punctuation. A dash here, a comma there, sufficed. One pictures her writing at top speed, knowing she has minutes, not hours, before the inevitable interruption. The letters retain her breathlessness.

June 13, 1843.

'I fear I have not time to give my own dearest Fed a long letter this post [twenty-three hundred words] at first I thought I had the week before me but it will not do to risk it beyond Thursday and this is Tuesday evening, you are aware that I am nurse in the true sense of the word and now dear Eddy is so lively and sleeps so little by day and moreover is so heavy that my arms ache and I am literally tired towards night . . . — yesterday I was busy as I could be all the morning, dusting and putting to rights with him in my arms. . . .' In an earlier letter she had reported to Featherstone that a certain McMann 'had been killed by a waggon going over him'—but 'it was a Papist in his neighbourhood' with a similar name and the inference is that his adherence to Rome diminished the tragedy. 'Not one individual has paid in any money [lent by Featherstone to needy parishioners] nor do I see how they can . . . everyone says *the times will be very bad*. Our little flock are all pretty well, I vaccinated E[llen] M[ary] again and she is poorly with it— the dear boys were so delighted with [your] nice little notes F[eatherston] was in ectasies, and B.B.'s quiet joy was not less evident. . . . The girls [domestics] and James [handyman] go on very good-humouredly but they none of them will be ill from overworking. . . .'

In one sentence Ellen answers the question 'How does your garden grow?'

'It is a backward spring but the mushrooms and the *weeds* . . . are very thick—we shall have no melons I am sorry to say, in the first place the hot bed did not heat properly, and the heavy frosts we had cut off the two or three plants that came up al- though they had been covered with the exception of one night that we did not think frosty—all the Indian corn is cut off and we put in oats today—the Egyptian wheat we have near the fence by the clover and it looks very well . . . the acasias have been weeded all the young trees are doing well, we have an abundance of currants and the gooseberries look remarkably fine. . . .'

Letters do not divulge who put the pressure on Ellen's uncle- by-marriage, Captain Britton, whose house had been her home for many years. 'I am not sorry,' wrote Ellen, 'that at last there is a satisfactory will made by the old gentleman—but I know him so well that I do not place the least dependance on him, what he was frightened into, he can as easily be frightened out of—Wills are easily altered, easily destroyed, nor would he scruple to do either if he was in the least annoyed—however for the present it stands good and it may be a benefit to our dear little ones, who I most sincerely hope will never have a

The Church at Tecumseth

large portion of this worlds wealth without a heart to spend it in the service of God.' Captain Britton undoubtedly became 'annoyed' as there is no record of the Oslers inheriting anything from England.

'I should like to be with you,' the letter continues, 'but I know that dear Mother and the girls will do all for you that I could in the way of attention to your wants and when you get not less than a Marchioness to take care of you I need be under no apprehension of your being slighted when away from home. ... After all the luxuries of English nobility how will you be able to return to your homely cottage in the far backwoods of Canada? I hope you will not lose all relish for a country life.'

One letter ends:

'I have not to complain of being ... solitary, but when you are from me I do feel desolate and think what a poor wretched creature I should be if God were to remove you altogether'; another, 'I am loth to say goodbye even by letter to my dear Fed, but must do so, praying always ... that God may cause His face to shine upon you. ... You have need to keep yourself humble amidst all the kindness shewn you for it is a more trying season than the day of adversity. I long to see you once more and humbly trust that God will spare us to meet. ... Believe me, my own dearest husband, to be ever your most affectionate wife

'Ellen Osler.'

Featherstone was welcomed home at the Holland Landing cross-roads by the same wagon-loads of people who, six months earlier, had wished him good-speed.

F. Osler to Proctor:

Oct. 2, 1843.

'. . . . Arriving at the Parsonage the people drew up on the lawn and standing on the verandah I addressed them. After returning thanks . . . and giving three hearty cheers for their Minister they departed. Yesterday I preached in West Gwillimbury church to an overflowing congregation from Gal. vi. 14—God forbid that I should glory etc. . . . The Methodists, my great opponents had been endeavouring to persuade my people, first that I would not return to them and then that I had become a decided Puseyite. Some of my people have died during my absence and the settlement of their temporal affairs in a great measure devolves on me.'

Pusey had recently preached his famous sermon 'The Holy Eucharist, a Comfort to the Penitent' and was barred from the pulpit for two years. The ensuing publicity sold 1,800 copies of the condemned sermon.

Featherstone expressed his anxiety in regard to '. . . a Newspaper which is published here called "The Church". Though not advocating the errors of the Oxford heresy, [it] continually excuses them and sets forth the Church instead of Xt set forth by the Church. The Editor is a Clergyman named Bethune, who like the Bishop with whom he is an especial favourite is ultra high Church. The paper has done much mischief but I hope there will be a change soon else there will be a split. . . .' Bethune succeeded Strachan as Bishop of Toronto.

A parishioner wrote:

'. . . When in Toronto this winter I was told by one who . . . goes there, that there was a day given out in Trinity Church to be kept for the Virgin Mary and that it was kept in the Cathedral also. . . . ' The letter ends, 'I hope soon to see your Reverence and have your pleasing company for one night and believe me to be Revd. Sir your affectionate friend until death when we shall all pay our vows. Then your Reverence I hope will receive a bright Crown.

'Ann McMannus.'

CHAPTER SIX

A New Generation

AND SO the busy years passed, churches and children multiplying and the bush being driven farther and farther north by the fat new farmland.

In 1845 Ellen bore her fifth child and fourth son, Edmund Boyd; two years later twins, Charlotte and Francis (Frank). Their mother blamed the subsequent troubles of the latter on her limited supply of milk. While Charlotte had enjoyed the home brand Frank had been put out to nurse with a coarse Irish-woman. William, the youngest son, was born on July 12, 1849, and Henrietta, who died in her third year, in 1851. Ellen was thirty-two years old when Featherston was born, forty-five when she produced her last child.

Featherstone had intended christening William, Walter Farquar, after one of his patrons, but the date of his birth decided his name. Every year on July 12 the Orangemen of the district gathered at the Corners for their annual fête. From here they marched to the steps of the parsonage, singing 'Teeter Tawter Holy Water', bodies decked with sashes and yellow lilies, their leader on a fine white horse. When Featherstone came out to greet them, holding the new baby in his arms, the crowd cried 'William' (Prince of Orange) and the name stuck. On subsequent birthdays the child was suitably dressed for his part in orange and blue and held up on the verandah railing to receive the cheers of his subjects. It was many years before he and his brothers and sisters realized the parade was not conducted solely in his honour.

The days of expansion were over, both in the parish and on the home front. It was a question now of consolidation.

Featherstone's work for God sometimes had the happy knack of fitting in with personal or domestic needs. By training men for the Church he was relieved of distant parishes. His interest in education came at a suitable moment—when his boys were in need of it.

He wrote to his mother on March 3rd, 1851, ' . . . Lately I have been much occupied in procuring an endowment for a Grammar School in this neighbourhood of about £75 per ann. Having accomplished this, a suitable school house is to be erected by private subscription. . . . In July or August next DV I hope to have a superior school in operation within a mile of the Parsonage. This will be a great matter for Ellen's troop of boys for I could not afford to send them all to . . . boarding school and have not time to attend to their education at home. I . . . hope my late assistant will take the head Mastership of the School and at the same time act as my Curate on Sundays which will enable me to supply some places with Sunday services which now I can only visit on week days. God has permitted me to see the accomplishment of more than my most sanguine hopes had anticipated and now that I am unable to travel much, at least compared with what I formerly did, I do thank God . . . for giving me strength when it was . . . needed. . . .

'. . . We have every reasonable temporal comfort we could desire . . . we live within our means and have something to give to the poor. My only anxiety in money matters is that when God may be pleased to take me, Ellen & her large family may have some provision. I am very thankful I purchased the farm. It is of material assistance, in fact supplies us with provisions and some to give away. We have fuel enough to supply two households . . . and the bees give us honey for ourselves and neighbours. . . . Ellen is a capital hand at giving and I rejoice at it. I leave her to tell you about the children. They are neither very good or very bad. One thing they can do well is speedily make a loaf disappear and a sheep lasts but a short time. I often think, since Ellen has proved such a breeder, what a mercy it was we did not remain in England, and yet there is no place like home. . . . '

While Featherstone was trying to organize an elementary school in the neighbourhood, he was faced with the emergency of Featherston and Britton, now thirteen and eleven years old. The Barrie grammar school, about twenty miles north of Bond Head, offered a solution. There they boarded for a year or two until Mr. Hill, an ex-curate of their father's, opened a school near Bradford.

In *Some Reminiscences of a Modern Do-the-Boys School*, the late Mr. Elmes Henderson described this odd seat of learning. Featherstone and Britton were among his fellow-students during the school year, 1853-4.

'Mr. Hill was a tall, handsome man with a cultivated voice, fresh complexion and fine bearing, quite an ideal English parson . . . the incumbent of the Church at Middleton, with charge also of a small station at Coulson's Corners, a little north of Bradford. [He] had a good parsonage house with fifty acres of Glebe land attached. . . .

'. . . Mrs. Hill was not so satisfactory, a large boned woman with a stoop and a somewhat cold and forbidding air. . . . I think none of the boys became attached to her or appealed to her in any of their youthful difficulties. . . . She gave us the impression of not being Mr. Hill's social equal and we gathered that his marriage was the cause of his immigrating to a new country. . . .

'Mr. Hill was the only teacher . . . [and his] duties as a clergyman in a large district entailed frequent absences from home. When the boys were left to their own devices . . . they naturally larked about and the school-room saw nothing of them and lessons were neglected.

'. . . Mrs. Hill was not, to say the least, a bountiful provider. . . . Our meals were meagre—no meat or butter for breakfast—porridge and milk only; for dinner, meat and potatoes—no second helpings, and frequently no puddings. . . . Our evening meal consisted of bread and butter with tea. . . . Mrs. Hill . . . went round putting on each boy's plate one piece only. . . .'

Whenever Mr. Hill needed extra hands for outdoor work he dismissed school and the boys helped in building fences, chopping wood and even killing and cutting up a cow or a pig for Mrs. Hill's larder.

From Mr. Henderson's report the boys were happy enough. They objected to the lack of food but not to the lack of book learning. He described Britton Osler as 'a very enterprising boy [who] conceived the idea of making some profit out of our general hungry state. There being no shop nearer than Bradford, three miles away, Britton once a week, on allowance day, opened a shop in the schoolroom. . . . He had a small cupboard in a corner with shelves filled with bread, cakes, sugar sticks, molasses and other sweets, and our weeks' allowances were soon spent—much to the satisfaction of the shop-keeper and his young customers.'

In October, 1854, Britton, in a letter to his brother, Feather-ston, who had since left school to study law in Barrie, gave a spirited account of school doings. The boys had raided a neighbouring farmer's orchard. The consequences were grave.

. . . When Hill Esq. came home . . . he would not give us any tea; next morning no breakfast and we were not to have had any dinner only Mama . . . came down—lucky [she] did for the boys were going to rebel at two o'clock. . . .
On Friday last Diny and I put some gun powder in Small's pipe and it blew up and sent the pieces all about, singed his eyelashes and set him crying. He threw a stick at Diny for doing it. Diny got up and gave him an awful licking. Miss Small came up to put Barclay's trunks to rights and to comb the bugs out of his head. . . .
Hoping you are quite well I remain your affec. brother,
                                        Britton Bath Osler.

P.S. I have to survey village lots for Robinson to-morrow or the next day.

This seems to have ended Britton's career at Mr. Hill's and for the next few years he attended the new grammar school in the vicinity of Bond Head whenever he could be spared from the family fields.

On October 30, 1854, he wrote from Tecumseth Parsonage to Featherston in Barrie.

. . . We have all the potatoes up, of which I dug half. We were three or four days at them. Sam [hired man] and I cleaned up fifty bushels of wheat this morning, twice through, which

Sam is going to take to the Landing tomorrow. He got $64.75 or £17.3.9 for a load he took out last week and it is higher now. We will finish the turnips in another day. . . . You have got out of this delightful work, slick what they call. . . .

Ned Battens shot a deer the morning the snow was on the ground, and shot at a bear, which latter mentioned animal seems to be very thick about here.

We have miss Skinshin [domestic] here now who is even worse if possible than Crather Bitch & Co. She is an awful thief and we have to watch her as a cat doeth a mouse. However Papa hired a first rate girl just out from Ireland to come here on Thursday and then this wee hussy will be off. . . .

Margaret MacCoy thought fit to elope with a young man . . . who had no intention of marrying her but Sam and I caught them, Sam having his bulldog with him (and Papa being at Toronto). We found them at Joe MacGowan's about ten o'clock. Sam, after . . . a raving and scolding and showing the mouth of his bulldog, scared Osborne so that he got a license and in about two hours I had the pleasure of seeing Mr. Swazee marry them. She is about fifteen. He is an awful drunkard.

. . . We have a new master at the grammar school . . . , a thorough Yankee but I believe a good scholar. . . . He is a black looking brute, as cross as X and having as beard, a stachios [mustache].

I remain your affec. brother,
Britton Bath Osler.

P.S. Charlotte had the top of her finger chopped off the other day by Master William with an axe. It is healing as well as can be expected. . . .

William was five years old and cutting faggots for the stove when Charlotte, seven, determined to tease him, kept putting her finger on the spot he was about to hit with his little axe. Finally William said, 'I'll count three. If you don't take it off, I'll chop it off.' And chop it off he did.

Ellen was away from home at the time. She had been ill and had gone to stay, first with the Henry Oslers at Thornhill, then with friends in Toronto.

In one of her rare moments of discouragement she wrote to her son Featherston (Nov. 13, 1854), '. . . Indeed the five weeks that I was from home was a time of much weakness and pain. There were seasons when I could not help thinking my race was almost run. . . . Since my return . . . I have gained strength slowly and am better now. . . .' The letter continues cheerfully, 'Sam has left us more than a week ago and Britty is head man . . . clearing the barn field ready for ploughing, cutting up all the wood that was in the yard ready for the saw. . . . He acted the good housekeeper . . . while I was away, making pies, cakes etc., with great skill, [and he] attended very nicely to the boys' lessons. Really I do trust that my two elder boys are growing up steady youths and will not let the hopes of their parents be disappointed. . . .'

Ellen had trouble to come with other sons but little to complain of in Featherston and Britton. Featherston worked industriously in a law firm in Barrie. He had already acquired the habit of intensive reading which later produced the scholarly judge. Britton, at fifteen, was capable as a man, excelled at books when the opportunity offered, could run a farm or cook a meal. As for Edward and Edmund, they 'must get on as well as they can, a little at the books and a little at outdoor work . . .'.

Ellen to Featherston:

Parsonage, Tecumseth, April 17, 1855.

'. . . Did you feel the storm yesterday morning? With us it was fearful . . . , the house was in such a state of confusion as I hope never to witness again. The hail shattered our windows wholesale. . . . Hail stones and broken glass were scattered all over the rooms, even on the beds. The young ones screamed, the girls were terrified, indeed it was . . . alarming. It was a long day's work for Britty, with Papa's help between services . . . , to glaze all the windows. . . .'

The Osler boys grew up, lords of their environment. Heat, food and shelter were home-grown, home-made elements. They cut the wood for the stoves which they themselves had set up and piped in readiness for winter; they raised and killed the sheep and pigs they subsequently devoured; they were carpenters and window glazers; at home on a horse or driving a team. And still they had time for sport: shooting, fishing, skating, swimming in the pond at the foot of the hill—all these things they mentioned in their letters and in later tales to their grandchildren.

Though work was expected of each and every member of the family, Ellen and Featherstone were not the rigid disciplinarians common to their time. '. . . Never was there a greater mistake than the idea that he [Featherstone] is a Tartar to the children. Aunt [Ellen] holds the reins far tighter than he does, and she never checks without absolute need': this was the opinion of their niece, Jennette Osler, in 1866.

But they were many, and endowed with extra vitality, a menace to at least one neighbour, a woman who would not allow her children to start for school until the Osler troop had passed the house.

Though spared the rod they were, as one of them later remarked, exposed to 'solid and indestructible blocks of divinity'. The Parsonage bookshelves sagged with theological tomes: Hooker's *Ecclesiastical Polity*, Bishop Burnet's *Lives*, Bunyan's *Pilgrim's Progress* and many others. The secular shelves held Locke, Addison, Macaulay, an early Tennyson, Hone's *Everyday Book* and one or two pious novels that had crossed the sea in missionary boxes, gifts of the S.P.G., and, to their pride, the works of their English Uncle Edward. Sunday reading was confined to the theological shelves. Morning and evening prayers, regular church-going, and constant, if gentle, reminders of their Eternal Home may have contributed to the later lukewarm attitude of the brothers toward the pulpit.

When Featherston was seventeen, a law student in Barrie, and, his mother feared, a backslider, she wrote:

'. . . I could not find a suitable opportunity while you were at home to ask a question or two, and have a little serious conversation. Having been Confirmed in the True Faith and having, I am sure, a correct knowledge of the main truths in the word of God, have you yet seriously thought of taking the Sacrament?

'It is a plain Command of the Saviour's, "Do this in remembrance of Me". Read carefully the latter part of your catechism . . . and I think you will see that is a duty required of you. . . .

'God enable you, my dear boy, "to fight manfully against the world, the flesh and the devil, and to be Christ's faithful soldier, even unto the end".'

Featherston, as is natural in a young man, was enjoying

his new independence. Too much, Ellen feared, and gravely reminded him of family loyalties.

(1855), '. . . I must say we were not a little disappointed that you didn't come down last week. Papa is half disposed to think "Where there's a will etc". It would grieve me if I thought you were in any way weaned from home, but knowing you find plenty of office work and like it, I am willing to make excuses for you. . . .'

B.B. kept the peace. Acting as go-between he warned his brother when a letter here or a visit there was needed to soothe ruffled feelings. Fen was chronically broke, B.B. usually solvent and always generous. '. . . I send you a dollar,' he wrote, 'and hope you will spend [it] properly like a good boy, ahem !' They corresponded weekly and usually there was an 'enclosure' from the younger brother. Once, when he too was cleaned out, he explained '. . . as I had none of the needful myself I spoke to Papa, said you were rather hard up. I enclose what he gave me, $10., he being rather jolly this evening. . . .'

He kept Fen posted on village news:

I have just come home from the woods where I have been making extensive preparations for sugar or rather mollasses. . . . I think I will tap this afternoon. . . . Mrs. Geikie, the doctor's wife, was delivered of a younker but it kicked the bucket. Mr. Thomas Gaviller is likely to be a papa within, at the most, two months. How proud he will be. The Miss Hills are both stopping at the Parsons' one teaching music, the other drawing. By the by, Mrs. Hill has let out her dress. Send down my watch the first opportunity. . . .

I remain yours
B.B.

Ellen made the clothes for the smaller children and shirts and nightshirts for the males of every age. She knitted their socks and it is a family tradition that at one time she even made their shoes though there is no reference to her cobbling in letters or journals.

By 1855 there was a local shoemaker, for on October 13th of that year Featherstone received the following itemized bill:

            1855   Tecumseth
                 Rev. F. L. Osler   due to John Mathews.

Oct. 13   Miss Charlotte one shoe one pice & pair silk lases   –6
Do. 25   Sir your son Frank one boot sold & toe piced   1–2
Do. 25   Your son Wm. pair of boots sold toe piced   2–2
Nov. 3   Mrs. Osler one shoe mended   –3
Do. 7   Your son Frank one boot sold & toe piced   1–3
Dec. 4   Edmund Osler pr boots sold heeled & toe piced   3–9
Do. 4   Your son Wm. one boot one pice mended   –11

1856.
Jany 11   one pump leather   1–11
Do. 12   Miss Charlotte Osler new pair boots   8–9
Do. 14   Edmund Osler new pair slipper shoes   7–0
Do. 21   Wm. Osler new pr. boots calf skin   7–11
Do. 25   Edmund Osler new pr Long boots   14–11
Feby. 1   Frank Osler new pr Calf skin boots   8–11
March 3   Mrs. Osler pair shoes mended   –10
April 29 Wm. Osler new Pair boots   7–9
May 16   Frank Osler „   „   „   7–10
Do 16   Miss Charlotte Osler pair boots sold &
               toe piced   1–9
June 2   Edmund Osler pr boots sold hilld one fronted   4–0
Do 9   125 cabbage plants   4–0
Do. 13   the Revd. F. L. Osler new pr slipper shoes   7–9

Do. 27	Frank Osler pr boots sold & fronted	2–9
July 10	Wm. Osler new pair calf skin Boots	7–9
Do. 16	Miss Charlotte Osler new pair boots	8–
Do. 17	Frank Osler new Pair boots	8–11
Aug. 1	Quarter veal 15 lb at 4½ per lb.	5–½
Do. 13	Frank Osler new pr Calf skin boots	8–9
Do. 20	Do. Do. Do. pr boots mended	1–3

$$£6- 9-\tfrac{1}{2}$$

| Oct. 8 | Frank Osler pair boots soled & fronted | 3–4 |

$$£6-12-\tfrac{1}{2}$$

settled in full Nov. 10 1856
John Mathews

When Edward, the third son, was sent to the Barrie grammar school in 1855, the family was already aware that he lacked the industrious habits of his older brothers.

Ellen urged Fen, also in Barrie, to keep an eye on this difficult one and to 'use his influence for good'; 'Britty,' she added, 'will not write this time for he is suffering today from the effects of Cal and Rhubarb which he took last night in two pills wrapped in brown paper—a novel way for the doctor to administer his drugs. . . .'

Of the other children in their last few years at Tecumseth there are few particulars. Ellen Mary seemed often to be ailing without any specific ailment; Edmund, not yet twelve when the family moved to Dundas, had been for some time past a good farm-hand, a reliable child. The twins, Frank and Charlotte, two years younger than Edmund, and the still younger William gambolled about the countryside, with only small chores for duties.

Featherstone knew the limits of a parson's purse and that it would not stretch to sending all his children to boarding-school. In 1854 he wrote to Bishop Strachan and asked to be transferred to a parish with more advanced educational facilities than Tecumseth afforded. In 1857 the parishes of Ancaster and Dundas fell vacant and the Bishop appointed Featherstone rector.

'It was one of the hardest trials of my life,' he wrote in his journal, 'to leave the place where I had lived happily nineteen and a half years . . . but I felt that the Church would not suffer by my leaving it. In the neighbouring townships many churches had been built, and in Tecumseth and West Gwillimbury, my specially licensed charge, where there had been neither church, parsonage, nor glebe, there were now six churches, two parsonages, and two glebes; the one in Tecumseth being especially valuable, consisting of 200 acres. I had 160 acres cleared.'

He mourned the parting with his people and the people mourned his going. But Ellen, the unworldly one, was hardest hit. Even the simple town of Dundas filled her with apprehension lest she become involved in 'social life'. She announced the news to her son Featherston in a letter written from Tecumseth, Dec. 1, 1856:

'Just as I was about to commence, Britty called me to admire Jessie [horse] drawing up a load of wood in company with Harry [horse]. She runs beautifully, quite to the satisfaction of her young master who will soon have to part with his pet for Papa is going to sell off all the stock and farm. More than that, it is highly probable, almost certain . . . that we are . . . going to remove from this to Dundas.

'It is by no means a sudden resolve. . . . As you may know, Papa has often talked of it. . . . Papa's work will be within a much narrower compass, and an excellent Grammar School with three masters will be close at hand for the boys. . . .

'I feel very very sorry to leave but your Papa commonly acts with judgement. . . .'

Britton added details:

'. . . Dundas, according to Papa's description, is an incorporated town from six to seven thousand inhabitants within four miles of Hamilton, connected to it by rail [and] within one hour and a quarter of Toronto by the cars. It has a rectory [with] four hundred acres of land attached. The salary . . . is double what it is here, the pew rents of one church being £175. Papa says it is a very go ahead place [with a] grammar school considered the best in Canada, [and] two foundries, each employing two hundred men. There is also a market place and Town Hall. It is connected with Ancaster, the other church four miles distant, by a macadamized road. . . .

'P.S. The town of Dundas is lighted by gas.'

With his father back and forth to Dundas and Featherston in Barrie, the arrangements for the two sales (one indoors, one out) devolved on Britton.

B. B. Osler to Featherston:

Feb. 23, 1857.

'We are in great confusion. Every room . . . is turned all about. Our sale takes place on Thursday next. . . . Edward and Edmund went with Papa to Dundas [on] Saturday. They're going to school at once. Mama and the three young ones go to Thornhill on Thursday morning where they stop a week. . . .

'There was a grand presentation of plate to the Gov. last

Tuesday, consisting of one waiter [tray], price £20, a coffee pot, tea ditto, cream jug, sugar bowl, butter holder, also a salver and kettle, something like an urn with a spirit lamp underneath. For Mama a pair of solid silver candlesticks, cost £20, from the ladies of Tecumseth. And from Joseph, the jeweller, a handsome cake basket, solid silver. The whole affair looks very grand. An address accompanied them. . . .'

Featherstone had acted wisely in asking to be transferred to a more populous centre. His boys and girls were growing up and their abundant energies demanded a wider stage than Bond Head offered. The Tecumseth days were over. But these formative years, even when far removed by time, remained an insistent echo throughout the Oslers' lives. The bush had proved good soil for tough seed.

CHAPTER SEVEN

Featherston and Britton

ELLEN reluctantly pulled up her roots and those of her children and prepared for the transplanting. She and the three youngest, Frank, Chattie and William, intended to go by rail from Toronto on March 12.* William mercifully developed croup and their journey was postponed. On the date they had chosen for the move the train never reached its destination. A bridge collapsed. Engine and coaches hurtled into the canal beneath. Britton, already in Dundas, supplied the absent Featherston with grisly particulars.

'. . . I suppose you have heard of the awful accident [that] happened last night. . . . Up to the present time they have 81 dead bodies . . . and when they get the cars out of the water they will get 40 or 50 more. . . .

'Mr. Zimmerman of Niagara was among the first to be taken out, with his head completely off. . . .'

The contractor, Zimmerman, whose faulty work—to increase his own profits—was the cause of the wreck, himself perished in it; a rare example of retributive justice.

'Folk about here and Hamilton think that the accident was entirely caused by the timbers of the bridge not being strong

---

* This was William's version but Ellen wrote to Featherston '. . . you will be uneasy on our account but the young ones and myself are still here, Papa not having come up for us yet. . . .'

Featherstone Lake Osler = Ellen Picton
b. 1805, m. 1837

- Featherston = Henrietta Smith
  b. Jan. 4,   b. 1839
  1838
  m. 1861   ⎫
- Britton Bath = Caroline Smith   ⎬ Sisters
  b. June 19,   b. 1836   ⎭
  1839
  m. 1863
- Ellen Mary = Alexander Erskine Wil-
  b. 1841, Falmouth   liamson
  m. 1868
- Edward Lake = Marion Wyld
  b. 1842
  m. 1868
- Edmund Boyd = 1st. Mary Isabella Lam-
  b. 1845   mond Smith
                  m. 1868, d. 1871
                  2nd. Anne Farquharson
                  Cochran
                  m. 1873
- Francis Llewellyn = Isobel Fowler
  b. 1847
  m. 1882
- Charlotte Elizabeth = Herbert Gwyn
  b. 1847   b. 1843
  m. 1872
- William = Grace Linzee Revere
  b. 1849   b. 1855
  m. 1892
- Emma Henrietta
  b. 1851, d. 1853

Henry Bath Osler = Harriet
b. 1815, m. 1844   Parsons

- Edward Henry
  b. 1845
- Frances Harriet
  b. 1847
- Mary
  b. 1849
- Emma
  b. 1852
- William Parsons
  b. 1854
- Ernest
  b. 1857
- Gertrude Ellen
  b. 1860

Edward (3) Osler, = 2nd wife Sarah Atkin-
M.R.C.S., F.L.S.   son, m. 1838

- William Henry, b. 1839 (?)
- Jennette, b. 1839, d. 1936
- Marian, b. 1841 = 2nd husband George Grant Francis

enough. In fact they were made of not the best of pine scanton.
. . . Among the slain [are] four clergymen, one Church of
England, [and] two members of parliament. . . . [I] enclose a
piece of splint taken out of Doyle's temple. . . .'

Their first house proved only a temporary dwelling place
but its modern conveniences and town elegance impressed the
youthful Britton.

'It is new brick, well finished,' he wrote to Featherston. 'The
two parlours are fitted with coal grates and gas chandeliers. . . .
There are altogether 14 gas lights in the house. . . .'

Ellen missed the parsonage but was happy to have a good
grammar school close by. Edward and Edmund could now get
regular book-learning. 'A woman's school' sufficed in the
meantime for the little boys, Frank and William.

Though she did not know it, neighbours were spreading
romantic rumours about her racial origin. When Featherstone
brought his black-eyed, dark-skinned wife from the backwoods to Dundas, many of the townspeople mistook her for
an Indian. Indeed, there were some who swore she was a direct
descendant of Pocahontas.

Ellen to Featherston:

March 26, 1857.

'We have been more than a week in our new abode but it
will be long before I feel thoroughly at home. We are in a
quiet part of the town, not far from the church and very close
to the school; the house . . . is well finished and comfortable,
two more rooms in it and a small garden would be desirable
but for the present we must rest content. . . . Papa has been busy
this week calling on the people and the people busy calling on
us. I am happy to say that as far as I can judge from present

appearances they do not seem a very fashionable set. They welcome us among them with seeming good will. . . .

'There are lots of young ladies to amuse Britty but I suppose he will soon be otherwise engaged in the flourishing city of Hamilton as he is now deep in Book Keeping, preparatory to setting off in life in some mercantile house there. . . .'

Featherston's style, his attitude 'all the world's a fool except thee and me', is reminiscent of his Uncle Edward. His insistence on what is due his station in life, as when, in a letter to Britton, he ends, 'F. Osler Esq. is my address', echoes both uncle and father. Britton shows no trace of small snobberies. He resembled his elders in his self-confidence, his capacity for work and his ambition. But his easy relaxed manner, both on paper and in person, rings a new note. There were, of course, 'jolly' Oslers as Henry proved and, no doubt, his brother Samuel, but Henry's jolliness inclined to be waggish, an altogether different type. Except for these letters written in his teens and twenties, there is a lamentable lack of material concerning Britton's life. But to those who knew him he appeared outsize; heart and body and brains in just proportion.

Life in Dundas was a world away from life in Tecumseth. Not only were the streets and parlours lit by gas but the social life was a cut above what the boys had been used to. The seventeen-year-old Britton entered into the new activities with gusto. Dundas had nicknamed the Osler boys 'Tecumseth Cabbages', only to find the cabbage a favourite vegetable.

Britton to his brother Featherston:

Dundas, April 10, 1857.
'. . . I have been playing cricket very extensively. We have three clubs . . . , a small boys', a big boys' and a men's. The

men's have a very slapup uniform. . . . The big boys (in which I am in) can beat them and did twice running.'

Dundas, May 26, 1857.

'. . . We kept her Majesty's birthday in style here yesterday, and the atmosphere is very hazy this morning from the effects of the cannonading which was kept up all day by the Artillery, which Co. together with the Cavalry Co. made the town look quite warlike. . . .

'I had the pleasure of taking the two Miss Hatts, Mrs. Crayton and Miss McCoy to see the fire works and I left them home at the hour of 12 midnight after witnessing the torch light procession. . . . I am engaged at the Hatt's this eve to play chess with Miss Ellen who is about the nicest girl in Dundas. . . .'

A few months later Miss Law had succeeded Miss Hatt in his affections.

'. . . I was out riding this morning with Miss Law of Hamilton. It was previously arranged that I should be one of a party of six but accidentally or on purpose Miss Law and myself had to go alone. She is 16 years of age [Britton 17] and when in Dundas the rest of the ladies may dry up. . . .'

November introduced Britton to the waltz, Sir Roger de Coverley and the Lancers and he became a member of a debating society where his abilities in oratory and argument were given their first expression.

'. . . I have been to two dress parties this season . . . and am progressing in the art of dancing. In that great institution the Pro Bona, an animated debate came off on Thursday last—(Subject) Whether morality increases with civilization—decided in the negative. . . .'

Once more Featherston called for help and Britton answered:

'. . . If before your instalment is due you cannot raise the tin, just write to me. I think as I have three watches I could easily raise from $15 to $20 at a week's notice, which I could advance to you on your own terms. . . . You would please Papa if you were to write to him about once a month. I think by his manner he is rather angry about it and rather than anger him you better write. Mamma sends her love. . . .'

Featherstone and Ellen, no longer farmers, remained good gardeners. They soon moved to a house 'much larger than the last we honoured with our presence,' wrote Britton, '[and] into the bargain we have one acre and a half of well laid out grounds . . . and a promise of a large harvest of fruit. . . .'

Britton had not yet considered law as a possible career and after a short course in book-keeping he went to work.

B.B. to Featherston:

June, 1857.

'. . . The business which . . . occupies my attention at present is to keep I. S. Meredith's accounts straight, in other words I am [his] book-keeper. He is a hardware importer and merchant . . . [and] he does a large business, keeps 2 salesmen and a man to do the dirty work. . . .

'We are most gloriously dull here at present. Owing . . . to the harvest, the source of money appears to have dried up. But we do credit enough to keep me on the stool from 8 to 7 o'clock. . . .'

In August he posted Fen on the latest births. It is impossible to tell whether Britton intended the three sentences in the following paragraph to be linked but he should be given the benefit of the doubt:

'. . . Aunt (Henry's wife) last Monday had her sixth young one. It is of the masculine gender. The Revd. A. Hill's wife had her third a short time since. We had a temperance lecture last night by Crawford. . . .'

(Aug. 9, 1857) Featherston replied, '. . . So my respected Aunt has presented another son and heir to the house of Osler. May her shadow never be less. They must be enjoying to their heart's content the music which some fool declared the sweetest in the world, viz a child's cry—thereby rendering it apparent to any reflecting mind that his auricular organs were decidedly out of tune. . . .

'. . . I am afraid you are becoming a most arrant Lady Killer. It seems Miss Law is at present the victim of your attractions. What has become of Miss E. Hatt? Have you "left her on the pedestal of grief and woe to stand"? My maxim is "War to the knife's point" with every mother's daughter of them, barring four.

'I paid Shanty Bay a visit the other day . . . but the women there, except Miss Ardagh, are engaged; and confoundly stiff, stuck up erections of crinoline they are. . . .'

It is usually the old or at least the middle-aged who discover that the country is 'going to the dogs'. But Featherston was not yet twenty when he wrote:

'. . . The world is evidently going to the bad. I never heard in all my life . . . such a fearful catalogue of corruption, embezzlements, murders, bank robberies etc. as are now daily committed and that by people whose integrity and standing hitherto has never been questioned. . . . Such is the U.C. Bank robbery in Toronto, and though it is said that the law will have no hold on any of the parties who obtained the money as it was or seemed to be advanced in the regular course of business, still the moral guilt is the same. . . . And the tale of murders, felonies and every species of crime, with which the New York and American papers teem is really frightful. Even here we have a man in gaol waiting his trial for murder & I am afraid the wretch [will] be hung here if convicted.

'Have the boys returned to school yet and are Frank and Willy still going to that woman's school? Those youngsters are getting pretty old now & I hope that if they are kept at one Grammar school they will get on well. . . .

'. . . I hope Mama has my shirts done. I am literally and really and truly out. . . . I have a most benevolent washer-woman who always manages to keep me supplied with stockings—first rate ones—she swears they are mine but I know better. . . .'

Featherston, like his Uncle Edward before him, wished to appear above the frivolous pursuits of his fellows. After a glimpse of a less conservative brother, he wrote, '. . . Edward is looking very "fast".'

Featherston to Britton:

Aug. 17, 1857, Barrie.

'. . . Miss Morgan arrived last Tuesday in "robustuous" health barring a sprained wrist—I expected some confounded accident or other would happen on carrying out that riding idea. She has now however quite recovered—Allah be praised! Not that I am particularly interested. Has any other young female been proposing to you or has your barbarity towards Miss Whats-her-name disgusted the feminine population? That brazen baggage (saving your presence) Miss M—— discovered the little flirtation on your part and seemed rather riled...about it.

'. . . There is to be a "circus" here tomorrow. I console myself with the reflection that I have done my best . . . to keep them away by refusing them the use of Patton's grounds. The women are to exhibit themselves most disgracefully. . . .

'A Regatta [comes off] . . . next Thursday and thereafter a "Grand Ball" if sufficient number of fools can be found to invest in $2 tickets. I am afraid Barrie must really incur the imputation and enjoy the unenviable distinction of being the *slowest* place of its size in Canada west. Although there are a pile of law students in the Town we cannot raise a Debating Society. . . . What, however, induced your club to call itself the *Pro Bona* . . . exceeds my not very brilliant imagination. . . .'

Barrie, Oct. 21, 1857.

'. . . If you feel particularly inclined to see an execution come up on the 17 Feb. 1858, on which day John Saltry, convicted of the murder of one Hogg, at the last Assizes will be *sus: per! col*; in other words, suspended by the neck. . . .'

Barrie's twenty-fourth of May festivities were similar to those Britton described in Dundas. The difference lies in the eye of the beholder.

Featherston to Britton:

May, 1858.

'. . . Did you celebrate the "Natal day of our beloved Sovereign" in a leal manner?

'We in Barrie did the thing rather *stylishly*, so to speak—we had *programmes* (which are considered aristocratic) of the day's proceedings. There were processions of rifle-men which I took the liberty of cutting—of fire & hook & ladder Brigades. There was then a "feed" to these valiant protectors of their

country . . . —[As a] result . . . many of them were rather off
their feed next day, having been gloriously "tight". In the
evening there was a torchlight procession, a bonfire and a
display of execrable fireworks. A Bazaar was open all day for
the benefit of the Church of England. . . .

'The Gov. wrote me . . . to say that he was going round with
the Bishop to the divers confirmations & among other places
to Barrie. Is Edward to be confirmed in—I was going to say
wickedness—for it is nothing else—this time? I don't see the
use of it myself, that's the truth of the matter.'

In the summer of 1858 Featherston left Barrie for a law firm
in Toronto. Britton wrote to him from Dundas.

Oct. 22nd.

'After some months deliberation I have . . . arrived at the
conclusion that my best course is to study law. As I have not
much time to spend I shall enter at the University and so get
through in three years from the date of examination. The Gov.
strongly approves of my determination and will do all in his
power to put me through.

'I want you . . . to post me . . . as to what is necessary to be
done, what I shall have to get up & when the examination
is to be. . . .

'Give me all the information requisite so that I shall be able
to go in the entire animal at once. . . . I am going into Notman
& Barton's office. . . .'

Featherston answered:

'I received yours of 22nd yesterday & . . . am glad to hear of
your determination to study law. I send you herewith a paper
shewing what has to be done re the examination which . . .

takes place in February. [The time] is short enough to give you as much as you can do to be ready . . . but a little hard work ought to accomplish it. You may leave out Greek, which I fear would prove a stumbling block, and take French. The Horace and Latin Prose translation will be most troublesome for you. If, however, the other subjects are done well, this, I believe, is not so much pressed. I think you might take one of the four scholarships . . . which would be a great assistance to you. . . .

'It is not necessary to take the L.L.D. degree to save two years. The L.L.B. is sufficient for this. . . . You should read . . . "The Common Law Procedure Acts" of 1856 & 1857—looking over this, even cursorily will tend to give you a very good idea of the practice of the courts. If, however, you find that you cannot go up [for] the Law (University) Examination in February—or can only take one of the two—you might defer the former till February 12 months—& you would then save *one* year—or you might take the University alone—*saving two years* & go up to the Law (Osgoode) examination in May. . . .

'Anything else you wish to know, or want to get, write & I will endeavour to supply as far as possible. . . .'

Britton to Featherston:

Dundas, Nov. 5, 1858.

'. . . Since Monday I have been at my books 9 and a half hours per day and am getting on better than I expected. The French master says I can easily do the French; I think Algebra and Euclid I can master. The balance, Latin and Blackstone are the stiffest fences I have to surmount. . . .

'From what Mr. Checkley said I should fancy Edward will

have a chance to pass at Osgoode on the 20th. If he does he goes at once to Notman & Barton office. . . .

'I have a most glorious study fitted up in a small stone out-building, in which, with my table, carpet, chairs and books, I am undisturbed except by the masters for lessons. . . .'

Britton's capacity for work then and later was phenomenal. In Jan. 1859 he wrote to Featherston:

'. . . I have added to my hours for study so that at present they are 14. . . .' And to prove he had not forgotten women:

'. . . Dick Thorne made his appearance on New Year's eve, which evening we had a select party of (unhappily) married individuals—which necessitated my flirting with a young pretty and married dame much to the annoyance of her husband "Ha hinglis mem". . . .'

The Oslers had been in Canada for more than twenty-one years when B.B. wrote,

Dundas, Jan. 6, 1859.

My dear Fen

Allow me to congratulate you on . . . attaining your majority. It must be [an] intense satisfaction . . . to be considered no longer an infant (in the eye of the law) and to know that you can sue and be sued. Did you receive the money the Gov. sent? If you did it would be policy to acknowledge the receipt thereof. . . .

. . . I have conceived the idea to go to Osgoode this term, unknown to anyone but you and the Gov—so that if I do get plucked no one is any the wiser and if I get through there is a good deal saved. . . .

If Edward gets through it will be but by chance. I do not really think he is as well up as he was last term. He will not work, do what you will. . . .

Britton made the grade but not Edward. The former wrote to Featherston with no false modesty.

Feb. 15, 1859.

'. . . Congratulations fall thick and heavy—more especially as Notman has blazed abroad the opinion of the benchers on my theme and says no one did their Euclid better. . . . I am most confoundedly tired and used up. . . .'

He handed on his recipe for success to aspiring law students: 'Get a good bench. If [they] know a bencher (like old Notman) let them join his artillery corps, tell him the last 18 pounder he got from the Govt. makes the loudest report of any you ever heard—and hint that in your opinion the whole Macdonald party [is] rotten, that Brown is a trump—and that it is no harm to drink Scotch whiskey going to bed. They will probably get the gent to assist them through and pass them even if they had only been studying Horace for 2 months and had a natural antipathy to it to commence with.'

With the examinations happily concluded, Britton started his apprenticeship with a Dundas firm. He and Featherston, devoted from childhood, had now the added bond of a common profession. They wrote weekly, often bi-weekly letters, filled with legal talk as well as gossip.

Britton to Featherston:

Dundas, March 21, 1859.

'Your welcome letter was received on Sunday morning. . . . It is an intense satisfaction to be through, high or low. . . . We are . . . busy preparing for the Assizes . . . [and] shall no doubt beat you on the case your office [is] defending. . . .

'I am glad to hear that you intend coming home on Thursday. I wish you would bring with you "Locke on the Human Understanding" as I want to read it for a debate which comes

off between the Hamilton Club and the Pro Bono on the 4th
of May next. . . .'

Work was the most reverenced virtue of the nineteenth
century and Britton and Featherston were of their time.

The letter continues: 'I have long hours—9 to 6 and as much
more as Barton can get. . . . This week I finish all my books . . .
for the second time and Williams for the third. . . . On Monday
I start . . . all through once more, digesting as I go along. . . . I
read from 6 to 11 without a break besides what I read in the
daytime. . . . I think the sole secret of success is *industry*. And I
do not think either you or myself are constitutionally idle. . . .'

Britton had the Osler capacity to recognize Osler worth.

B.B. to Featherston:

May 23, 1859.

'. . . We had our debate with the Mechanics' Debating Club
on Wednesday last, myself leader of the P.B. as I have some
gift of the gab. . . . I spoke for one hour and ten minutes . . .
and left them nowhere. We gave them a most complete beating
and had a jolly shine afterwards.

'I received congratulations from all present, was toasted as
hero of the evening and received a letter of thanks from the
club. . . .'

A scribble on the back of the letter may refer to the subject
of the debate: 'Are the inequalities of Rank (& Condition)
in Society favourable to the advancement of learning?'

'. . . A very extensive picnic takes place here tomorrow under
the auspices of the Upper-ten (such as it is) of Dundas. I shall
be home for the dance in the evening. On Friday week there
was a large party at Notman's which I attended and came out
very extensively in the dancing line. . . .'

Britton came out no less extensively as host:

'We had Col. Cotter of Irish notoriety . . . here this week. The Gov. was away but I did the honours of the house, I think to his (the Co's) satisfaction, for when the last glass of whiskey & water (not water and whiskey) found its level with the preceding 6, he exclaimed, "Pon my soul (hic) Britton (hic) you are (hic) the best judge of (hic) good whiskey (hic) I know. Give us your hand old fellow, I guess I'll go to bed."'

Britton had met his future wife when he wrote:

'I spent one of the jolliest days, among the prettiest and most intellectual girls, yesterday . . . [at] Captain Smith's of Hanford. Ellen Mary is staying there. There are four young ladies and it is rather difficult to say which is the best—so different from our misses in Dundas of whom it is hard to say which is the worst—tho as yet I keep on very fair terms with most of them. . . .'

Eventually he fixed his choice on Caroline Smith and Featherston chose Henrietta. Thus, characteristically, the devoted brothers married devoted sisters, another link, rather than a break in their relationship.

Featherston moved to Dundas and joined a local firm in 1860, but the brothers were reunited only a few short months before Britton was temporarily transferred to a Toronto office.

They were courting now in earnest though Featherston may have been slow in coming to the point for Britton wrote, '. . . You'd better hurry up or it may be considered that you have been flirting. I have good authority for saying that you will have *no trouble*, [but] rather *assistance* from the parents. . . . Christmas will bring about a crisis in my case. . . .'

While Featherston and Britton were preoccupied with law and love, Ellen catered to a still large houseful of young.

Ellen to Elizabeth Osler:

Dundas, Aug. 4, 1860.

'. . . I often feel a strong inclination to sit and have a long chat on paper but you cannot imagine how little time I can find for either reading or writing. Sometimes when all have gone upstairs and my work is put away ready for bed, I take up a book and indulge for an hour—the consequence is I am lazy next morning and resolve not to indulge again. . . .

'The holidays are nearly over for which I am really Thankful. We are always in a Whirr when the children are in all day—the little fellows have not found the time hang heavily for they have had . . . many delightful drives with Papa and our garden is so pleasant for them. They have a fine playground with Gymnasium poles and a swing which all enjoy. . . . Dear Fed has taken such pains to have . . . things comfortable for us —and Fen and B.B. who had been . . . long separated were so happy in being together again. Now Britty is off, . . . perhaps no more to be an inmate of his own family—I do miss him very much. . . . I am sure [his] removal to Mr. Pattons office in Town [Toronto] will be desirable in a professional way. His habits are formed—he is steady & a complete book worm.'

CHAPTER EIGHT

William, Edward and Frank

THE population of the Dundas rectory began to dwindle in the early sixties. Edmund, not yet seventeen, set out to make his fortune. He started in Toronto, modestly, as a clerk in the Upper Canada Bank, where he remained until its loud crash a few years later. In 1861, Featherston married Henrietta, the fourth daughter of Capt. Henry Smith, formerly of the Hon. East India Company's Service. Two years later Britton married Caroline. Edward and Frank came and went, as did the jobs procured for them by more industrious members of the family.

Many tall tales of William's school days have survived. Some he told himself to amuse a younger generation, others were remembered and repeated by his school-fellows.

The Dundas grammar school, his first serious institute of learning, unfortunately shared a building with the common school, the latter on the ground floor and the former upstairs. A quite natural and continuous state of war existed between the two. William had been general of the grammar school gang for some years before he was expelled in 1864. No one is certain which crime sealed his fate. It may have been the flock of hissing geese that greeted the principal of the common school when he unlocked the door one Monday morning;

or perhaps his patience came to an end when he found the desks and benches removed from his classroom. Some painstaking person had unscrewed them from the floor and they were discovered in a garret, to which the only means of access was a step-ladder and a trap-door.

Another version of the dismissal is found in an article on William Osler by his nephew the late Dr. Norman Gwyn (son of his sister Chattie). He claimed that William and nine other boys caught their master using a latin crib and shouted their jeers through the keyhole. As there were many offenders Featherstone maintained that it was Methodist deviltry (there were Methodists on the school board) to expel only one, the son of the English Church clergyman.

William was unperturbed by his banishment. In high feather he galloped home and greeted his sister Charlotte with the joyful shout, 'I've got the sack'.

Doubtless Featherstone and Ellen made suitable gestures of parental disapproval but after all the Methodists were to blame and it was next to impossible to punish this gay, affectionate creature, who, below the level of his mischief, was a bright, if not yet extra-industrious boy. They packed him off to board at the Barrie grammar school where Featherston, Britton and Edward had been before him.

But William did not change with a change of scene. Before long he and two special friends (Ned Milburn and Charlie Locke) were known as Barrie's Bad Boys.

On one occasion when the B.B.B.s had been 'gated' a week for the small matter of robbing a neighbour's melon patch, William retaliated by climbing up to the school-house roof where he covered the smoking chimney with a board. He watched with glee when the Barrie Hook & Ladder Co. came charging up to put out the non-existent fire.

Another day he and a friend answered the advertisement of a farmer in search of a wife. The friend was a blonde and William a decided brunette. They dressed themselves as girls and met the farmer on the platform of the Barrie station. The farmer chose the blonde, promised to write the following week and set the wedding date. But he had not fallen deeply in love for they heard no more.

Ellen to William:

Dundas, October, 1864.

My dear Willie,

I can excuse you if you begin to think of yourself in a small degree slighted, for I ought to have written last week but could not manage it. . . . I am sorry to find you have had such a bad cold but hope it will not wind up with another attack of intermittent. . . . Charlotte has written you all the news and the Pater told you how well the Ancastrians did at their Bazaar—$400 was more than any of us expected to make. . . . I bought a winter necktie for you which I will try to enclose. . . . Both Papa and I think it will be useless to send up a box, as apples are scarcely to be had and Frank's expedition for nuts . . . was only productive of *one quart* so if Papa sends you up a dollar it must do instead and I daresay you could get a tooth brush and a packet of slippery-Elm (not Elem) bark at Barrie— nor can we find "Horace" in the study to send up. I am glad your clothes suit. Frank went down by Boat last week to Toronto and got a suit of clothes at Walkers and Felt hat; they make him look quite the young man. Nothing yet has turned up for him to do, but all are looking out for him. . . . Edmund has his holiday. He was with us for a day or two and has now gone duck-shooting. . . . Give my kind regards to Mrs. Chickley and love to Mrs. Stewart when you see her and with my best love to you hoping that you are on terms of love and affection with your books,

I am ever

Your affectionate Mother

Ellen Osler

P.S. Frank left his skates at Barrie. Mind you take care of them to bring home at Christmas.

A new school in Weston, started by the Rev. William Johnson, attracted the notice of Ellen and Featherstone. The prospectus advertised music, painting and dancing for the senior boys but that can hardly have been a factor in the plain-living Oslers' decision to enter their son William, in the autumn of 1865.

Considering his views on the Oxford Movement Featherstone's choice was surprising. Father Johnson, as he was commonly called, stood for Puseyism in its most extreme form. He was a thorn in the flesh of even the High Church Bishop Strachan who had been forced to move him from parish to parish. Johnson ended as rector in a tiny village near Weston where his people loved him despite his Romish views. It was here he started his school. It had already been incorporated with Trinity University when William arrived and was known then as it is today as Trinity College School, though its site is now Port Hope.

Johnson had retired as principal but remained as warden. The headmaster, an Englishman, determined to model his school on the lines of Eton and Rugby. Top hats were the rule, outlandish as they must have looked against the rough Canadian landscape. The cane, a concrete symbol of discipline, was wielded often and with verve. The headmaster is forgotten but Johnson lives as a man who stirred the imaginations of boys and particularly of William Osler.

Johnson had a second god, biology, or natural history as it was called in those pre-Huxleyan days. William became his disciple and before long a first-class assistant, competent to prepare specimens for the microscope. Together they roamed the countryside, finding precious loot in swamp and field. Everything dazzled the eyes of the old and the young naturalist; a hair from a squirrel, a piece of moss, the molar of a cow or the wispy anatomy of a butterfly.

Because Father Johnson was his hero, William also absorbed his religious views, and under this influence chose the Church as his future career; not the evangelical message of his father but the High Anglican drama with its frankincense and myrrh.

Here, too, William met James Bovell, a friend of Johnson's and a frequent visitor to Weston. A physician by profession he was a biologist by inclination and became another enduring influence on the student Osler. It is strange that the inspiration aroused by this man who left medicine to be ordained in the Church of England, a convert to the Oxford Movement, decided William to forsake the Church for medicine.

There remains only one more tale of William's school-boy derring-do. On April 8, 1866, the Toronto *Globe* carried the story under the headline, 'School Row at Weston. Pupils Turned Outlaws. Fumigate the Matron With Sulphur'. There were several culprits, among them Johnson's eldest son, but William was the leader. He conceived the plan and led the campaign.

The matron was unpopular, but it was for some specific injustice that she was barricaded in her room by William and his followers. They then concocted a mixture of pepper, mustard and molasses which they placed on the stove below, directing the fumes to a pipe whose outlet opened into their victim's room. The desperate woman stuffed the hole with clothes but the boys' long sticks soon pushed them out again. She screamed for help and eventually was rescued, alive, by the headmaster. The culprits suffered from the hickory stick but that proved insufficient to appease the matron. She demanded nothing less than their arrest for assault and battery. And so it came to pass that William and his accomplices spent several days in the Toronto jail. When their case came up they were ably defended by William's brother Featherston. A reprimand and the payment of one dollar and costs ended the matter. But the victory was theirs for the matron departed in search of purer air. Ellen took the escapade with her usual equanimity:

Dundas, April 19, 1866.

My dear Willie,

I heard from Hennie that you had been there on your way to Lloydtown—and I suppose that you will be journeying back to school again this week. . . .

It was an unfortunate affair that of all you boys being brought into public notice in such a disreputable manner and although I do not think it was meant to be more than a mere school boy prank, such things often tell against a person long after, and I hear many say they think it will injure the reputation of the school. We are told to do unto others as we would wish them to do unto us. . . . We heard from Mr. Badgely the same day we had your letter last week telling of the matter, and since then we have had the school report which on the whole was satisfactory.

Could you only know how earnestly my heart longs to see

you walking in the paths of holiness, you would, I think, strive
to do well. . . .

This warm weather is making everything start into fresh life.
We have begun gardening in earnest. Papa is up every morning
early at work; the things in the hot bed are growing beautifully. Your sisters send their love and believe me

Your ever loving mother
Ellen Osler.

Enclosed you will find $2. & a stamp.

In spite of his propensity for practical jokes, William had not
lost his teachers' confidence. He was made head prefect and
topped his year scholastically.

After the annual sports day Ellen wrote in a postscript:

'Mine dear Willie, I must just scribble a line to tell you how
proud we all were to see "Osler 1st" so many times in the paper
today. . . . You will have a long letter from me as soon as I can
find time for such a proceeding. Bye Bye darling.'

Strange to relate neither Featherstone nor Ellen were enthusiastic about William's decision to study for the Church. Was
Featherstone at heart a disappointed man? Or did he fear he
would be succeeded by a Puseyite? Ellen gave guarded advice.

Dundas, May 30th, 1866.

'. . . And now my dear boy let me have a little serious chat
with you about entering the Church which you say you have
made up your mind to do. My first impulse was to thank God
that he had heard my prayer and inclined one of my six boys to
make choice of that as his path in life—it is a matter not to be
decided on hastily any more than is any other profession. Take
your time for consideration and above all search your heart for

the motives inducing your decision, for remember that God always judges of us by our motives while Man can only judge our actions. If you ask of God He will guide you in the right path—and without His guidance in all things we are sure to err. If you do seriously and in earnest desire to be fitted for the service of God in His Church Papa will do all he can to help you forward by giving you a liberal education and both of us will bid you God speed. . . .'

While William was distinguishing himself at school, Frank and Edward were grown, but not in grace. The family was inclined to lump these two together: black sheep amongst the spotless white. In fact they were quite dissimilar; failure in the eyes of the world and in their own, the common factor. When his cousin Jennette first met Edward in the sixties she remarked on his good looks, found him an amusing and altogether charming companion. According to letters he possessed a quite adequate intelligence but, as Britton expressed it, 'work he will not'. Only three years younger than Britton, he may have realized, even as a small boy, that he could not compete with his older brothers' ability and drive. Surrounded by a family of moderate achievement it is possible he might himself have attained a modest success. A sense of his own inadequacy perhaps paralysed his growth. Though his prospering brothers helped with jobs and money they appear to have had little affection for him. How could they understand a man who wouldn't (they didn't believe in couldn't) strenuously apply himself to the work at hand? Both Ellen and Featherstone sorrowed, and with understanding, over this unhappy son. Featherstone wrote later with real perception to Britton, then on his way to Winnipeg, asking him to be good to Edward who was trying, without success, to practise law in that frontier town. He made it clear that Edward was not only lonely but bitterly discouraged by repeated failures. Some believed he was Ellen's favourite child. Certainly she felt his need and responded to it.

Frank's troubles were of another nature. Physically and in manner he bore a remarkable likeness to his younger brother William. The resemblance went no farther. Evidence suggests that he had considerably less than average intelligence. This, in combination with a merry, totally irresponsible disposition led to endless scrapes. He helped himself to whatever took his fancy. His jobs were many and, except when at sea, short lived. From hearsay it would not seem he brooded over his shortcomings. And yet, despite his apparent light-heartedness he too must have been an unhappy man, for among his many weaknesses the greatest was drink. One letter survives and is proof that Frank had moments of remorse. It is undated and probably contained the first news the family had received of the wanderer for months, possibly years.

Liverpool

Dear Father and Mother

I received your kind letters shortly after my arrival in Liverpool. If only you knew how sorry I am for not having answered your letters sooner I am shure you would forgive me. The G Ammo [his ship] arrived about a month ago after a long and rough passage of 109 days. . . . I am living in hope that this will be my last voyage. I would rather do anything than follow the sea. It's such a rough and comfortless life I feel quite shure that if I had the opportunity of remaining home again I would lead a life altogether different to my past life. Pleas tell Chatty and Willie that I have delayed

writing so long that I have not time to write but will write
them from the coast. Tell Ellin Mary to write me. I should
like a letter from her very much. . . . Believe me Dear Mother
& Father to be your

Affectionate Son
Francis Osler.

While Ellen used almost no punctuation, Frank put full
stops anywhere—in the middle of a sentence, between Francis
and Osler. He appears to have stuck the dots in at random
when he had finished writing, knowing they were needed,
but not where.

In letters to the schoolboy William, Ellen expressed something of her anxiety.

Jan. 1866.

'. . . Frank is wandering about . . . trying to get employment
and we have again to supply him with the money to return
home. . . . I do not see what he will be fit for or how get
employment. Write soon and tell me all about your dear
self. . . .'

In February:

'Frank came home last Friday, as yet with nothing to do. . . .
Papa has written to Mr. Bath about his going to sea in his
Service and I dare say when he once gets fairly at Sea he may
do very well. I dread his being in idleness all this time however
we must hope for the best for him, poor boy. . . .'

May, 1866.

'Edward is going up soon for his Exam. [law] which I
sincerely trust he will pass this time. It will be such a relief
to us all. . . . I send you a note from Frank. You will see that

he has foolishly been running in debt at Melville and has left the place to go to Sea. He did not mention the name of the vessel but Papa has written . . . to make enquiries. . . . Poor unfortunate Frank—he will I trust learn wisdom by experience but it will also be with much trouble to himself. God, I hope, will watch over him and guard him from all adversities that may happen to his body, and from all evil thoughts that may assault and hurt his soul. I can never cease to pray for him. Indeed, my dear Willie, it is what I constantly do for each and all of you. . . .'

Edward eloped with Marion Wyld the following autumn. It is probable that neither family would have given their consent to the match as Edward had not the means to support even himself.

CHAPTER NINE

Visitors

In 1866 two young women and a little boy came to stay at the Dundas rectory. Their names were Jennette Osler, Marian Bath and the latter's two-year-old son, Percy. Jennette and Marian were the daughters of Featherstone's brother, Edward, by his second wife, Sarah Atkinson.

Jennette was twenty-six, Marian, already a widow, twenty-five. Marian had married an elderly first-cousin-once-removed, Henry Bath, a nephew of Mary Paddy Osler. Two years later he was dead.

An invitation to stay with Canadian cousins came as manna to these lively, intelligent young women. An ocean voyage and a sight of the new world held higher attractions than the provincial society of a Cornish town.

Their first trip was a visit of less than a year but they returned in 1869 and settled permanently in Canada. For many years their lives were closely linked with the young Oslers. For William in particular they were the principal female influence during his McGill period.

Jennette was small and slight, endowed with both intelligence and a remarkable heart. Marian, too, was small (later prodigiously fat), light-hearted and known for her rare and often ribald wit. Their father Edward had not neglected their education. Widely read and, according to Dundas standards, sophisticated, they put the local belles to shame. Featherston, Britton, Edward, Edmund, Frank and William had not met their like before. They fell in love. Married, unmarried or schoolboys—age made no difference, or circumstance. Age and circumstance continued to be irrelevant as far as Marian was concerned. She is said to have had admirers at her death-bed. And on her death-bed her mind still clung to the delights of living. Coming out of the world of anaesthesia she was asked if there was anything she wanted. After a pause, so long that her questioner presumed she was not conscious, her voice carried across the room: 'A bottle and a bird'!

When Marian, Jennette and Percy sailed for Boston in August, 1866, their father Edward had been dead for four years and their only brother had settled in Bombay. They had far more 'family' in Canada than in Falmouth. Jennette kept a journal of the voyage and was more than delighted with a young man, 'Colonel Holmes, son of O. W. Holmes, the author; . . . handsome, gentlemanly and clever. . . .' They sat at the same table in the dining-saloon and therefore 'meals were a pleasure'. But Marian, accustomed perhaps to all the attention, disapproved 'and,' Jennette complained, '. . . dragged me away as soon as her bare hunger was satisfied, saying, "Don't cultivate him, Toddles, he is only an American."'

Jennette wrote of their landing in Boston at night and in the rain; how forsaken they felt until 'Suddenly a tall figure came forward in the darkness saying, "Well Jenny dear, how are you"? and kissed me before I had made up in my mind who he was. It was Brick [Britton], and we were happy and safe at once. . . . With a sound like an earthquake two great vehicles, drawn by a pair of horses, came rumbling over the wooden floor of the wharf. These were the carriages from the Hotels, & England was instantly 10,000 miles off. Finished like a private brougham, high, hooded, hung on leather springs, light and swaying with every turn of the wheels, they were as unlike an English Hotel bus as anything made to be drawn by horses could seem. Into one of these vehicles we packed after an unwilling "good bye" to my young American, and at midnight we arrived at the Revere House, and went in at "the ladies' entrance", specially designed to give passers-by a view of their ankles, since a steep flight of about 20 stairs ascended directly from the street. . . . Next morning, we had [an] American breakfast. 1st a glass of iced water and some raw sliced tomatoes, 2nd. water melon. These cold comforts refused with a shudder, we were then supplied with meat, eggs, vegetables, and bread in many forms, and with dishes of unknown nature, such as clams, a kind of shell-fish, boiled beans, dry & yellow, Indian corn, succotash, &c; sweet cakes, known as Graham bread, peaches, pears, and iced milk, concluded this curious meal. Each person had each thing on a separate & small dish; the courses were not cleared as we finished, so we were crowded by 26 little plates till there was hardly room for a tea-spoon between them. . . . We sat down with the first hungry Americans and rose with the last, while languid delicate ladies on every side cleared their plates before we fairly attacked our food. There were very few handsome men to be seen; tall & gaunt, or short and slightly made, with hollow cheeks, deep-set eyes, loose limbs, goat beards, & keen restless, inquisitive expressions, they were as different as any Anglo-Saxon could well be from the fair, frank-browed, broad-shouldered, ruddy Englishman, with his bushy whiskers,

Group of Oslers and Perrams in 1854 or 1855

L. to R. William Osler, Francis (Frank) Osler, Edmund Osler, Edward Osler, Ellen (Nellie) Osler, Charlotte (Chattie) Osler, Ellen Perram, Lydia Perram, Henrietta Gavillar, Mrs. Perram, Walter Perram

stiff joints, and trim fresh look, satisfied with himself, filled
with his own little world and supremely indifferent to everything beyond it. The young ladies were mostly pretty; dark,
slender, stylish and self-possessed, with brilliant eyes and
sharply cut features; they were very attractive while sitting
in silence, but O the walk ! O the hoops ! and doubly O the
voices ! ! Even the heavy awkwardness of a shy school girl
seemed preferable to the wiggle waggle that was for ever
saying "Come, look at me !"—still there were none of the
silly baby faces that one often finds among our fair Saxon
girls; every woman looked intelligent, and looked too as if
she had a will and opinion of her own. After breakfast . . . I
sat in the ladies parlour and looked out of the window. . . .
The view . . . was not unEnglish at first. Solid stone houses,
London roads & pavements, and a cloudy sky over-head.
Bye & bye a great street-car came lumbering on; then various
negroes and mulatoes passed and nobody stared at them, then
gentlemen brought chairs out on the Hotel steps and sat there
smoking as comfortably as if they were not in the public
street. Moreover the pedestrians had neither the easy lounge of
an idle Englishman, the erect satisfied swing of a merchant,
nor the cowed hurried scuffle of an artisan; with few exceptions they got over the ground with long loose strides, head
thrown forward, chin in the air, and with wide-awake
eagerness on their faces. Dr. Peebles arrived at eleven, and in
due time, Brick, Marian and the luggage came, after which
we went for a walk through the city in all the luxury of clean
garments. . . .

'Next morning we had a small levee, Mr. Boyd, Doctor
Peebles, Colonel Holmes, my friend [and] opposite neighbour

L.W.—10

at meals in the steamer. He was always attentive to us and we had some nice chats but he did not know my name nor I his until we said good-by finally. He is young and handsome & a thorough gentleman; don't imagine that all Americans are full of brag and bad manners; a well-educated one is just like an Englishman except that he is far more at ease without being forward, and he is sure to have a foreign accent, not necessarily American as we understand the term. They [the Holmeses] have a beautiful country place just out of Boston and are some of the best people there. We grew very friendly on our voyage and parted with mutual regret. Mr. Quincy Browne, an American gentleman took us for a long drive round Boston. . . . On our way back we called at Mr. Browne's house, a very pretty place, his wife & two sisters welcomed us, elegant pretty women, but with a sharpness & hardness about them uninviting to an English mind. They were very kind, and made us more at home than English ladies could; they were intelligent & lively too; I don't know what it is that one misses; but I shall never like a true Yankee lady, though the gentlemen, judging from Colonel Holmes & Mr. Browne are quite equal to Englishmen. . . .'

With Britton as escort they travelled by train from Boston to Stonington and there embarked on a steamer for New York, which, wrote Jennette, 'is a great noisy dirty bustling busy money-making advertising place, as different from Boston as Billingsgate from Belgravia . . .'.

After two days' sight-seeing they headed for Dundas; first by steamer a hundred and fifty miles up the Hudson River, then by rail to Rochester where they changed trains and continued to Niagara. Here Carrie (Britton's wife) met them. 'I think

we shall get on very well,' wrote Jennette. 'Brick is almost
perfection. I suppose he has faults like other mortals but they
don't appear. . . .' The next day brought them to Dundas, the
end of their journey.

'We arrived at 3.p.m. & on getting out a stout kindly looking gentleman [Featherstone] in clerical costume came forward
& welcomed us to Canada. I should have known him, he is so
very like Aunt Lizzie and his voice is like Papa's and is full of
English tone, the most home-like since we left Swansea; We
felt . . . happy at once; he is always reminding us of Papa ! It is
a long drive from the station, but as we neared the house we
grew eager, and lo at the gate stood a pretty dark girl with a
fair little boy in her arms; Charlotte & Hal [son of Featherston];
then a tall elegant very pretty girl came down, Ellen Mary,
then at an upper gate stood a dear little dark woman in a nice
little cap tied under her chin and this was Aunt Ellen. They
welcomed us most warmly, we felt at once as if we had known
them for years; they are all dears. Edward is very handsome,
tall & gentlemanly, a person to be proud of. Willie is at school
& Frank has just gone to sea, to China, so we shall not see him
at all. Willie will come home at Christmas, Edmund is in
Toronto. Featherston and his wife mean to come on Saturday,
with their two little children. We are going to dine at Brick's
at 1 and it is ½ past 12 now. His house is very near & very nice.
The two girls are most lovable and Uncle & Aunt are like our
very own people already. They seem not to know how to
make enough of us nor we of them. Ellen Mary & Charlotte sat
on our bed till 12 last night talking, and we were down at 8 to
breakfast ! We are too excited to feel tired but, I suppose it is
all to come. . . .'

A few weeks later Jennette wrote to her brother, William, a reporter in Bombay.

Dundas, Oct. 9, 1866.

'. . . Uncle's house & Bricks are two among the nicest in the place; they are large & comfortable & beautifully situated. You would like Edward. . . . He is strong & active, and a good cricketer, the only one of the boys who cares for the game; he skates, rides, fishes and shoots. . . . It is a fortnight since the last letter so I will try to go back a little.

'On Saturday evening Edmund came up from Toronto. He is six feet high and stout in proportion; he is nice looking, (but not so handsome as the elder boys) fair, & clever-looking; not at all shy, less conversational than Brick & Edward, who are full of fun & chaff. He is steady and gets on well at the Bank; unfortunately it has just failed and Uncle has lost his share profits; he has been paid his deposit entirely in cents, 100 in 4 shillings English, he has 20,000 of them tied up in little bags, 200 in each. Edmund is promised a better place in another bank.

'. . . Fen came in the evening and we went to tea at Carrie's to meet him. He is very gentlemanly, quiet, & agreeable; clever-looking, handsome, but less so than Brick & Ned, and we like him exceedingly. Brick & Fen are devoted to each other [and] Edward & Charlotte pair off. . . . Frank has a situation in Boston, he is going to sea in the spring. Nellie is very delicate and Charlotte does not look strong.'

Ellen wrote to William of the new arrivals:

Dundas, Oct. 1, 1866.

'. . . Our English relatives are now quite at home with us, and so far are pleased with Canada, and not I think displeased with their Canadian cousins. Of course Brick [B.B.] is their standard of perfection. Edmund . . . goes to Montreal, Quebec and Kingston to wind up the affairs of the unfortunate U.C. Bank. I hope the shareholders will not eventually lose by it. . . .

'I am glad that Frank wrote to you. B.B. saw him in Boston and thought him improved. We are all sorry he has not gone to sea again. . . .'

Ellen should have been warned that a school that advertised music and dancing might countenance graver follies. When William had returned to Weston after the holidays she wrote, 'Were you glad or otherwise when the Theatricals were given up ? I know who was glad—I can never fancy they can do good to anyone but have a tendency to do ill. . . . I am sorry Mr. Badgely advocates the evil . . . but truly thankful that it is . . . for the present set aside. . . .'

Ellen Mary (Nellie) and Charlotte (Chattie) were as enthusiastic as their brothers about their English cousins. Together they went to Weston to see Willie on sports day and he 'won four of the games. Leaping, racing and throwing weights were the chief amusements. . . .' In the evening they attended 'a capital dance . . . & slept in the drawing room on shake downs. . . . Willie,' wrote Jennette, 'is the handsomest of the family except that he is not tall & graceful like Ned & Edmund. He is extremely dark; a very nice gentlemanly boy.'

From Weston the quartet moved on to Toronto where they stayed at the now vanished Queen's Hotel. The Osler wives may well have been jealous for they 'dined at Fen's on Friday and Sunday', on Monday they lunched there, on Tuesday ate another dinner, 'and,' wrote Jennette, 'he and Edmund come to see us every day. Edmund spends the evening here when we are not out. . . .'

She found 'Toronto very English. There is less wood & more stone used than in Dundas or Hamilton. The people look like old country folk too, though not entirely for we are "spotted" (Canadian slang) for English wherever we go. There are some fine public buildings. Osgoode Hall, the law place, is splendid; a massive stone erection with a Hall up to the roof pillared and vaulted; tesselated pavements, carved work & pictures on all sides. They say there is no Court house in England to match it. On Saturday the Mathematical Professor at Trinity College invited us to lunch with him, so we went and saw the place, it is built in Gothic style but is small and poor; there are only 45 students. . . . After this we walked in King Street, the fashionable promenade, and in the evening Edmund fetched us to his lodgings where we met three friends of his, one of them a young Englishman, had an oyster supper and came home in good time.

'We are going to Bricks early in December and to Fen's after that. Henrietta is pleasant & kind; I think we shall like her; neither she nor Carrie are warmhearted to anyone but their husbands; just those self-contained natures that one likes & respects without growing fond of them; not a bit like the cousins . . . who are very affectionate. . . .

'Uncle is very nice; a large hearted considerate liberal minded man, unselfish & truly good. The more you know him the more highly you learn to appreciate him.'

A Canadian Christmas brought fresh excitement to the English cousins. All day until 11 o'clock on Christmas Eve they decorated the church. 'Willie & I,' wrote Jennette, 'cut the letters for four long texts in scarlet & gold, pasted them on plaid calico & edged them with wreathing. Marian covered numerous devices with green. Frank ran all the errands, and Edward & Edmund lent a fitful hand at odd times. Uncle procured the necessaries and was as over driven as most ministers at Xmas. . . . Aunt & Charlotte prepared food for the mighty household—the cook is only a kitchen girl, just for the heavy work. . . .' Fourteen were staying in the house and on Christmas Day twenty-three sat down to dinner, 'eighteen in the parlour & the rest in the kitchen. . . .' They drank the health of 'all friends to the North', 'and then,' Jennette wrote, 'had some music. Mr. Stratton sang some comic songs in character (they don't keep Xmas Day like Sunday here), Marion Osler, Edward's wife, sang old Ballads, and the rest did their little best; then we acted charades, & after all outsiders were gone, gathered round the kitchen stove with our feet up on the plate, to eat cake and drink a drop of comfort before parting for the night. Edmund gave us each a lovely little trinket made from the green brazils. . . .'

Henry Osler, their other parson uncle, expected a visit from his nieces. With his daughter Fanny he called on them at Dundas extending his invitation in person. Before he arrived Charlotte had described him to her cousins as a 'gay old bird' and Jennette wrote, 'it is quite true. He is most comical; a little springy active man, very like Aunt Etta in the face, but not in manner, saving a strange reticence at times.'

Marian and Jennette accepted his invitation and in February moved from one rectory to another. Jennette was delighted with their novel vehicle, ' "a jumper", that is to say a crockery crate cut down and laid on wooden runners, the basket work

[is] two feet high; half fill your crate with pease-straw stuffing (some like a cushion at the back); throw on a buffalo robe, get in and curl up on it, cover yourselves with more robes and you ride as warmly & easily as in the best London brougham with patent springs.' In this the sisters set off for the post office. 'Marian sat in front to drive and went on gallantly enough, till we came to the gate . . . [and] caught on the post. Out we were all tossed into the snow; the horse dragged the jumper upside down for a few yards, then the whipple-tree broke & he galloped to the stable; we picked ourselves up somewhat shaken but little hurt. . . .'

Life in Lloydtown resembled the later years at Tecumseth. 'The longer I am here,' Jennette wrote, 'the more I am surprised at the work that Uncle Henry gets through and the usefulness of the two little boys. Willie, 13, takes the entire charge of the two horses, cleans, feeds and harnesses them, prepares their food and makes himself useful in many ways besides. Ernest 10, has 5 sheep, two cows and a calf, 2 pigs and 3 rabbits to keep entirely, excepting the milking. Moreover he pumps all the water and brings in all the wood which Uncle chops. Willie drives the pair of spirited horses alone any distance; but Nellie has just been telling me that when Brick and Fen went to school as weekly boarders they would wake up poor little Edward then eight years old, drive off to school six miles at four in the morning and send him back in the dark with the pair of horses, driving through the bush, baby as he was for such work as that! They one & all here & at Dundas handle the reins as if they were born with them. . . .'

Marian's son Percy had not been included in the visit but 'dear Aunt Ellen with only one servant & plenty to do . . .

found time to write every other day to tell of [his] welfare. She is one of the blessed of the earth; one does not know how to respect & love her enough. I verily believe she has not a single proud or selfish thought. She just lives to do good.' So ends a letter of Jennette's.

At twenty-seven Britton supplemented his income from an already lucrative law practice by shrewd investments. He and Carrie were established in Staplehurst, a house large enough to boast a ballroom, when the English cousins came to stay. The hour-by-hour routine of the female members of his household is closer to Jane Austen's eighteenth century than to the backwoods the Oslers had so recently left.

'. . . We are very happy here,' Jennette wrote. 'Carrie is extremely kind; you need know her well to appreciate her; my first prejudice is rapidly wearing off. This is my usual day. Up at half past 7, then Carrie, Marian & I have a little scrimmage between our room & Percy's, that little man being usually in his bath . . . finally Brick's big voice is heard saying "Now you girls if you don't go to your rooms and dress like a streak of lightning I'll come & pull Carrie in by main force. I'm coming now" ! Of course we scud away to our proper quarters and in due time are ready for Prayers to which Percy comes in, behaving splendidly, & then breakfast. Brick goes to the office immediately after, and I give Percy his reading lesson. . . . This brings ½ past 10 after which we mostly work or write till one, when Brick returns to dinner bringing the daily papers. He just snatches his meal and goes off again like the cheery, happy, hardworking man he is, & then if the weather suits we go out and mostly stay till five, making a long visit at the Rectory on our way home. Brick comes home at six, and after tea, reads

aloud for an hour or so. We are having Dante's Inferno and
some Odes from Horace now, translated, of course. Then we
have some music or perhaps a rubber of whist. Supper at half
past 9 with Prayers first, and bed soon after 10. There are many
varieties and interchange of visits between this & the Rectory;
Sunday & one other day there, & some or all here twice a
week or oftener besides the daily calls. . . .'

May was a month of gentle dissipation.

'. . . My last was written from Toronto to where we pur-
posed staying a few days longer, but Lo ! four letters and a
telegram summoned us home instantly to attend a party given
in our honour, which would not be delayed; Dundas is in
little fits for such a quiet place. Carrie gave a croquet party two
days after; there was a large dance at Mrs. Geddes last week,
another croquet shine here; tonight one is to be at the Rectory;
we have a picnic in store for the Queens birthday with fireworks and a bonfire in the evening, & Carrie is going to give a
grand Ball before we go up the Lakes; three more parties at
other places are talked of, so you see we are somewhat gay—
These croquet parties are pleasant institutions. About a dozen
meet early & play croquet until seven. (Brick has two lawns &
a double set) then we have a high tea, & others drop in till perhaps 20 are there, when we dance, sing part songs, & generally
make ourselves happy till eleven, when cake & wine is handed
round, we have an 8 hand reel and "Sir Roger", sing "God
Save the Queen", in full chorus with the Colonial verse, &
then break up. . . .'

Carrie's ball ended the Dundas season. 'There was a nice
Quadrille band, and we danced through the program, 25
dances, breaking up in broad daylight soon after 4. The night

was mild & fresh, we paced the wide verandah or wandered among the beautiful trees in the moonlight between the dances; I have never enjoyed a party more. Charlotte was the belle and Alice Gwyn the most stylish. No gentleman looked better than Edmund; the girls raved over him. We had to be down as usual next morning after two hours' nap, but did not spend an industrious day. Mr Stratton is staying here, a most pleasant gentlemanly man. . . .'

Jennette, Marian and Percy returned to England in August, 1867, taking Charlotte with them for a return visit.

There was a general weeping and wailing at their departure.

William wrote to Jennette from Dundas, Aug. 6, 1867:

Dear Old Ὑιγγρος [Jennette]
How are your pocket handkerchiefs are they dry yet, none of mine are fit for use, and now when I want to have a good cry I have to bring the table cloth. It is very hard to wring out. After I saw the last wave of your handkerchiefs I left that wharf very sorrowful. . . . Your stock of snakes has increased, you have a black snake now. I killed one in the marsh. It is about three ft long and very thick. I just this minute caught a moth, a pretty little white fellow. I am writing in the study, it is about $\frac{1}{2}$ past eight p.m., the paternal and maternal, Fenn, Hennie and Nellie are sitting in the parlour talking away. . . .

Now Jennette good bye come out again to us soon for we miss you very much.

Believe me ever your aff. cousin,
Willie

Love to Mammy Muff [Marian] and Percy.

(William wrote 'Ὑιγρος' but probably meant 'Ὑιγγρος'—a Phoenician flute or pipe with high pitch and plaintive tone.)

Marian was also loved, particularly by her male cousins. Of

the two sisters, her reputation as enchantress rated even higher than Jennette's. But Marian destroyed her letters. Soon after her return to England she married George Francis, the same young man who had seen them off on the boat for Canada. After the wedding Jennette wrote to Britton asking him to make her will. He replied,

Dundas, 1868.

'As to your little will I enclose a draft founded on your [letter]. What a hopeful little Aunt it is & how encouraging must be the prospects when the watch & trinkets are to go, not to the daughter (as of one) but to the eldest living daughter (as of many) What faith! What cradles! What night watches! What measles! What a proud & happy Aunt!!'

They all confided in Jennette, even Featherstone, who confessed himself a stranger in an alien land.

'... Your Uncle Henry calls himself a Canadian and Canada his country and truly it is a very good one and perhaps as a whole there is no country which has greater advantages and fewer disadvantages; but with me England is home and I love the very name and in my heart I yearn to see it. Whether I shall be able to do so this summer is yet uncertain. I feel that I want a little change which is not unnatural after twenty four years hard work of body and mind with one week's holiday during the whole of that time. I propose sometimes to your Aunt that I should be superannuated but she says "you are not yet worn out" and I suppose I must believe her.

'I cannot tell you how your letters make me long to be with you . . . , to see the sea, to wander by the rocks and to feel as if there were no duties pressing upon me. . . . God bless you all, my dear Jennette. . . .'

Featherstone often longed for England but probably never more than in the year 1868. Thomas Devey Jermyn Farmer in a privately printed book, *A History of the Parish of St. John's Church, Ancaster*, 'with numerous poetic allusions and quotations' by the author, describes a rebellion that surely produced a gnashing of teeth from the Rev. F. L. Osler. Mr. Farmer wrote with great delicacy: 'Let me just mention as briefly as I can . . . how it came about in 1868 that Mr. Osler severed his connection with Ancaster. Immediately after the fire (in which the church was destroyed) . . . prompt steps were taken to rebuild, and many vestry and other meetings were held. Differences arose between the rector and some of the more headstrong of his people over the style of the new church and over the subscriptions to the building fund. No doubt there were faults on both sides, as is usually the case in such disputes—perhaps an inclination to tyrannize on the clergyman's part and a desire and a determination to rule in matters not properly within their province on the part of some of the congregation. It is neither seemly nor necessary here to mention any names to this ordinary church "row" looming so large then to those concerned. . . . At the bottom of it all was . . . a desire on the Ancaster people's part to run their own parish in the future disassociated from Dundas, and no doubt had any other clergyman than the Reverend Canon Osler been rector of the two parishes, the same result . . . would have happened. . . . And so, after a more or less unfortunate display of hostility on both sides an arrangement was happily and finally come to by which, . . . subject to the approval of the bishop, St. John's vestry were to be allowed to select their own incumbent or vicar. Mr. Osler was to receive $300 a year from Ancaster so long as he lived or contin-

ued rector, and for this sum he gave up entirely all connection with St. John's except that he still retained the title of rector....'
Even Mr. Farmer's restraint cannot conceal the fury of the battle. The people of Ancaster won but what a price they had to pay for victory ! $300 a year and Featherstone banished, but still nominal head of the parish.

It is strange that no mention is made in letters of either the row or the exceedingly odd bargain that settled it. Perhaps the evidence was destroyed when his son Featherston acted as self-appointed censor to a large collection of family correspondence.

In a *Sketch of the Life of Featherstone Osler* written by himself, no hint of discord appears. 'So soon as the leases of the Rectory lands expired,' he writes, '. . . I relet on improving leases, giving up for nine years the rental which I might have received, for the general improvement of the property. So much was it improved that when the property was sold, it realized $600.00 instead of $60.00 which it was worth when I took possession. From the increased income of the parish I was enabled to engage the services of an assistant minister to reside in Ancaster, and so give a morning and evening service there.' This was the version he wrote for the benefit of his descendants.

CHAPTER TEN

Family Affairs

IN THE autumn of 1867, a few weeks after the cousins returned to England, William started a new life at Trinity College, Toronto.

Though the Church was still his chosen future he devoted ever increasing hours to the microscope.

Ellen Mary wrote to Jennette:

June 17, 1868.

'. . . I thoroughly enjoyed your rave over Willie, it was so like you, Oh Jennette of visionary ideas. Unintentionally I must have mislead you as to Willie . . . entering the Ministry of his own free choice. Papa would prefer his becoming almost anything except a misunderstood poorly paid backwoods parson. No, my objections were that Willie was neglecting the works that from choice and his own will he chose to take up and instead of reading for his scholarship and honours, wasted his time over intricate Theological controversies.

'When in Toronto I made a point of speaking to Dr. Bovel (Willie's greatest friend) to ask his candid opinion as to the boy's future . . . and which way he would advise me to throw my influence. He said by no means dissuade him from the Church; underneath the surface his feelings were deep & sincere and the boy, having varied talents, was never likely to strikingly excel in any one thing. . . . Willie has been reading very hard this last term & I hope may come out well at the examinations. My argument is that he should not attempt two good things at once, thereby spoiling both. . . .'

Bovell had no inkling that his favourite pupil would soon dedicate his life to the art and science of medicine, content to leave theology to others.

Bovell had helped to organize the medical department for Trinity College of which he became both Dean and Professor of the Institutes of Medicine. When the school closed he joined the Toronto Medical School Faculty but retained the Chair of Natural Theology at Trinity where he lectured on physiology and pathology. His *pièce de résistance* was a course entitled 'Physiology as Related to Theological Conceptions'.

No wonder William was confused. Science was shaking the dogmas of religion, religion confusing the new dogmas of science.

Sir Thomas Browne's *Religio Medici*, a book first introduced to him by Father Johnson at Weston, made a lifelong impression on a boy torn between the two words of its title. He bought his first copy in 1868 and in 1919 this same volume lay on his coffin in Christ Church Cathedral, Oxford. Between these dates he collected at least one of every edition of his key book.

William returned to Trinity for his second year in Arts but after a week announced his intention to enter Medicine. From that day on the youngster whose talents were so varied that he 'was never likely to strikingly excel in any one thing', became a directed and concentrated force.

During the winter of '69 he stayed with Dr. Bovell and

Featherston Osler

Britton Bath Osler

William Osler

Edmund Boyd Osler

here, for the first time, lived in close association with a large and catholic library. From Bovell and his books he learned more than from the lectures at the then uninspiring Toronto Medical School. But the following spring Bovell returned to his previous home, the West Indies, and at his advice William left Toronto in September, 1870 and entered McGill University. Montreal was then the centre of the Canadian medical world and to Palmer Howard, Professor of Medicine, he handed a letter of introduction from his departed teacher and friend. Howard became the third father-teacher of his student days.

Christmas brought William home for a brief visit. 'They were all very swell last night,' Ellen Mary wrote to Jennette, 'dress suits for the gentlemen. I wore my grey . . . which is liked better than any other I have, the waist being very much trimmed with scarlet velvet. . . . Edmund brought our immense wild turkey and Brick the champagne.' Featherston's present to Nellie was Jean Ingelow's *Story of Doom*. It is pleasant to read that 'Edmund gave Mama a most lovely bouquet' and that 'Willie, who lives in the Red Chair [Featherstone's], kept repeating "I wish Υιγγρος was here, blame it Jennette has no business not to be here!"'

Time: the day after Christmas. Scene: the Rectory breakfast room. 'Mama [is] packing mince pies & cake, jam etc. in Edmund's valise; Willie & Marion [Edward's wife] are sitting at the end of the table devouring all they can get. . . . Edmund & Willie are never to be seen without a mince pie. . . . Willie has eaten a dozen this morning, & raisons, but not warm ones. . . .'

Jennette was perhaps the first person to recognize William's potential ability. Intelligent herself she encouraged the wakening intellect of her young cousin. Whether she too revelled

in 'hunts for "beasts"' or whether she assumed an interest for
his sake is not known. Most young men of nineteen fall in
love. William's choice remained a lifelong friend.

William Osler to Jennette:

Dundas, Jan. 1, 1868.

I was just asking Nellie to give me a start as I am a gnat
stupid at letter writing. But I am going to try to write a good
long [one] to little Ττγγρος. In the first place many thanks for
the beetles. . . . I was so rejoiced to see those big fellows pop out
of the parcel. The little mother immediately began to kiss and
hug them as though they were human beings. They are such
beauties. I had heard about them but I had not seen them. . . .

Nellie, mother & myself are . . . sitting round the table
writing English letters. Nellie has got a bad cold and has been
drinking Port. She says that she's drunk. She is acting as if she
was for she is lecturing me about my letters and accusing me of
eating too much cake.

I am getting on very well at college. I attend the Medical
School every afternoon. . . . At Dr. Bovell's every Saturday we
put up preparations for the microscope. I am grinding at
Lyells Principles of Etiology this vacation and I hope to get
through it before term begins. . . .

I would throw out here, my Ursula [another nickname for
Jennette], that I might give thee warm raisons though raisons
are scarce this year. . . . Do you know whether Uncle Edward's
works "On Burrowing and Boring Marine Animals" and on
the "Anatomy and Habits of Marine Testaceous Mollusca" are
published or not ? If they are please tell me . . . where I can get
them. . . .

Believe me ever your affec. cousin,
Willie

The bread-and-butter letter was one of the family's sacred
cows and its neglect called forth from Ellen a sterner rebuke

than the fumigating episode that landed her Benjamin in jail. William had returned to Trinity after (presumably) the Easter holidays.

Ellen to William:

Dundas, March 27, 1868.

My dear Willie

If you erred through ignorance I freely forgive, especially after receiving your nice letter yesterday, but know now and forever, that it is a long established custom in the polite world, (to say nothing of stronger home ties) that when an individual has been an inmate of a family for a season, to intimate to that family his safe arrival at home or elsewhere—so I hope you'll understand for the future. . . .

. . . We have heard of Frank (not from him though). The Captain very kindly wrote to tell us they had arrived safely at Caldera. . . .

I am going to ask Belle Smith [Edmund's fiancée] to spend Easter with us and I hope Edmund may come up too. . . .

After the failure of the Upper Canada Bank, Edmund joined forces with Henry Pellatt, father of Sir Henry whose dreams of glory turreted into Toronto's only castle. Their partnership in the brokerage business lasted until 1882 when Edmund Osler and H. C. Hammond founded the still existing firm, Osler and Hammond.

At twenty-three Edmund was well able to support a wife and in 1868 he married Isabella (Belle) Lammond Smith, an event approved of by both families.

The same year Nellie eloped with Alexander Erskine Williamson. Perhaps he was a Methodist, reason enough not to ask or expect parental approval. The family found no good in Mr. Williamson but his wife thought otherwise and when he died a few years later she mourned him exceedingly, blaming their infant, Alex, for his death. Suffering from a heavy cold Williamson had gone to fetch the doctor for his child's delivery. The father died. The baby barely breathed. Ellen took charge and wrapped him in cotton wool. Safe in her tender care he lived, a future grief to himself and to those about him.

Marian, her new husband and Percy and Jennette settled in Canada in 1869; the Francis family in Montreal and Jennette back and forth between the Dundas Rectory and her sister's house. Back in Falmouth, Samuel Osler, the 'tindery' one whose love affairs had so incensed his elder brother in the twenties, continued to rile Edward's daughter in the seventies.

Marian Francis to her aunt, Elizabeth Osler:

Montreal, Feb. 25, 1870.

'. . . I can not see that you are at all bound to help Uncle Sam in *any* way. If a brother had behaved to me in the manner he has done to you & also had disgraced himself & invariably acted with such deep hypocrisy—I should hold no further communication with him, let him be 70 or 80. I believe him to be the most designing hypocrite. It is not long since he tried to influence William Henry [Marian's brother] to league with him to *do you* out of everything—trying to persuade him that as the eldest son of the eldest son he could make a claim & wanted to institute legal proceedings. Do *keep entirely clear of him* & don't believe his protestations of want. He made the same to Papa [Edward] & when he pinched himself to spare him . . . money, Uncle Sam spent it at hotels & on Prostitutes. I have heard things of him . . . which make one's blood curdle & I trust you will not let your sisterly feeling lead you away. . . .

'I hope you will write to the Exiles sometimes. . . . It seems strange in all this great city to have no relatives or friends. . . . I am longing to behold one green leaf—only perpetual snow. The winters are twice as severe here as up west with Uncle [Featherstone].

'Everything—poultry, meat etc. in the market is frozen like a rock. Our butcher killed three hundred sheep in one day—it saves their feed. He keeps them frozen and chops off an ugly joint for you. The meat is very inferior, especially down here among the French farmers. Two thirds of the population . . . are Roman Catholics & it is a hot bed of Jesuits. . . . I have a bigoted Roman Catholic cook but a very good servant [and] a Highland Scotch Presbyterian housemaid. . . .'

George Francis travelled. Why or where remains a question. William's arrival in Montreal brought cheer and a welcome male to Marian's frequently manless household.

Jennette to Ellen:

Montreal, Jan. 16, 1871.

'. . . Willie shed the light of his face on us this evening, with the English letters to ensure him a double welcome. I cannot tell you what a pleasure it is to us to have the dear merry fellow coming in & out. . . . We hear his praises on all sides and from those whose good opinion is hard to win and well worth having. Your Benjamin is pronounced "thoroughly reliable", "as good as he is clever", "the most promising student of the year", & finally, from a learned Professor, slow in approbation, "a splendid fellow". Now little Mother, purr over that; we did! Willie says nothing himself and does not put on airs at all.

He took me to Church last night and we got well drenched in coming home; then frost followed and the milkman had to crawl up the steps like a four-footed beast or creeping thing. . . .'

Ellen passed on the good news to her sister-in-law, Elizabeth Osler:

Jan. 18, 1871.

'. . . I will send you [a photograph] of Willie as soon as I get them from Montreal. He is going on there in a very satisfactory manner, a great favourite with everyone, the leading Medical men especially, so I ought to be thankful; indeed I have been very lovingly dealt by in every way, all the past years of my life, and only wish I had a more grateful heart. . . .'

Except for William's success at McGill Ellen had little to be grateful for in the year 1871. Frank's whereabouts were not known. Edward deserted his wife and two small children. His elder daughter never forgot her mother's frantic search for a note of explanation. No note was found. They shook the piggy bank in vain for Edward had shaken it first.

Edmund, prospering financially, was stricken domestically. His first son, born in 1869, died seven months later; his wife and second son the following year. The proud family man found himself a childless widower at twenty-six.

Nellie had fared no better. On July 3, 1872, Charlotte married Herbert Charles Gwyn, a barrister in the same firm as her brother Britton. Chattie, like her mother, proved a good breeder and produced five sons and four daughters. But money did not grow for Charlie. There is an occasional glimpse of him in Ellen's letters to her daughter. One ends 'love to Charlie and the *other* children'.

After his sister's wedding Edmund sailed for England, taking his youngest brother along as company on the voyage but principally to give the newly graduated doctor an opportunity to work in London hospitals. Study abroad was the immediate necessity and Edmund made it possible.

CHAPTER ELEVEN

The Young Doctor

THEY toured together in Ireland before Edmund visited Aunt Lizzie in Falmouth and business called him to Manchester, Liverpool and London. But the prime objective of his trip was Aberdeenshire, Scotland, where he stayed with relations of his late wife. There he met Anne Farquharson Cochran, whom he married a year later, in Sept. 1873, and henceforth, until her death in 1910, Edmund had his fair share of domestic good fortune. But his early grief had accentuated or produced an ever-present anxiety concerning those he loved, and though often free from care he was rarely free from apprehension.

In London William received pungent whiffs of the Rectory air through letters from his mother.

> Dundas, Autumn, 1872.
>
> My beloved Benjamin,
> This is a scrap to thank you for the nice letter of Oct. 2 and to say that I cannot write much this week having a pan of citron waiting to be transformed into jam. Don't I wish I could transport you a jar full when it is made.
> . . . Aunt Lizzie writes with much purring over Edmund and wants very much to know Willie. . . . You had better write the dear old soul and give her your address. Chattie keeps well and saucy. She often runs up to see us and as a matter of course no one goes down town without running in to see her. . . .

You want Frank's address—Mud River, Winnipeg, Manitoba.

Father has sent him up $200 to take up his farm then comes another $100 for the winter supply of provisions. Poor boy he promises well and we must still hope on. God love and bless you my dear Willie. Ever your loving mother in a whirl of hurry.

In October, 1872, William received a letter from McGill offering him the Chair of Botany which he refused on the reasonable ground that he knew little about the subject.

To Jennette or Marian from William:

London, Oct. 1872.

This private and confidential.

McGill College was foolish enough to offer me about six weeks ago the Chair of Botany at the University. Botany is a thing I know next to nothing about and is a subject I could not get up with my studies—consequently I have sent a polite refusal. I am afraid from his letter . . . that Dr. Howard expected me to accept it but really I would have made an ass of myself in so doing and that is not to my mind. . . . I hope Dr. Howard did not tell anyone but yourselves and pray that you have not sent [the news] west. Of course the Paternal as well as many others will think I am just as well fitted to take Botany as anything else, but I should feel like an imposter. . . .

I shall . . . return to Montreal but it will probably be as a private practitioner unless some further offer is made which I do not expect . . . in connection with McGill. I do wish you would not build upon me for doing anything beyond my fellows. My abilities are but moderate and I can feel bitterly sometimes that deficiencies in early education and want of thoroughness drag me back at every step. In addition to all this I have my bread to earn and . . . general medical studies demand the time which might be spent in acquiring a reputation. One thing is certain,

the cultivation of these scientific pursuits at the expense of paying ones is an injustice to oneself and, if he ever has one, to his
family.

On prayers for the dead I will write in my next but it has
always seemed to me a doctrine which commended itself to the
affections rather than the reason.

With much love
Yours Willie.

William then proceeded to spend the greater part of his life
in 'the cultivation of these scientific pursuits at the expense of
paying ones'.

When Jennette's brother, a newspaper reporter, died in Bombay, his letter of sympathy began 'I hardly know how to write.
... You understand my undemonstrative nature, but know also, how underneath it, my feelings are as deep as any, though I
may be and am, slow in expressing them . . .' and ended
'Write to me often and remember always that though your
natural brother has been taken from you I trust you will allow
me as far as possible to occupy his place. . . .'

His London letters, less vivid than those written more than
fifty years earlier by his Uncle Edward, are concerned with the
same subjects, science and religion.

To Jennette:

'London Nov. 9, 1872.

'. . . We were able to see a good number of the animals before five o'clock when the [zoo] closed. As you may imagine I
was delighted with everything from the little water pidgeons
to the gigantic elephants. I had not time to see the monkey
house. Not liking to do my nearest relatives in a careless manner I have determined to take a special afternoon at them. They

say the new chimpanzee has made many converts to the Darwinian theory, from its horrible likeness to some men. . . .'

With one foot resting on Darwin, the other on the Oxford Movement, William found his balance precarious. The letter continues: 'I shall be quite spoilt for the singing in Canada . . . I was even beginning to like anthems, though I object strongly to them on principle. . . .'

And to his sister Chattie he wrote: 'Christ Church, Albany Street, which is almost within a stone's throw, is not nearly so high [as All Saints], no vestments, incense or the like, but I do not want to become enamoured of those as I will not get them in Montreal nor can I quite forego the notion that they are not orthodox (Johnson and Bovell to the contrary). . . .'

William left London for Berlin in September, 1873. There, and later in Vienna, he studied under the great medical men of the day. He returned to London in April, '74, and a short time later sailed for Canada.

William to Chattie:

April 16, 1874.

'I am still in London having postponed my Cornwall visit. . . . Prof. Sharpey, the Vice-President of the Royal Society, kindly gave me an introduction to their Soiree which comes off next Wednesday and as it is a very swell affair—swell in my line—I shall wait for it. . . .

'I have got very low church lately and am afraid Father Johnson and Wood [of St. John the Evangelist, Montreal] will be horrified. . . .'*

Among other notables at the 'Soiree' William met Charles Darwin.

* Cushing: *The Life of Sir William Osler.*

He returned to Canada with a fine store of knowledge but with no money and no prospects. For a few weeks he relieved the local practitioner in Dundas, then worked with Dr. Charles O'Reilly, resident physician at the City Hospital in Hamilton.

In July he received a letter from Palmer Howard, Professor of Medicine at McGill, offering him the office of lecturer of the Institutes of Medicine (pathology and physiology). Nothing could have suited William better.

He moved to Montreal in August, 1874, and a year later, at 26, was made a full professor. His industry became a byword among his colleagues. The microscope, teaching, small-pox wards, his innumerable scientific papers—everything occupied him except private patients for whom he had neither the time nor the inclination. He lived frugally, undisturbed by poverty.

Marian Francis and her children supplied his domestic needs. Jennette joined them when she learned of her sister's illness.

To Miss Jennette Osler from W.O.:
'Dear Janet, Marian continues poorly, but nothing definite can yet be said of the nature of her illness. Fever is the chief symptom, though it has never been high. She is easier than she was & takes plenty of beef-tea and milk. Her spirits are good. If it is to be Typhoid it will in all likelihood be a very mild case. Howard is looking after her with me & tomorrow if any decision is arrived at & you are wanted I shall telegraph. . . . I look after Marian at night, running up & down at intervals, & taking a nap on the chair or couch. She is a good patient and no trouble. . . . Love to all yours etc. Willie.'*

Marian recovered but not before Jennette had packed her

* Cushing.

bag and left for Montreal. The next sixteen years of her life she
devoted to the Francis children. Their numbers increased until
Marian had given birth to seven boys and four girls. Marian
produced but she left it to Jennette to bring the produce up.

How prophetic Britton had been when he wrote his cousin
about her 'little will', and ended, 'What faith ! What cradles !
What night watches ! What measles ! What a proud & happy
Aunt !'

Marian (Francis) Osborne described the young McGill professor in *Recollections of Sir William Osler* '. . . My brother and
I used to watch for him to come home from his lectures. He
always came down the street at a swinging pace with the spring
on the ball of the foot, which he kept till the day of his last
illness. He entered the house with a cheerful whistle . . . "O, the
darlings", he would call out gaily and wave to us in greeting.
Then he would put his hands lightly on the dining-room table
and vault across its width. To us it seemed a marvellous feat. . . .

'When Uncle Bill first had to lecture . . . my mother
[Marian Francis] spent many hours in practice with him that
he might train and pitch his voice so that it could be heard. He
had trouble, too, in preparing his lectures and my Aunt, Miss
Jennette Osler, who lived with us, used to proof-read them with
him and help him towards a literary style. It is typical of the
man whose "Master-word" was "Work" that he strove until
he had overcome his lack of elocution, his shyness and Osler
reserve, and had attained a masterly simplicity of style. . . .'

When Jennette was an old woman she wrote the following
note about their household:

'While we were living in Montreal Willie was a frequent
visitor, especially during his later student years and his pro-

fessorship. We were then living on McGill College Avenue and he would look in almost every afternoon for 5 o'clock tea with Marian and the baby and dowager baby—successively Brick, Willie, Gwen and Bea—this explains the interest and affection he has always shown for them—not so much for Brick who was . . . my special boy and who usually preferred to stay with me and the other older children. . . . He was my dearest friend as well as cousin; we studied German together for a time, but the children left me little leisure or quiet and he very soon distanced me. He was the Well-beloved of the whole family and Willie F[rancis] adored him from his babyhood. He went regularly to church (St. John the Evangelist) and spoke of things religious with unfailing reverence.'*

During his lifetime William never forgot Willie,† Gwen and Bea and after his death they were remembered in his will. But his interest in the Church declined. By the end of his Montreal years it was hard to guess what if any were his opinions on theological questions.

* Cushing.
† Dr. William Francis, librarian of the Osler Library at McGill.

CHAPTER TWELVE

Lawyer and Judge

IN 1877 Edward was trying, unsuccessfully, to practise law in Winnipeg, a new boom town that optimists predicted would soon become the navel of Canada in more senses than the geographic. He found his profession only too well represented. Twenty-three lawyers had settled there before him. His father and mother must have suffered something graver than their chronic concern when Featherstone made the long journey west. 'It was an effort,' he wrote to Jennette, 'to leave the mother for nearly a month. Our time now in which we can be together must necessarily be short, but my heart yearns to see and encourage Edward. . . .'

While Featherstone commands respect for a certain tough courage, an unwavering determination to act according to his own uncompromising lights, one seldom warms to the man, as revealed in letters and journals. His most endearing quality lay in his affection for Ellen and his children and grandchildren. He found Edward 'looking well' but 'depressed'. Frank he could not visit for he was 'nearly a month's journey from Winnipeg' [in British Columbia] but 'many persons here speak of him. He was a general favorite, kind to everybody but himself. . . .' Featherstone enjoyed the trip, much of it by water, though not salt.

F. Osler to Jennette:

Winnipeg, Aug. 1, 1877.

'I left home on Saturday week last, the trip up the lakes was delightful. Weather fine and water smooth. We called at the Bruce mines where everything is dull as . . . can . . . be. . . . Prince Arthur's Landing . . . was our next stopping place. Here we found disappointment and depression among the people. They had hoped and expected [Prince Arthur to be] the terminus of the Pacific railway . . . but the Government located at Fort William; consequently many who gave large prices for land and built expensive houses are heavy losers. Our next stopping place was Duluth, a town at the extreme head of Lake Superior. Here we arrived too late for the train and were consequently delayed . . . for two days. Like Washington, this may be called the city of magnificent distances; the population is about 2000 and the houses scattered over the face of a hill. Two years ago $100 a foot was asked and paid for building lots on the front street. Now land is not saleable, like many American towns on the prairie. . . . Lake Superior City, about 5 miles distant, which was to rival Chicago, has . . . not one house in twenty occupied. Here ends what might be termed comfortable travelling. . . .'

Featherstone continued by rail, '. . . the road follows the course of the [St. Louis] river which at one place for nearly four miles was a succession of cascades. The trestle works over some of the gorges seem too fragile to be safe. They ranged from 80 to 100 feet in height and on either side were banks of rock and a man on each bridge ready to put out any fire which from the engine might drop on the bridge. The diner is changed each 270 miles. At nine o'clock in the evening we had supper at one place and at 4 o'clock next morning we were called to have

breakfast in another. . . . Here we crossed prairie country; as
far as the eye could reach . . . an apparently boundless plain
with red wavy grass. . . . Our next stop was Fisher's Landing
. . . a rowdy frontier village, the resort of rogues and gamblers.
Here we were delayed for hours while the steamer put on her
cargo. I was fortunate enough to get a . . . berth but at least
40 had to sleep on the cabin floor.

'The steamer which is flat bottomed, propelled by a wheel
at the stern, is nearly as long as the river is wide. On Saturday
evening we sighted Fort Pembroke, the American side of the
boundary line. As we approached there were many officers
and women . . . who seemed to be very polite, everyone wav-
ing a handkerchief, but on coming nearer it was found that it
was not politeness to us but [to ward off] mosquitoes. . . . At
nearly midnight we reached the first village on the English
side, called Emerson. . . .'

. . .

In 1879 Featherston, forty-one years old and the father of
seven children, left the bar for the bench.

Sir John A. Macdonald to Featherston Osler:

Ottawa, February 28, 1879,
House of Commons
Confidential.

My dear Osler:

I want a judge and it has occurred to me that you would
make a good judge. I have not mentioned your name to the
Minister of Justice or to my colleagues until I knew whether
you were tired of the bar and would not object to the bench.
Of course I mean the Superior Court bench.

Let me know by tel whether you will accept the judgeship

if offered. Yes or no will be sufficient. Remember the appointment must be made for the Spring Circuits. I remain

Yours faithfully
John A. Macdonald.

Featherston could not make up his mind. A series of telegrams ensued. Amongst them:

To Featherston Osler:

March 3, 1879.

Have you received my letter. Please answer.

John A. Macdonald.

To Featherston Osler:

March 3.

Certainly consult your friends.

John A. Macdonald.

On the 5th Featherston replied, 'I would accept if offered'. His elevation to the bench was only the outward symbol of the inner man. His critical nature had been judging human frailty since the days of his youthful letters to B.B.

He wrote a characteristic letter to his parents announcing the appointment.

March 6, 1879.

'You will probably have seen in the papers some indications that I was to be appointed to the vacant Judgeship in the Court of Common Pleas. I believe it is true that I am to receive the offer and having consulted some friends on the subject I have determined to accept it. The income derived is rather less than my present professional income but at my apt considering that I should find a continuance of my present work tell upon me too severely I think I shall be doing better even in a pecuniary sense by accepting the offer—the honor is one which I value as much for your sakes as anything else and I can only hope that I shall prove equal to the weight of it. Professional friends are kind enough to speak well of it and I believe that the appointment generally will be a popular one. I shall run up to see you soon and with love to Nellie who I know will be as much gratified as yourselves.'

Britton's spontaneous note of congratulations illuminates the differences in the brothers' temperaments.

Osler, Gwyn and Teetzel
Hamilton, March 7, 1879.

My dear Fen

I received your telegram at 7 p.m. and answered it—I have to extend my hearty congratulations and well wishes over the event and to say that you will only regret the change for a short time. The appointment is well received here on both sides of politics and those who do not know you will, when they do, be satisfied. . . .

The call has been pretty sudden and loud but the swear in tomorrow is, I suppose, a necessity. . . . I send down by C[arrie] my new coat and vest as the one in the Hall is pretty shabby. Smart is bringing me out a new silk which you can have and I will send for another. If you are not coming up I will send 'Corc Principles of Punishment', a good book for leading ideas in measuring out sentences, one of the most difficult branches of your . . . work.

Goodby Barrister, welcome Judge

Ellen was gratified, and said so in a letter to Featherston's wife, but not overwhelmed. Practical matters still existed, such as her need for lace to trim muslin pinafores.

Dundas, March 1879.

'A little scrap dear Hennie by way of telling you how pleased we are to hear of dear Fen's promotion. You, I'm sure, will be fully satisfied that Fen is truly appreciated by his fellow men. I do hope he will not now have so much strain and mental work day by day and night by night. . . . The Office will be the greatest sufferer, if any do feel sad about it. I know he will be at times inclined to take his bag and be off after breakfast to the familiar spot. . . . I saw Carrie for a moment yesterday, she says you are likely to be up next Tuesday. Will you be troubled to get for me a couple dozen yds. of lace edging for muslin pinafores not too wide or too expensive, it is for Bazaar work. . . .'

Four years later Featherston was offered a seat in the Court of Appeal. Again he hesitated.

From Sir Alexander Campbell to the Hon. Featherston Osler:

Ottawa, Nov. 10, 1883.

My dear Sir:

With the entire concurrence of the Premier I write to propose to you that you take a seat in the Court of Appeals. . . . We are quite satisfied that such a transfer of your services would be attended with very great advantages to the public service and I . . . hope to hear favourably from you on Monday.

Perhaps you will be kind enough to telegraph a few words on receiving this and if . . . the reply be in the affirmative I will prepare and submit to his Excellency in Council my recommendation for the appointment at once. With great esteem,

Faithfully yours,

A. Campbell

From Sir A. Campbell to the Hon. Featherston Osler:

> Department of Justice,
> Ottawa
> Nov. 14, 1883.

My dear Sir:

Your second telegram from Owen Sound has just reached me and I write a few lines . . . before you answer my proposal, to express the anxiety of both Sir John A. Macdonald and myself that you should accept the offer which my letter made.

It has become of the greatest moment to strengthen the Court of Appeal and we are persuaded that this can be done better by your going there than in any other way which can be adopted, and he desires therefore to submit it to you as a matter of duty as well as obligation which it will confer on Sir John and myself. He has asked that this as regards himself should be specially mentioned to you. . . .

> Faithfully yours,
> A. Campbell.

From F. Osler to A. Campbell:

> Toronto Nov. 15, 1883.

My dear Sir A.C.

I have to acknowledge the receipt of your letter of the 10th & 14th inst. which convey in much too flattering terms the proposal that I should take the seat on the Court of Appeal, created by the recent vacancy. With the greatest hesitation and, I may add, reluctance and entirely in deference to this so strongly expressed wish of the premier and yourself, I have determined to assent to the proposal.

I am conscious that this is but a grudging and ungracious acceptance of such an offer made in such terms as you have been pleased to employ. My present position is however one which in regards my colleagues and the nature of my duties accords so entirely with my own feelings that any change must inevitably be distasteful.

I have a strong conviction that I can be more useful as a member of the High Court than the Appellate Court. If therefore the seat can be filled by any other way than by my removal from the C.P. I beg that my telegram and letter may be considered as cancelled. . . .

Featherston moved to the Appellate Court but would go no farther. When still greater honour was offered five years later he turned it down.

From Sir John A. Macdonald to F. Osler:

Ottawa, Sept. 28, 1888.

My dear Osler,

After conference with the Minister of Justice I desire to offer you a seat on the bench of the Supreme Court of Canada, vacant by the death of Mr. Justice Henry.

I hope you will be able to accept it. Will you kindly let me know by telegraphing yes or no and not mention the fact of the offer until I inform you that your name has been submitted to the Governor General.

Faithfully yours,

John A. Macdonald.

From F. Osler to Sir John A. Macdonald:

Toronto, Sept. 30, 1888.

Dear Sir John Macdonald:

I have to thank you for another instance of your too flattering considerations. I sincerely wish, so far as complying with your desires is concerned, that I could accept the very great honour that you offered me. It is however out of the question. Apart from private considerations, in themselves conclusive, my knowledge of the French "Language & Institutions" is altogether too limited to warrant me accepting a position in what is or ought to be the great Court of the Dominion, and for this reason as well as the private objections referred to, I am compelled to decline the high professional & personal advancement which you have thus placed within my reach. I am dear Sir John etc.

It is not known what 'private considerations' prevented his acceptance. In Featherston's obituaries much is made of his exceptional modesty. True, he lacked the exuberant self-confidence, the unselfconsciousness of William and Britton. Neither Featherston nor Edmund enjoyed the limelight but Featherston's mania for 'no publicity' had its roots in something other than humility. Reserve or pride or both would have been fitter words. Preoccupation with health, dislike of change, a reluctance to take on further responsibility, these may have been the lions in his way.

In 1892 Trinity College, of which he was a trustee and councillor, conferred on him the degree of Doctor of Civil Law. For many years he served as a senator of the University of Toronto, his white Jehovah beard adding its weight to the councils of higher learning.

At seventy-two, a mature age for the switch from justice to finance, he retired from the bench and became president of the Toronto General Trusts Corporation.

CHAPTER THIRTEEN

Ellen and William

FEATHERSTONE achieved his holiday at last and in the summer of '79 he and Ellen sailed for England. The former's homesickness for Cornwall was soon appeased by days of rain or drizzle. He wrote minute instructions to Nellie for the care of his garden and assured her that 'we miss you . . . so much, though here the people do all they can to spoil [us]. . . .' Ellen added, 'Thank God for good tidings from home and we will still hope all may be well, but when there is no letter I cannot help feeling somewhat fidgetty. . . .' It is obvious that neither contemplated spending their last days in the country of their birth. Edmund was in Falmouth the same year, and probably Featherston, for their Aunt Lizzie wrote, 'The dear Willie [seems] almost lost sight of. No one mentions him until the father [Featherstone] . . . speaks of his world-wide reputation. . . . Fen and Edmund, such fine specimens of men they are—the English gentlemen with American energy. . . . I hope we may see some of them again next summer. . . .'

By 1882 Featherstone's health had deteriorated sufficiently for Ellen to think him 'worn out' at last and he retired. With Nellie and Alex they moved from Dundas to Toronto where their house, 83 Wellesley Street, became the focal point of the ever-increasing clan.

The same year Frank married Isobel Fowler and it was to

her that Edmund entrusted their quarterly allowance. From now on Frank rarely felt the touch of cash in his hand. Only William occasionally relented and slipped his brother enough for a modest spree.

B.B., who had left Dundas for Hamilton in 1874 when he became Crown Attorney for Wentworth, in 1880 joined a Toronto firm, subsequently known as McCarthy, Osler, Hoskin & Creelman. Featherston and Edmund had long been established in the tory and provincial city of Toronto, the now obvious centre of the family circle.

Featherstone had retired but not Ellen, according to her breathless letter to Jennette.

83 Wellesley St., Feb. 15, 1883.

'I tried to get a short note written last night but by the time I had two letters for England and one for Dundas, Nellie out all the afternoon and evening, Rachel [a grandchild] to bathe, and numberless items to see to there was no time left and today has been a continual whirl, Nellie came home with a bad head-ache last night and has been in bed all day (I hope only a temporary bilious attack) there was a parcel to make up for C[hattie] to send by Ex[press], Belle [Frank's wife] came early to stay to lunch, there was a small pig in process of cutting up and the lard to be rendered, then two letters to write and before all could be done, in came two sets of callers, and Carrie to stay for a couple of hours, so you may judge that I have not much time on hand. . . .

'I ought to be feeling at home . . . and perhaps I am. The house is very comfortable and warm as we can wish but after 25 years and more in one place it takes time to settle down in another—

I miss Chattie too as might be supposed. Meantime I am kept very busy and take the days as they come and find them not long enough for all that I would like to do, for I have not the energy or ability of bygone years. . . . I seem to have been living in one perpetual whirl . . . and my daily negligences are many. . . .'

William shocked the Canadian medical world by proclaiming useless ninety per cent of the current drugs. Ellen, too, was abstemious in regard to medicine. But she had a small pot-pourri of household remedies and was fond of prescribing for her physician son. William was still in Montreal, a distinguished member of his profession, when she wrote, 'I could not help feeling worried about that horrid carbuncle though I felt you were in the best of hands for treatment and nursing at Dr. Howard's. . . . We shall look for a note to-morrow and hope to hear . . . you are . . . better—would not Preparation of Weiths Beef, Iron & Wine, be good for you to take & no trouble if you kept it at hand. . . . If you indulge in boils you ought also to take the remedies required to heal them. . . .'

Whiskey was cheap when she described the Osler cure for the common cold.

'. . . On Monday I went to see Carrie & in some places the sidewalks were more than ankle deep with water. . . . Of course I changed everything when I got back & bathed my feet in whiskey, hoping to escape any ill effects but the cold came on and I dare say will run its course. I am swathed in cotton wool & vaseline and stayed in bed till 10.30 today—am taking great care of dear self. . . .' For earache, too, she had a remedy. 'Ethel had a very bad cold all last week. . . . Inflamation of the ear came on and Nellie was in requisition from 12 till 6 applying leeches.'

When William went again to Europe in 1884 his trunk may well have contained a jar of Ellen's oft-mentioned ointment and a bottle of Wieth's Beef, Iron & Wine. He stayed for six months, learning and listening and attending medical meetings. It was at Leipzig that he received a cable offering him the Chair of Medicine at the University of Pennsylvania. Many years later he recounted his indecision and his means of resolving it.

'I was resting in a German town when I received a cable from friends in Philadelphia, stating that if I would accept a professorship there I should communicate with Dr. S. Weir Mitchell who was in Europe and who had been empowered to arrange the details. I sat up late into the night balancing the pros and cons of Montreal and Philadelphia. . . . I finally gave it up as unsolvable and decided to leave it to chance. I flipped a four-mark silver piece into the air. "Heads I go to Philadelphia; tails I remain at Montreal." It fell "heads". I went to the telegraph office and wrote the telegram. . . . I reached in my pockets to pay for the wire. They were empty. My only change had been the four-mark piece which I had left as it had fallen on my table. It seemed like an act of Providence directing me to remain in Montreal. I half decided to follow the cue. Finally I concluded that inasmuch as I had placed the decision to chance I ought to abide by the turn of the coin, and returned to my hotel for it and sent the telegram.' In a farewell address before his departure for England fifteen years later he referred again to the event, possibly with a slight stretching of facts.

'Dr. Mitchell cabled me to meet him in London, as he and

his good wife were commissioned to "look me over", particularly with reference to personal habits. Dr. Mitchell said there was only one way in which the breeding of a man suitable for such a position, in such a city as Philadelphia, could be tested: give him cherry-pie and see how he disposed of the stones. I had read of the trick before and disposed of them genteely in my spoon—and got the Chair.'*

McGill regretted his departure. Dr. Palmer Howard wrote from The Saint Louis Hotel, Quebec, no date.

'. . . I don't know how to speak my own sentiments and those of the entire Fac.; the thought of losing you stuns us, and we feel anxious to do all that we can as sensible men to keep you amongst us, not only on account of your abilities as a teacher, your industry and enthusiasm as a worker, your personal qualities as a gentleman, a colleague and a friend; not only on account of the work you have already done in and for the school, but also because of the capabilities we recognize in you for the future useful work, both in original investigation which shall add reputation to McGill and in systematic teaching of any branches of Medical Science you may care to cultivate; and finally because we have for years felt that vitalizing influence upon us individually exercised by personal contact with you—analogous to that produced by a potent ferment. . . .'*

On William's departure for Philadelphia, Marian, her children, and Jennette left Montreal and settled in Toronto. George Francis, the traveller, was no longer an intimate of their household when they gravitated back to the family centre. '[Jennette],' Ellen wrote, 'needs a change and perfect rest, but what they would do without her is hard to say for in common par-

* Cushing.

lance she runs the house yet is content to be in the background.
. . .' Featherstone and Ellen celebrated their fiftieth wedding
anniversary among a sizable host of descendants and relations.
William was absent but his mother sent him a message on the
day, Feb. 7, 1887.

'Very many thanks for your *golden* note . . . more welcome
to us than a nugget of Californian gold. . . . We had a very
peaceful Jubilee. . . . The family dropped in by twos & threes
to offer kindly greeting to the . . . very much married people
and there were some little golden gifts in the shape of flowers,
and a jar of ginger found its way to the after dinner table to the
satisfaction of some of the juveniles. Hal and the two boys
[grandchildren] were at dinner, Clara, Fen, Marian [Francis]
were afternoon callers, Grant [Francis], Beatrice [Francis], the
two small boys at tea, Annie and the little girls after morning
Church and Edmund, Annie, Jennette & Gordon at supper.
B.B. has been from home for some days but is expected back
tomorrow. . . . Carrie is miserably poorly. . . . Chattie sent me
half a dozen very pretty Tidies from you for which many
thanks. . . .

'I am glad you wrote to Alex and to Nellie. I know she feels
badly at times about Alex and he is trying now and then—if
the bank fails him, or he leaves the bank I cannot see what else
he is fitted for. He wants to make money fast and is forever
counting up his gains etc.

'Father manages to prowl out a little nearly every day. . . . '

A month later Marion, the wife Edward had left fifteen
years earlier, died of some infectious disease at 83 Wellesley St.
Their elder daughter Isobel remained with Featherstone and
Ellen. Ethel went to live with her maternal grandmother.

From letters and hearsay one must indeed conclude that Ellen was 'one of the blessed of the earth' but the sweetness of her nature did not express itself in syrup and those who knew her say that her tongue was quick and to the point. But Ellen in a worldly mood, as when she wrote to William of the engagement of an English cousin, Emma Dash, produces a (not unpleasurable) sensation of shock.

1887.

'. . . she is likely to be married next May—old Dr. Truran . . . so admired her kind attentions to her uncle in his illness that he has made her an offer. His wife died . . . last spring so he waits the year before taking his second. . . . He has no family or outside relatives so all he has will be Emmas, £15000—he has almost retired from his profession . . . [and] must be past seventy—' Two months later she referred to the matter again. '. . . Aunt Mary's opinion of him [Dr. Truran] was by no means flattering as to his appearance or general bearing and [she] did not like the idea of him as son-in-law—though being a good man with a heavy purse & no relatives who could blame E[mma] for taking him?'

Ellen had a lurking sense of mischief and took obvious delight in her enterprising granchildren. (To William) '. . . Chattie is quite herself again & ran down to see us one day last week—of course it was the old game of Cats away, mice will play. The two little fellows [Chattie's] were happy all day painting the ballroom floor with mould, shoe polish & water. . . .' Others 'played Indians with shingles sharpened for axes with which they tracked a barrow load of beets to make it appear they had been scalping their enemies. . . .'

There was a stir of excitement in medical circles when

William, a Canadian not yet forty, was appointed professor of medicine to the new and subsequently famous Johns Hopkins University. One suspects that Ellen thought the world made too much of Benjamin. True, he was one of God's creatures, but so were Edward and Frank. On hearing the news she wrote her usual weekly letter. 'Chattie has been very poorly ... but is mending now. .... I fancy there has been something of inflamation of the lower bowel. .... Did you hear of Carrie's trouble in addition to her chronic ailments ? Ingrown toenails. .... I had no idea that the nails had to be removed ... only fancy the agony she must have endured. ....

'Thanks for the Baltimore paper. How proud I ought to be of you. I wonder, am I ? Perhaps so—this I do know—that my heart is full of love & thankfulness to Him who has showered so many blessings on my life in the matter of dear precious sons and daughters. ....

'Father keeps about the same. He is in the garden now, grape-gleaning. As days go on I see him more helpless & still so patient. His feet and legs swell a little more of late. I am going to give him the digitalis again—10 drops I think you said before each meal. ....'

In another letter she tempered enthusiasm with a word of warning, 'Father thanks you for your letter received a day or two since and we congratulate you on the prospect of taking another upward step on the ladder. Only, dear Willie, take heed that as you climb and step firmly on this ladder you get nearer and nearer to the golden gate of the Heavenly City and "so pass through earthly things, that you lose not the things that are eternal". There is a jubilant feeling amongst us all in hearing that honours are thrust on you in comparatively early life—may many of your fellows be benefitted as well as your-self. . . .'

Ellen was again, or perhaps always, worried about Edward and the contrast between the fortunes of these two sons only made her pain the more poignant. '. . . We hope Ed[ward] will be able to come home for a while . . . ,' she wrote to William. 'It is a grief to me his being so lonely and far away from any of us. He has not . . . many friends being naturally reserved and nothing seems to prosper with him—it is true that two thirds of our troubles are bred within ourselves but they are none the less hard to bear and call for sympathy from our fellows. . . . A mercy it is that they are often over-ruled by our Heavenly Father for our best interests—May it be so in his case—Thanks for your note. I am a neglectful mother and do not deserve to get many letters but my thoughts are often with you and my heart always. . . .'

Though William had been appointed professor to Johns Hopkins in 1888, his department did not open until the following year. Ellen's reference to 'the honours thrust upon him' in this case refer to Philadelphia's burst of farewell praise.

> 83 Wellesley St., Toronto,
> Jan. 17., 1889.

'It is a shame to have been so long without writing but you know how this house jogs on with the many interruptions of every day and with a very inefficient help in the kitchen. . . .

'Thank God you are not lifted up with pride at all the honours thrust upon you. Knowing how well deserved it all is I feel in some danger myself of indulging in the haughty spirit. You must not overwork yourself meanwhile else you'll

Jennette Osler
Taken probably in the 1870's

not be in good heart when you take up your new position in
Baltimore. . . .'

Had William ever before received such extravagant praise
from Ellen? To have forced 'the little mother' to indulge, even
momentarily, in 'the haughty spirit' was surely as rewarding as
all the fine speeches made in his honour.

After his usual Easter visit to Toronto, Ellen wrote:

'. . . The house has been cruelly dull all the week, we sadly
miss your chirpy voice coming in and out one day after another.
. . . The everlasting dinner-table is needed and I finish in haste.
Do you smell the bread-cakes I have been making & buns?
Would you like one for lunch? Do you want ointment? . . .'

And waiting his return,

'. . . Father looks well and keeps much as usual in health but
becomes more feeble as days pass on. He will be glad to see you
once again and would like you to bring up *just a few seeds*, for
as long as he is able to move about, the garden will keep up its
attractions for him . . . the look of the papers and the handling
of them will do him good. . . . You will be glad to see that Fen
gets an additional $1000 to his income. . . .'

In 1888 or thereabout (the year is omitted in the letter),
Featherstone suffered his first stroke. His mind and speech were
unaffected but henceforth he was a feeble and, according to
letters and reports of grandchildren, a patient old man.

Ellen to William, Dec. 7:

'The morning after I wrote my last note Father had a fall in
his dressing room. Just as he was . . . turning round to put the
towel out of his hand, he fell. . . . Of course he went back to
bed and seemed much shaken, with pain in his loins & down
to the left knee. . . . Dr. Burritt still thought nothing more was

the matter than the twist and nervous shock which a good rest would make all right, so I quieted my fears. . . . He seems to enjoy the moderate meals he takes [and is] patient as usual . . . —"when I am gone", he said, "you will have to adopt a child to care for instead of me—it was an apoplectic warning I had— I went down as if shot." Do you think it so? I have said nothing to anyone. . . .'

A few weeks later she asked William to make 'all reasonable excuses for the old Mother not writing as often as she ought to her dearly beloved. Some days "The grasshopper is a burden" and then I do as little as possible. There is a hum of Xmas-tide in the air . . . children are on the alert making their little plans and having private converse with the old Santa Claus as to presents etc. The elderlies are aware that they must wake up and bestir themselves. . . . As I want to give each of the grandchildren a small gift there is no time to lose. . . . I asked the boys the other day if I might be excused making the mince meat and the Xmas pudding but was not allowed to think of such an escape. . . .'

Edward's daughter Isobel produced the first great-grand-child. Ellen to William (Nov. 11, 1889):

'I meant to have written last week but am glad now I waited as we had your letter to Father this morning. No congratula-tions to me as the *great-Grandmother* and as it is the one and only way in which I could attain any honour or distinction it is just mean of my Benjamin to pass me by. However I am very proud all the same but have not yet been able to get to Collier St. to see this new arrival. . . . If you write a line to the proud mother give . . . sage advice as to keeping the little thing warm and quiet . . . which as far as I can learn they do not seem to consider necessary. . . .'

CHAPTER FOURTEEN

Britton and Edmund

IT WAS as a criminal lawyer that Britton's name became known to the public. His gift for oratory gave him colour; mastery of argument and the wingspread of his knowledge impressed his fellow-practitioners.

Though he ran as the (unsuccessful) Liberal candidate for Welland in 1882, he was generally regarded as an Independent in politics, the only Osler of his generation who did not embrace the Conservative faith.

A month before Britton's death Professor Goldwin Smith praised his eloquence at an annual bar dinner.

'I have not often attended courts here, but I have read reports of trials, and, comparing the speeches with those with which as a literary man I am naturally familiar, namely, those of ancient and modern orators, there are one or two speeches—Mr. B. B. Osler especially on the Birchall and Ponton cases, worthy to take high rank among the classic orators.

'As a lawyer prominently before the public his name has become a household word. That this is so is partly to be accounted for by his great force of character, a large fund of hard common sense [and] no small supply of that indescribable gift which goes by the name of personal magnetism. . . . That the better mental attributes of humanity are distributed in such proportions in him as to form a well-balanced whole is, perhaps, the explanation of his own understanding of his fellowmen. Placidity, except upon occasions when calmness of temper would be out of place, such as in the cross-examination of an untruthful witness, or the denunciation of injustice, is one of his characteristics. This, with the absence of formality, and an easy, matter-of-fact and patient manner, will be . . . recalled by those who have had occasion to consult him, rendering him one of the most accessible of men.

'His long study and knowledge of human nature, his power of expression to render himself intelligible to men of all classes, an even, well-controlled temper, and perhaps, beyond all else a persistent and intelligently directed industry, are some of the characteristics which have brought Mr. Osler the honors he bears, and to which none of the profession questions his right.'*

Ellen's letters give occasional glimpses of Britton's activities. Ellen to Chattie:

Dec. 12, 1887.

'. . . B.B. entertained a Legal party at dinner on Friday—18 of them. On Saturday next another of 20 (more mixed) is to come off. Fen was one of seven Judges at the last; Edmund is to be at the one this week. There is one perpetual whirl in this Society Life. I look on and wonder—Is it well ?'

Eleven years after Featherstone's long journey to Winnipeg by water and rail, then water again, his son travelled in style by the now completed Canadian Pacific Railway.

Ellen wrote to Aunt Lizzie, her sister-in-law in Falmouth:

* From an article in the *Canada Law Journal* also written before his death.

March 1, 1888.

'. . . B. B. goes off . . . in the morning for a six day railway
journey to British Columbia on some govmt. Law business
in connection with the C.P.R. This is only a preliminary trip
to a longer one in the summer. He will be 18 days away, 12 of
which will be on the Railway. But all the fittings . . . are
luxurious to a degree. . . . Not the usual sleeping berths but a
whole car divided into rooms with [the] ordinary beds and
furniture of a house. Another car is the large dining room and
a third the drawing room, another the kitchen and again
another as bath rooms and lavatory. A party of about 8 go in
this style, then the ordinary cars for the regular passengers
and freight. . . . What would you say to a journey of over
three thousand miles ? Some 20 years ago I should have enjoyed
the trip but now—no thank you. . . .

'. . . [Chattie's] two elder boys go into the High School . . .
in Hamilton. . . . B.B. always gives them school tickets for the
journey in and out by the St. Railway. He used to own the
railway for some years after he built it, but it has passed into
other hands. . . .'

Britton and Carrie had no children. Soon after their marriage
Carrie felt the first pains of arthritis. The disease progressed
until she became permanently crippled, an invalid until her
death in 1895. Her misery runs like a black thread through
many of Ellen's letters.

Ellen Osler to William:

Oct. 16, 1886.

'. . . None of us think Carrie any better than when she went
to England. Indeed I'm quite sure her old enemy has a firmer
hold on the system—I feel quite distressed to see her, and she

fights so with all she has to bear—it is an effort to move from room to room. Brit is away from home almost constantly or only home late in the evening. . . .'

When Carrie could not sleep Britton sometimes read to her the whole night through; starting at the end of a heavy day and continuing until the dawn of another. He is said to have killed himself with overwork but work may have been the opium necessary to dull the distress of his unhappy house. It was, at least, an escape.

Hector Charlesworth in his *Candid Chronicles* paid tribute to the lawyer.

'In the nineties the man who really dominated the Canadian scene as facile princeps in his calling was the late Britton Bath Osler, Q.C., by many regarded as the most brilliant of the four eminent sons of Canon Featherstone Osler. . . . Before his death he was internationally recognized as the peer of any pleader in the world. . . . He . . . was frequently sent for in connection with litigations in the United States, where, because of his transcendent abilities, he was permitted to practice in the courts of several States. . . .

'The sober but thrilling oratory of B. B. Osler; the penetrating shrewdness of his cross-examinations, in which he was never the forensic bully; the cogency of his arguments; and the scientific care with which his cases were prepared—all these elements were largely lost on the kind of persons which constitute the average jury in a Canadian criminal trial. But they were extremely valuable to the country in cases where it was necessary to speak to a vast public beyond the courtroom. They were also a great intellectual stimulus and an education to his rivals at the bar. . . .

'In argument Osler was complete master of the Socratic method. His case was unfolded to the jury in a lengthy series of questions, which he insisted that the jurors must answer to themselves before rejecting the view for which he stood. . . .'

The trial of Reginald Birchall, an Oxford graduate, for the murder of an Englishman named Benwall attracted attention beyond the borders of Canada. Britton was retained by the Crown.

Of the Hymans case, another murder trial, Charlesworth wrote, '. . . I can still see the majestic Osler, talking to the jury with the shattered skull held aloft in his hand, tracing for them the technical causes of death; and the nervous, ingenious Johnston confusing the issue with all the resources of a Scottish metaphysical mind. . . .'

Meanwhile Edmund kept pace with the booming business world of Canada. During the eighties he devoted himself to railway and navigation promotion, generally with a view to the absorption of these systems by the Canadian Pacific Railway which had received its charter in 1880. As a director of the C.P.R. his interests expanded to the west and he opened a Winnipeg branch of Osler & Hammond under the charge of A. M. (later Sir Augustus) Nanton. How he rose so quickly in the mysterious realm of finance is a question for which the answer seems to be lost. But like his brother Britton (who could, if that had been his aim, have made a reputation in the same field) he was alert and in his young days adventurous. His nose, guided by intelligence, led him to rich pastures. A fifteen-year-old grandson, sitting at Craigleigh with his uncles after

Edmund's funeral, listened while they discussed their father. They credited his switch from speculation to a conservative brand of finance, not to middle age, but to the knowledge that as family banker his responsibilities were endless. He became 'safe' because so many depended on him. But one suspects that after the death of his first wife and their two children, safety was what Edmund wanted.

In these crowded years Ellen had all she could do to keep track of her busy sons and their widespread activities.

Ellen to Chattie:

83 Wellesley St., Toronto, Nov. 9, '86.

'. . . Edmund was away nearly all last week and went from New York one day to dine with Willie in Philadelphia. . . . They rush round at a great rate in all directions, a kind Providence caring for them and keeping them in safety. . . . Edmund had a letter from Frank and he told him they were coming down for Xmas . . . *much to Nellie's disgust* (this between ourselves). . . .'

Ellen to William:

Sept., [1886 or 1887]

'Edmund returned yesterday from his ranch in the far N. West. He had nine long days of travel and nine consecutive hours on horseback—stiff and tired he was, but looks well in spite of all. He saw Frank but not Edward. He was but one day in Winnipeg and I fancy Edward was at the lake about the time he was there. . . .'

Apart from believing in all conservative doctrine Edmund had little appetite for politics. It is therefore strange to picture him as M.P. for West Toronto in the Federal Parliament from

1896 till 1917. That he was not contentious is proved by a newspaper headline, 'After seventeen years in the House Osler speaks'.

Some years earlier he ran for mayor of Toronto. A few details of the event are found in Hector Charlesworth's *Candid Chronicles*. E. E. Shepherd, editor of *The News*, and Goldwin Smith, whose house became the nucleus of Toronto's Art Gallery, 'staged the first and last attempt in modern days to run a business man of the highest eminence for Mayor of Toronto in the person of the late Sir Edmund Osler, who at that time had not been knighted. There were committee meetings of the "intelligentsia" every day or so in the office of Mr. Shepherd, at which Goldwin Smith usually presided, but as the event proved they were quite out of touch with popular opinion, then as now, inimical to a "silk stocking" candidate. . . .'

During the campaign Edmund went about his usual business. The fact that business meant a month or two abroad did not perturb him. A daily paper printed a verse entitled:

Mr. Osler's Parting Address
TO HIS COMMITTEE UPON HIS DEPARTURE FOR ENGLAND.

'I am going away to England on important business bent,
To leave my boom in faithful hands I'm very well content;
There's no need for me to stay here, for my name, as well you
    know,
Will carry all before it—'twas yourselves that told me so.
'You only need to say that I give my consent to run;
No need of vulgar hand-shaking—the fight's already won;
Inferior men may take the stump and canvass for support,
But dignity demands that I do nothing of the sort.

'There are self-seeking intriguers who, I'm told, do not refuse
To appear at public meetings and elaborate their views,
And will go among the people and mean-spiritedly deign
Their future plans and policy to outline and explain.
'Now gentlemen, I'm sure that it would pain you very much,
Supposing that your candidate were classed along with such;
I occupy much higher ground—I should be doing wrong
To take into my confidence the low and vulgar throng.
'A dignified aloofness is the *role* that suits me best—
A sort of "press the button and leave you do the rest"—
My name is E. B. Osler and I'm candidate for mayor,
Now surely that's sufficient to elect me to the chair!
'And this is my position, it is just as plain as day
That it makes no sort of difference that I shall be away;
Just mention to the public that I'm in it till the last,
And cable my majority when the election's past.'

———

Ellen wrote to Chattie:

Dec. 18, 1891.

'. . . You see by the papers all the Pros and Cons about the
Mayoralty. I shall be more pleased than sorry if he is not
returned. It will save him any amount of worry. . . .'

When his opponent, R. J. Fleming, was elected Ellen may
have rejoiced at his defeat but it is likely she was surprised.

There was one discernible blemish on Edmund's life as a
public man. As a governor of the University of Toronto
during the 1914–18 war he insisted on the dismissal of German
professors. Others on the board were more charitable. Edmund
resigned in protest.

CHAPTER FIFTEEN

Domestic Details

NELLIE lived under the parental roof from the date of her husband's death until her own in 1902. Her marked executive ability went into work for the church, perhaps the only outside activity permissible at that time to women in her circumstances. She was among the founders of the Women's Auxiliary and lived her life in and for this organization. A niece remembers her as 'very pious', a term no one ever used to describe her mother who had piety but was not pious. Chattie (Mrs. Charles Gwyn) was the only member of the family whose daily life remotely resembled the younger days of Ellen. She bore nine children, raised them on a small income and proved an expert at the household arts. Staplehurst, bequeathed to the Gwyns by Britton when he left Dundas, was big but not too big for such a family. Chattie's hand was firm, her sense of humour robust. As soon as her children could walk, and until they reached an age of discretion, she dressed them in 'turkey red', the more easily to spot and count them from the windows of the house. '. . . I hear now and then of someone who has nothing to do, cannot tell how to . . . get rid of time,' Ellen wrote to her sister-in-law, Elizabeth Osler. 'That is not you, nor me, either. Chattie's little party will always find me employment while I can use a needle & if not, there is the Women's Aid, the Infants' Home,

The Children's Hospital . . . and friends that . . . always give one plenty to do. . . .'

Sewing was not Ellen's only occupation. Her weekly letters to Chattie give domestic details.

'. . . I found a basket of quinces waiting for me and got through peeling yesterday, the preserving this morning, 7 bottles—added to those I had before and your JAM make my stock 75—small compared to many but all I mean to do unless it may be some apple-marmalade.

'I have had ever so many hinderances as usual and now have to go over to pay Mrs. Vicars for 20 lbs of butter, 16¢ per lb. I packed it in a stone-jar this morning & it will not be my fault if it does not turn out well—no going to hunt up butter for a time. These 20 lbs make a good show. . . .'

Another week she wrote:

'I had a long afternoon at gardening yesterday, putting in the plants we brought from Annie's. Thrice I had to come in to visitors—which means washing of hands, taking off rubbers etc. . . . but I did not like keeping them out of the ground. They look very well and I hope will shew themselves to advantage when the "beloved Physician" sees them. I go round this afternoon . . . to pay the monthly bills and then . . . to see Carrie. Love to all your belongings. . . .'

When she and Featherstone returned from a visit to Chattie in Dundas, her bread-and-butter letter ended, '. . . if the chicks continue to be blessed with good health you will be happy as a queen. . . . I left [behind] three things, I am sorry to say— "Voices of Comfort", rubbers, & watchkey. Rubbers in the cupboard, book on the library table, key under the toilette-cushion. Take care of them for me. . . .'

With 83 Wellesley Street as their beating, communal heart, the Oslers had no need of telephones to keep the various members up to date on family affairs. News travelled by the grapevine. After the birth of Chattie's eighth, Ellen wrote to the mother:

'I was wondering how I could let interested members of the family know of the event—Fen came in this evening to tell us that Hennie was going tomorrow to Quebec to meet Georgie, so he took the News; Marian's [Francis] work-girl called with a pattern and was to go to the Island this morning so they are in possession of the News—and quite late Annie and Edmund walked down—of course they were very glad to hear it. . . . Such a delight for you to have a *girl* after those three boys— kiss the weeskey crumb for Granny. I would so like Nellie to have gone up this week to congratulate you and welcome the little lady but it does not appear practicable. *Mary has gone!* I told her it was not the thing after living here so long to go until we had another girl . . . but she was off as soon as she finished the ironing. . . .'

A number of months had elapsed when she wrote:

'Your letter on Saturday aftn was very welcome. It was so newsy "it did my spillet good". . . . The first tooth does not lose interest even when it shews itself in the eighth baby. May the sweet pet get her mouth full without trouble to you or herself. . . .

'I want to know if you will have knee bands of Calico or of same material as the drawers—I wish you did not like them—I think them very bad for the poor little legs, girting them so when they sit down. . . . The wedding [a grand-daughter's] will occupy all spare thoughts of the juveniles till it is over—dress your girlies very simply, they will look so much better. . . .'

Of the bridesmaids she wrote after the event: '. . . there was a discussion as to which of the elder maids carried the palm of good looks—I have no doubt that each mother [decided] her own crow to be the whitest. . . .'

(List of contents of parcel sent by Ellen to Chattie)

10 prs of stockings	4 collars—pr extra cuffs
2 nightshirts	1 tin of cocoa
1 made-over suit (white)	2 cakes soap
1 velveteen suit	1 pail of sweeties
1 nightdress (repaired)	1 basket ditto

'. . . I can only find the time to thicken 2 prs of Trevor's stockings but send the wool. . . .'

'There were lions in the way two or three times last week when I was about to write to you. . . . Alex I feel sure is wearying of the Bank—or *it may be the bank of him*—I don't know which. I'm very sorry and know it worries Nellie though she says nothing. . . . He has always tired of everything after 3 or 4 months. Could he only be kept at this till he felt the benefit of sticking to one thing I should be thankful. . . .'

Chattie may have been troubled over some family irregularity when Ellen wrote, '. . . The skeleton more or less hideous in every house, and the Thorn, sharp or blunt in every Parish, has been the rule for centuries. The exceptions are few, but can be found at discretion—or the skeleton can be well draped & the Thorn touched up with silver or gold tipping and not be so hideous or so painfully sharp. Frank & Belle got off on Friday evening. . . .

'Willie's meteor-like visit was pleasant while it lasted. . . .

He is lamentably thin—I do wish he had a nice wife to attend
to little home comforts for him. . . . [He] is sure to have sent
you a copy of his Address. Of course you, like the rest of the
tribe, will say that you think it very good even though you
have reserve thoughts in your mind of a different type. But
then it does not follow that they would convince anyone to
the contrary. . . .'

'Teacher and Student', the address referred to, stresses the
need for young teachers. After forty 'the change is seen in
weakened receptivity and in an inability to adapt oneself to an
altered intellectual environment . . .', said William from the
platform. Ellen, at eighty-six, did not agree.

CHAPTER SIXTEEN

William and Grace

WILLIAM spent the greater part of 1891 writing what became the most widely read medical text-book of its time, *The Principles and Practices of Medicine.*

He wrote to Jennette from Baltimore, 1891,—'I was very glad to have your nice letter last week and to have . . . news of the children [Francis]. It did me good to have a peep at you all. . . . I am . . . hard at work again. Hospitals two and three hours a day and writing every night. My book makes slow progress as I have two or three other things on hand and I hate to put off good . . . progressive work for such a hack labor as text book writing. I miss the chickens. . . . I would like to run up every Saturday. I enclose a letter for Jimmy, the dear fat lad. Love to Jack & Willie and the girlies. . . .'

When the book was finished, so the story goes, he took a copy fresh from the printer and threw it into the lap of his future wife, saying, 'There, take the darn thing; now what are you going to do with the man ?'* The recipient of the book took the man as well. Her name was Grace, daughter of John and Susan Revere of Boston, and great-granddaughter of the fast-riding silversmith, Paul. Grace was the widow of a friend and colleague of William's, Dr. S. W. Gross of Philadelphia.

* Cushing.

Featherstone Lake Osler

William was forty-two and Grace five years younger when they were married in Baltimore, May 7, 1892.

'... I'm sure you heard from Willie of the new life opening before him with a Lady Help at his side—' Ellen wrote to Chattie, 'he let Father and me into his secret when he was up, but we were not at liberty to make known the fact—these young things always think their love affairs are secrets to the outside world, whereas lookers-on often see things plainly enough. So it may have been in this case—however I think we all feel glad at heart that there is good hope of Willie having a loving wife to care for him. When you see Grace I think you will bid her welcome as a Sister-in-law. I feel quite pleased to have her as a daughter-in-law and Father is right glad that Willie is likely to have such a good life-partner. The event will make quite a stir in the family. . . .

'Tell Marion [grandchild] that Mary Lammond [grandchild] brought me in some lovely wild flowers gathered by herself in Rosedale. I feel as if I would like to don an old sunbonnet and take a lot of the little ones and go gathering the beauties myself, even though I could find neither primroses nor daisies. . . .'

William's son, Paul Revere, was born on Feb. 7, 1893. Ellen wrote the next day to Chattie.

'Unquestionably you had the joyful news flashed over the wires last evening. We had 4 words which told of mother & boy all right and we are hoping there may be a tel. today confirming the same. . . .'

But there was no happy confirmation of the child's wellbeing and Paul Revere died before his tenth day.

'You will have written to Baltimore I know and . . . shared with us all in the first glow of gladness and then in the deep wave of sorrow . . . dear Willie, it will take some time to bring back his chirpy ways. . . .'

Edward Revere was born two years later. This only child became the deepest personal love of William's life.

From Grace Osler to her mother-in-law Ellen:

> No. 1 West Franklin Street
> Baltimore
> Jan. 3rd, 1896

'. . . Just as B.B.'s telegram came yesterday saying that he would be here in the afternoon, one came calling the doctor off to Pennsylvania. He was obliged to leave at midnight, but had time enough to take his brother to the Club and have some lawyers to meet him at dinner. He will be back this evening, when Major Venable, a Narragansett friend of B.B.'s will have a dinner for them. It is nice to see him [B.B.] looking so well and he has promised to take you good news of the small boy. I have only one disappointment and that is that you cannot see him while he is so tiny. . . . You must excuse the proud father if he leaves unsaid what you want to know, for he is really very much excited. . . . He brings all his medical friends up to look at him. . . .

'I hope you will be pleased to hear that we have decided to call him Edward Revere Osler. We were thinking . . . seriously of it and Brit has clinched it by telling me that he knows you will be pleased. My younger brother is Edward and I am particularly attached to him. Willie is very anxious to have Revere in the name. . . . At first I was anxious to call him Palmer Howard, for Dr. Howard but now I am more satisfied, as I hear that this will be the fifth generation of Edward Oslers. . . .

Tell the little Auntie [Jennette] that Willie says she is to feel a
particular share in the boy, as he will have her father's name....'

Ellen knew William's way with children and was also aware
of the concentrated love he would bestow on this only child.
As Revere grew from a baby into a small boy she sent the
father little messages of advice. In one sentence she speaks a
truth that has not yet been superseded by the wisest psychia-
trist: 'Pet him, love him, but do not spoil him.' On occasions
she rebuked the Professor of Medicine:

'... I have my [picture of] dear Revere smiling at me on the
table.... He used to have something of a little Samuel about
him but of late seems to have another spirit. Perhaps he was
laughed at when he said his childish prayers and resents it, but
he is one of the Lambs of the fold—in my prayers, night and
morning, I bring all these family little ones to the Saviour and
ask Him to take them in His arms . . . and bless them. . . .'

At other times she shared the blame.

'... As to Master Revere, he seems to be outgrowing babyhood; a boy now most decidedly, indebted to his father I fancy
for some of his odd speeches. I charge you to bring him up in
the Faith and fear of God. If there is one petition in the Litany I
take more to heart than others it is "forgive my negligences and
ignorances" (in the bringing up of my family), I always add in
my heart. . . .'

Ellen must have thanked her God for supplying Grace to
balance William. She wrote to her daughter-in-law: '. . .
[Revere] will not be behind his age in boyish tricks. He has two
(one is William, other unknown) tutors to lead him on, and
well it is he has a sober minded mother and a staid Scotch
nurse to keep [him] in check.... Bless the precious little lad. ...'

The man who had once been a member of Barrie's Bad Boys could still revert to his youth. When Revere received his first set of carpenter's tools, father and son were discovered by Grace, joyfully hammering nails into the drawing room floor and, according to Ellen's letter, the furniture.

'. . . I wonder has that precious Revere given up the musical hammer and nail amusement. If indulging in it still, Willie had better let Morris get him brass-headed nails to ornament the furniture in the drawing room—perhaps this nail-driving may indicate a firmness of purpose in anything he undertakes. Bestow many kisses on the dear boy for me and tell Willie to study up some of the precepts of Solomon about the bringing up of children—but there is a proverb of later date about pebbles & glass houses etc. So I will say no more or may get the worst of it. . . .'

CHAPTER SEVENTEEN

Deaths in the Family

FEATHERSTONE died in his ninetieth year, on February 16, 1895, eleven months before Revere, his last grandchild, was born. Some weeks before his death, Ellen wrote, '. . . When I see dear Fed sitting day after day utterly helpless I am amazed at his true submission to God's will. . . .'

Ellen to her sister-in-law, Elizabeth Osler of Falmouth:

Feb. 21, 1895.

'I wrote last week that your dear brother was suffering from a bad cold—I had a feeling that it was the beginning of the end & so it proved. The oppression of the chest and symptoms of a cold passed away. For two nights he breathed freely and rested quietly, got up on Saturday as usual, took a little, very little porridge for breakfast—then was made ready to be brought into the sitting room, but signified to the nurse that instead, he would lie down again—I went to see if he was ready, as I always helped to bring him in, but found him resting very quietly, and sat down beside him taking his hand in mine, but there was not the loving response as usual. He seemed to be in a sweet sleep & I knew the end was not far off. . . . Nellie read the 23rd psalm then telephoned for Jennette. . . . The Dr. came . . . but could not reassure us. . . . Soon there was a gentle sigh, and without the slightest distress . . ."His soul returned to God who

gave it" . . . "The peace of God which passeth all understanding" has kept him through these years of helplessness. He was
waiting, watching for the Master's call. . . . There is a sad blank
in my heart and in all the house. . . .

'. . . Long ago he requested that when he should die he
might be buried in his surplice, and thus with Scarf and Bands,
resting in a plain black coffin, "he yet being dead" preached to
all who saw him true submission to God's will. . . . I believe the
impression made on the dear grandchildren will be lasting—
they all loved him as did his children and his life example will
hold in their hearts as in the hearts of old parishioners in Tecumseth & Dundas, from whom have come genuine expressions of
love & sympathy. . . .

'. . . Good bye dear Lizzie for another week, if I live till
then—I am a wonder to myself, I had a bad cold but it has
gone. . . .'

Chattie came from Dundas; Edward returned from the West.
Children and grandchildren gathered about to warm her.

'. . . Such unnumbered mercies I receive day by day, all so
unmerited. Could I only have a more loving grateful heart for
temporal things and the still richer blessings of Grace it would
be well but I feel so dead as regards spiritual things that sometimes, "when I consider I am afraid", yet I pray to God to help
me to "lay hold of His strength".'

These words, infinitely sad coming from Ellen, were written
to Elizabeth Osler, one of her few surviving contemporaries.

After his father's death, Edward settled permanently at 83
Wellesley St. He suffered from chronic gout interspersed
with acute attacks. Ellen felt easier about him when she herself
could attend his misery. This son of many troubles became the

object of her devotion and filled the gap left by Featherstone.
Spring brought another loss to the family.

Ellen wrote to Carrie a few days before the latter's death in
May of the same year. Somehow she managed to seed the
letter with life.

'My heart has been with you and sorry I am to know that
you have been so poorly lately. Now that bleak March is
over I hope the Spring-tide will brighten up all invalids,
especially your dear self—and B.B. I hope will not have to
make long journeys from home. After a while you may be
able to drive out and enjoy the fresh air, hear the robins chirp
their spring notes and from your window you can see or smell
the green buds shewing new life and the promise of summer. . . .

'I have been enjoying a half glass of the good port that our
dear B.B. sent over, it is my 11 a.m. draught, far nicer than
the dose of whiskey that I only take now in 2 teaspoonsful
twice a day. . . .'

Ellen imbibed at William's advice. Approaching ninety
when he first suggested whiskey, she demurred, 'But Benjamin,
if I should get the habit?'

Two years after Carrie's death in 1895, Britton married
Elizabeth Ramsay of Montreal. Their time together was short.
In April, 1900, he became critically ill. *'At this point the engine
breaks down on the track and has to go to the repair shop for
rebuilding and overhauling' was the last entry in his little fee
book. He appeared to recover and spent the summer at Keo-
nonta, a house he had built some years before near Colling-
wood.

Britton was hard at work again in the autumn but collapsed

* From *A Sketch of the Osler Family* by W. A. Craick.

a second time a few months later. He died in Atlantic City on Feb. 5, 1901, two days after writing to a member of his firm announcing his regained health and imminent return.

The first of the six brothers was dead and at the shockingly early age of sixty.

'The symptoms of his collapse came in the form of amnesia at Philadelphia whither he had gone in connection with some important litigation. He returned to the hotel where he always stayed . . . and asked the clerk his name and address. His mind was blank to his own identity. He was put to bed, and Dr. William Osler was hurriedly summoned from Baltimore. With the help of the best specialists in the United States he was restored to health and resumed practice. After a few cases in which he showed undiminished powers, he broke down again. . . .'*

In a letter to a friend, William wrote: '. . . I have just returned from Toronto. B.B. went off with coronary artery disease. He has had a slow pulse with syncopal attacks for a year. 'Twas a mercy that he died suddenly as he dreaded a long illness. . . .'†

Ellen wrote to Britton before his death.

My own dear Brick:
You are in my mind continuously but to think of going over to see you seems beyond my ability. Truly I cannot be thankful enough to God that you have such a nurse and treasure in our dear Lily; this time of rest will I trust soon renew your strength and it will not be lost time either for much can be done in quietude. . . . You will not worry I know about outside work for what cannot be done is not required of us. Shall I not be glad to hear that you are downstairs and making good progress.

* From *Candid Chronicles* by Hector Charlesworth.   † Cushing.

God bless thee my precious son and renew you in health of soul and body.

Ever your loving mother
E. Osler

Best love to dear Lily.

The Oslers, a close, united family, mourned for Britton. Edmund expressed what they all felt: 'When B.B. died half my life went with him.' Nellie's death a year later shook for a second time the family's belief in their indestructibility.

CHAPTER EIGHTEEN

Esteem and Notoriety

WILLIAM had been Professor of Medicine at Johns Hopkins for fifteen years when he was offered the Chair of Regius Professor at Oxford in 1904.* 'Thank heaven relief has come' was his wife's reaction to the letter. William's fame had increased and with it private patients who stole his time from the essentials: teaching, investigating and writing. Doctors called him in consultation from the ends of the continent and when, as often was the case, the patient was a member of a doctor's family, he could not refuse to go.

When faced with a similar decision twenty years before he had been driven to flipping a coin. To leave Baltimore for the cloistered Oxford seemed to William almost a renunciation of life. Probably the influence of Grace, who feared his present pace would kill him, decided the issue.

As he was going to London in the summer he asked that the matter be left open. While he was there he made up his mind.

In a letter to his predecessor at Oxford, Sir J. Burdon Sanderson, he wrote: '. . . While very happy here and with splendid facilities . . . I am over-worked and find it increasingly hard to serve the public and carry on my teaching. I have been in harness actively for thirty years, and have been looking

* Cushing.

forward to the time when I could ease myself of some of the burdens I carry at present. With the income from my book we have a comfortable competency, so that I am in a measure independent. . . . I should miss sadly the daily contact with students, unless I could arrange for clinical work in London. On the other hand, I have a mass of unfinished literary material on hand which the academic leisure of a new place would enable me to complete. . . .'*

Before he sailed for America he had accepted.

It takes a number of private saints to make a public one. At some point in his Baltimore career William was canonized— by students, colleagues, and in a measure, the general public. Many saints made possible his grace. Ellen, first in time, had steered the child. Her hand was firm and therefore able to relax on the reins she held. William's warmth and sympathy toward each sufferer he met (and he met them daily) came from his mother's genes as well as her example. And how could he have escaped humility with Ellen always there to remind him of the transient nature of even the highest earthly endeavours? Edmund's generosity made possible William's lifelong indifference to money—an indifference essential to any self-respecting saint. Next comes Jennette. Her faith in his exceptional ability acted as a stimulant to one capable of fulfilling high expectations. She encouraged the schoolboy, taught the medical student how to express himself on paper (his early letters show no sign of the later proficient writer) and remained throughout his life a close and loving friend. Her sister, Marian Francis, wore her halo at too rakish an angle to be included in a calendar of saints, but she was an intelligent

* Cushing.

and exceedingly attractive woman. Attractive women were necessary figures on the landscape of the Osler brothers.

William's good fortune in his choice of wife can be compared with the good fortune of his father Featherstone. From the day of their marriage Grace expanded rather than reduced the radius of his freedom. The wheels that ran his household never betrayed themselves by the smallest squeak. And William brought home droves of friends—students, doctors, relations. But he was a busy man. After dazzling the company for five minutes he retired to his study and to work, leaving his wife to entertain his worshippers.

When they were about to move from Baltimore to Oxford and the moment came to dismantle the house with all the hundred and one decisions and chores that a change of countries involves, William packed a suitcase and was off. After attending a medical meeting he joined his wife and son on the dock in New York. 'Willie's motto,' said Grace, 'may well be aequanimitas.' But Grace knew William was right. Tiresome mechanics must not interfere with his contribution to life.

The strain of parting with colleagues and friends, the innumerable public farewells, left him in greater need than ever of Oxford quiet. Cushing in his *Life of Sir William Osler* wrote: 'Such an unrestrained outpouring of appreciation for what he had done, of regret at his departure; such a demonstration of love and affection on the part of students, alumni, faculty, and community few teachers have ever received. Most men would have to live after death to know how others really regard them but it fell to Osler's lot several times in his life to have paid to him in public the embarrassing tributes usually reserved for obituary notices. . . .'

On Feb. 22, 1905, William gave his valedictory address in McCoy Hall, Johns Hopkins University. The revered doctor woke up the next morning, not famous but infamous. Headlines crossed the continent: OSLER RECOMMENDS CHLOROFORM AT SIXTY. It was a dull season and the controversy blazed for days. Osler's house was inundated with abusive and threatening letters. A new verb was coined: to Oslerize. His address touched on many subjects but one section only caught the reporter's ear:

'I have two fixed ideas,' said William, 'well known to my friends, harmless obsessions with which I sometimes bore them but which have a direct bearing on this important problem. The first is the comparative uselessness of men above forty years of age. This may seem shocking, and yet read aright the world's history bears out the statement. Take the sum of human achievement in action, in science, in art, in literature—subtract the work of the men above forty, and while we should miss great treasures, even priceless treasures, we would practically be where we are to-day. . . . The effective, moving, vitalizing work of the world is done between the ages of twenty-five and forty—these fifteen golden years of plenty, the anabolic or constructive period, in which there is always a balance in the mental bank and the credit is still good. In the science and art of medicine, young or comparatively young men have made every advance of the first rank. Vesalius, Harvey, Hunter, Bichat, Laennec, Virchow, Lister, Koch—the green years were yet upon their heads when their epoch-making studies were made. To modify an old saying, a man is sane morally at thirty, rich mentally at forty, wise spiritually at fifty—or never. . . .

'My second fixed idea is the uselessness of men above sixty
years of age, and the incalculable benefit it would be in commercial, political, and in professional life if, as a matter of
course, men stopped work at this age. In his "Biathanatos"
Donne tells us that by the laws of certain wise states sexagenarii
were precipitated from a bridge, and in Rome men of that age
were not admitted to the suffrage and they were called Des-
pontani because the way to the senate was per pontem, and
they from age were not permitted to come thither. In that
charming novel, "The Fixed Period", Anthony Trollope dis-
cusses the practical advantages in modern life of a return to this
ancient usage, and the plot hinges upon the admirable scheme
of a college into which at sixty men retired for a year of con-
templation before a peaceful departure by chloroform. That
incalculable benefits might follow such a scheme is apparent to
anyone who, like myself, is nearing the limit, and who has
made a careful study of the calamities which may befall men
during the seventh and eighth decades. Still more when he
contemplates the many evils which they perpetuate uncon-
sciously, and with impunity. As it can be maintained that all the
great advances have come from men under forty, so the history of the world shows that a very large proportion of the
evils may be traced to the sexagenarians—nearly all the great
mistakes politically and socially, all the worst poems, most of
the bad pictures, a majority of the bad novels, not a few of the
bad sermons and speeches. It is not to be denied that occasionally there is a sexagenarian whose mind, as Cicero remarks,
stands out of reach of the body's decay. Such a one has learned
the secret of Hermippus, that ancient Roman who feeling that
the silver cord was loosening, cut himself clear from all com-

panions of his own age and betook himself to the company of young men, mingling with their games and studies, and so lived to the age of 153, puerorum halitu refocillatus et aducatus. And there is truth in the story, since it is only those who live with the young who maintain a fresh outlook on the new problems of the world. The teacher's life should have three periods, study until twenty-five, investigation until forty, profession until sixty, at which age I would have him retired on a double allowance. Whether Anthony Trollope's suggestion of a college and chloroform should be carried out or not I have become a little dubious, as my own time is getting short. . . .'

These are the words that caused a furore that did not wholly die during his lifetime. They were said half jocularly with the intent of easing his own regret and the regret of his students and fellow-doctors at his departure.

He took the storm with his customary equanimity, refusing to read the newspaper reports or the stacks of letters that continued to come, week after week. When he came to say good-bye to Ellen her parting words contained a gentle warning, 'Remember Willie, the shutters in England will rattle as they do in America.'*

* Cushing.

CHAPTER NINETEEN

One Hundred Years

ON ELLEN's one hundredth birthday (Dec. 14, 1906) she had six living children, twenty-six grandchildren and twenty-one great-grandchildren. The majority were present at her party. William, Grace and Revere came out from England; granddaughters married and living in the United States returned with husbands and young.

The birthday cake, lit by a hundred candles, had five layers, representing the five reigns of her century: Georges III & IV, William, Victoria and Edward. Its size required two men to carry it. 'Telegrams and cables came from all quarters of the globe,' wrote a grand-daughter: from Johns Hopkins, the Archbishop of Canterbury, the Governor-General, Earl Grey, the Conservative Members of the House of Commons and many letters from old parishioners of Bond Head and Dundas.

> The Rectory, Bond Head
> Dec. 20th, 1906.

Mrs. F. L. Osler,
Toronto

Dear Respected Friend:

The members of the various branches of the Women's Auxiliary in the Parish of Tecumseth, desire to convey to you an expression of their hearty congratulations on your attainment and enjoyment of another birthday, and . . . an assurance of their sincere sense of gratitude for your long and faithful services in the work that lies near their hearts. Would you be so kind as to accept at our hands this little gift (a Tecumseth turkey, grown on the seventh line of Tecumseth) with the hope that the coming Christmas may be to you one of great joy.

Believe us to be, dear Mrs. Osler

(sgd) Mrs. Coffey

Mrs. Watt, Presidents of Branches

P.S. (Parcel sent by express tomorrow the 21st)

A daughter of Dr. Orr, possibly the Bond Head physician who had prescribed pills wrapped in brown paper for the youthful Britton, wrote:

'I was so delighted to see a notice of your one hundredth birthday, that I couldn't refrain from sending my sincere congratulations. Perhaps you will remember me as a girl in your class in Sunday School in Bondhead some fifty years ago—Maria Orr, the youngest daughter of Dr. Orr. The precious lessons learned at your side have never been forgotten. Oh, for a return of those lovely Sabbaths, to listen to the collects as only you could explain them, what a help and comfort to me through all the changes and chances of this mortal life. I can recall your face as though it were but yesterday. . . . I would love to have a photo of you as you are. Would it be asking too much ? . . .'

Further back in memory than Bond Head lay Cornwall with its echoes of childhood and youth. The Cornish Society of Toronto in a letter of birthday congratulations, added, 'With the consent of your son, Mr. E. B. Osler, M.P., we are exceedingly glad to say that arrangements have been made with the Choir of our Association to sing two or three Christmastide

selections about the hour of 8 p.m. to-morrow night, in front
of your residence, which we trust will be appreciated by you
and yours. . . .'

Thus Ellen went to sleep with Cornish tunes ringing in her
ears. She lived to eat the Tecumseth turkey on Christmas Day
but the climax had come and gone. She died, quietly, a few
months later, on March 18, 1907. William in a letter to Dr.
White attributes the immediate cause of death to worry over
Edward.

Sunday

'Dear White, Thanks for your kind note of sympathy. The
cable was very unexpected as we had only a day or two before
a letter saying that she was keeping so well. A brother had been
at death's door with acute gout & as he lived with her she had
insisted upon going to his room very often & it worried her
greatly. She had a fine outlook on life—ohne Hast, ohne Rast—
and even the vagaries of her sons did not disturb her tran-
quility. . . .' *

'The Osler family,' someone said, 'was matriarchal,' and so it
seems to have been. Featherston, B.B. and Edmund, when not
away on business, rarely spent a day that did not include a
visit to their 'little mother'. She was the source to which her
sons and daughters, all equal in her presence, returned for
replenishment.

* Cushing.

CHAPTER TWENTY

Honours and Losses

EDWARD died two months after Ellen, presumably of gout. Jennette, who had lived with Ellen since 1894 moved on to care for great-nephews and nieces. Gwendolyn Francis and Bertram Andras were married in 1906 and the 'little Auntie' spent the rest of her days tending their offspring. She almost equalled Ellen's flight of time, living until her ninety-eighth year. William remained 'her dearest friend'. After hearing she had suffered a slight stroke, he wrote,

13 Norham Gardens, Oxford,
Nov. 5, 1909.

Dear little Auntie,
We heard sad news of you and were much worried. . . . What a shock it must have been! Do be careful. You are the prop of the family! I am glad to hear that dear Gwen keeps well.
I enclose you your cheque. Let me know . . . should you want anything extra and get any little things Gwen or the baby need . . . and charge them to me. All well here. Revere grows rapidly—he is up to the top of my ear. He is a dear lad but no student—except the family fondness for natural history. . . .
Your affec cousin
Wm Osler

In the autumn of 1910 Edmund's wife died after a long illness. Edmund had visited Egypt before. In the winter of 1911

he organized a second trip and William, his chosen companion
when he sailed for England after the death of his first wife,
again accompanied him.

Travelling up the Nile in their dahabiah William had for
once leisure enough to write long letters. His wife (they never
left England together unless with Revere), friends and relations
received vivid accounts of tombs, temples and sand. In Cairo
he visited hospitals and the Khedival Library. From Luxor he
wrote to F. L. Barker. 'Such weather! such Monuments! such
a revelation of the intellectual development of man, 6000
years ago! I am a bit bewildered. I have just come from paying
my respects to Dr. Imhotep, the first physician with a distinct
personality to stand out in the mists of antiquity. I am brown
as an Arab. The country has one God—the sun; & two devils—
dust and flies; the latter responsible I am sure for 2/3 of the
disease. . . .'*

William was made a baronet soon after his return to England. Before the coronation of George V the papers published
the usual list of honours, which included his name. When the
offer arrived in a letter from 10 Downing Street his wife asked,
'What excuse are you going to give for declining it; you
always said you would,' and he replied, 'I think I'll have to
accept—Canada will be so pleased—there's only one Canadian
baronet.'*

He wrote to Chattie:

June 21, 1911.

You must have had such a shock yesterday morning when
you saw Bill's name in the Coronation honour list. We had
word about ten days ago from Mr. Asquith, but nothing could

* Cushing.

be said. I did not know when it was to come out—I thought
not till after the coronation, but yesterday before I was out of
bed the telegrams began to rain in & there has been a perfect
stream—more than 100 from England, & 49 cables, U.S. &
Canada; two from India. Letters galore.

 . . . I have had rather more than my share, but these court
honours mean so much here. And when in the swim we must
take what comes. These things have never bothered me, &
we have so much & have been so happy, that we really did
not need it as much as some poor fellow who had done more
but who has not caught the public eye. I am glad for the
family. I wish Father & Mother had been alive & poor B.B.
& Nellie. It is wonderful how a bad boy (who could chop
off his sister's finger) may fool his fellows if he once gets to
work. Nona looks so well [Chattie's daughter]. Her presentation picture is . . . good & as for Grace—it was her regal
appearance that settled George R. Love to Charley & the girls.

Your affec bro.
Sir Billy ! ! ! ! !

If Ellen had been alive she would certainly have been pleased
but he knew she would have tempered her congratulations
with a reminder that these are but worldly honours and as such
not to be overestimated.

Six months later Edmund was knighted. But he was a
widower, his children were married. A title could not mitigate
his loneliness.

William had played the Pied Piper since boyhood. One
whistle and children followed wherever he led them. But he
was forty-four before he had a son he could call his own.
Revere became the indispensable human being in his life: a
gentle, blue-eyed boy, a passionate fisherman, a mediocre
student. As he grew older he acquired, perhaps to please his

father, his father's bibliomania, concentrating on the Tudor period. William's letters to friends and family as well as to his professional colleagues always included some doting reference to Izaak (Walton) or Tommy, as he often called him.

Revere was eighteen and about to enter Christ Church, Oxford, when war was declared in August, 1914.

His father wrote in a New Year's letter to an American friend (Mrs. Brewster): '. . . We are having a very happy holiday with Revere—such a chip of the old block in his devotion to books. He has developed so rapidly & you never met anyone with a more delightful taste in literature. It is a shame to have his studies interrupted, but he goes on with the military training & will take a commission when ready. My library grows apace—all sorts of treasures come in—a beauty this week, the Editio princeps of Aristotle 1495 bound by Derome. My bountiful brother E.B. sends an occasional fat cheque to meet my extravagances, as he knows my medical and scientific books are being collected for Canada. . . .' This shared interest added an extra radiance to the relationship between father and son. Revere wrote:

'. . . Dad has given me (I am telling everyone I meet this, out of joy) a first edition of Iz. Walton's life of Herbert—a perfect gem of a book, uncut, unsoiled and just as it left the hands of the printer and perhaps of Walton himself. . . .'*

Revere served first with the McGill Hospital Unit—this at his father's persuasion. He transferred to the British Army in March, 1916, no longer able to bear his relatively sheltered position. There were already eighteen Canadian Oslers in France.

* Cushing.

William's house, 13 Norham Gardens, Oxford, earned its title 'The Open Arms'. Canadian relatives on leave, medical officers from McGill and later, when the United States entered the war, one-time students from Philadelphia and Baltimore, filled his expandable house. William again returned to a life of almost superhuman activity.

From William Osler to W. S. Thayer:

Oct. or Nov. 1916.

'We have had an anxious time of course—so many of the family are here, & in the fighting line. My bro. Frank lost his only son, such a fine fellow who had been Shaughnessy's (Canadian Pacific Railway) private sec.' (Chattie's youngest son Campbell was killed in action in April, 1917.) 'Norman Gwyn has been doing good work at No. 1 General near Boulogne. Revere is on the Somme in a dug-out, just 100 yds from the German lines, & the chief occupation seems to be the exchange of gas bombs. He has taken to the practical work very kindly, writes . . . cheerfully & seems keenly interested, but as a disciple of Izaak Walton the whole business is very distasteful. . . . Dirty business for a decent lad, but they have to go thro. with it. Of course we are terribly anxious but—the seen arrow slackens its flight, as Dante says, & we are steeling our hearts for anything that may happen. . . .' *

On Dec. 28, 1916, William wrote:

To my son on his 21st birthday.

First—regrets that you are not with us—but these are the only ones; and the most satisfactory of all the feelings I have is that no regrets cloud the clear past of 21 years—and that is a good deal to say. You have been everything that a father

* Cushing.

could wish, a dear good laddie. And it is not often I am sure
that father and son have been so happy together. . . . For the
Future—everything is too uncertain to make plans. We can
only hope for the best. . . . Many, many happy returns of the
day and I hope when this tyranny is overpast we may have
more . . . days together—you and I and Muz.

Your loving Dad.*

On the same day Revere wrote to his father. The letter ends:
'I can't help feeling that at this time next year we will all be
together again. I hope Lloyd George doesn't stop us buying
books ! I have no regrets except for my own shortcomings,
only endless love and gratitude for you both.'

Revere died of wounds on Aug. 30, 1917. He was hit at 4.30
in the afternoon and survived for only a few hours the operation performed on him at midnight. Harvey Cushing, his
father's past student, great friend and later his biographer, was
with him at his death.

'We saw him buried in the early morning. A soggy Flanders
field beside a little oak grove to the rear of the Dosinghem
group—an overcast, windy, autumnal day—the long rows of
simple wooden crosses—. . . the boy wrapped in an army
blanket and covered by a weather-worn Union Jack, carried
on their shoulders by four slipping stretcher-bearers. A strange
scene—the great-great grandson of Paul Revere under a
British flag, and awaiting him a group of some six or eight
American Army medical officers—saddened with thoughts
of his father. Happily it was fairly dry at this end of the trench,
and some green branches were thrown in for him to lie on.

* Cushing.

The Padre recited the usual service—a bugler gave the "Last Post"—and we went about our duties. Plot 4 row F.'*

William wrote in his notebook, squeezed between engagements and consultations,† 'I was sitting in my library working on the new edition of my text-book when a telegram was brought in, "Revere dangerously wounded, comfortable and conscious, condition not hopeless." I knew this was the end. We had expected it. The Fates do not allow the good fortune that has followed me to go with me to the grave— count no man happy till he dies. . . .'

That William might have one day alone, Grace wired, cancelling his engagements. A Swiss doctor, failing to receive the message, came to lunch and stayed until late afternoon. Only on his way to the station did he learn from the chauffeur of Revere's death.

William wrote the next day to Jennette:

13 Norham Gardens, Oxford,
Aug. 31st, 1917.

Dear Little Auntie,

Our dear boy has gone and we are left desolate. The one comfort is that such a . . . friend as Harvey Cushing was with him. We had hoped to have him back on leave next week. Poor Laddie ! He hated war and he is now at peace.

William hid his sorrow from the public. At no time did he evince personal animus toward the Germans, nor would he allow others to do so in his presence. To him the enemy was war. He worked as hard as ever and superficially appeared his cheery self. Alone in his room at night he wept.

* From Cushing's Diary.   † Cushing.

Grace wrote to her sister:

Jan. 11, 1918.

'. . . I thought Willie would give out on Christmas day. . . . He was like a ghost and he is so thin. . . . We had all the American doctors who are working here at supper and they seemed happy enough . . . [Willie] sobs his heart out nearly every night and mourns his darling every moment. . . .'

Only his books and the small children of friends remained to comfort him. His staunch wife in her efforts to alleviate his loss, forgot her own. William's friends (they were numbered in the hundreds) felt for William something more acute than friendship. A magnetism, indescribable and known only to the eyewitness, produced in men, women and children a state of love. Many (particularly women) became fanatical worshippers. Therefore, though thousands were losing only sons, Revere's death came as a personal blow to his father's disciples. Everyone dreams that some man may live a perfect life. William had come so close. His had been golden, blessed both by his own efforts and talents and a fate friendly almost to the end.

In 1919 he wrote to a friend of an honour that made a fitting climax to his life. 'I am struggling with an address which I hope you will like—as President of the Classical Association—a body composed of all the professors & teachers of Greek & Latin. Every other year they have an ordinary citizen—that is how I came in; but as Bryce, Morley, Balfour & Asquith are my predecessors I am a bit nervous. . . .'

In a scarlet gown and velvet cap, 'looking medieval and wonderful' according to Grace, he gave his Presidential Address, 'The Old Humanities and the New Science'. His former Hopkins colleague, Professor Welch, was among his audience and described the occasion.

'There have been physicians, especially in England, well known for their attainments as classical scholars, but I am not aware that since Linacre there has come to a member of the medical profession distinction in this field comparable to Osler's election to the presidency of the British Classical Association. It was in recognition not merely of his sympathetic interest in classical studies and intimate association with classical scholars, but also of his mastery of certain phases of the subject, especially the bibliographical and historical sides, and the relation of the work and thought of classical antiquity to the development of medicine, science and culture. . . .

'. . . The distinguished company, the brightly coloured academic gowns and hoods, the traditional ceremonies for such an occasion in Oxford, the figure of Osler himself, the charm and interest of the address and its cordial appreciation and reception by the audience, all combined to make a scene of brilliancy and delight. . . .'*

Sir Frederic Kenyon ended his tribute, 'Osler himself was a well-nigh perfect example of the union of science and the humanities, which to some of us is the ideal of educational progress; and his address embodied the whole spirit of his ideal.'*

William had been subject to bronchitis since childhood and several times during the war years his old ailment developed into bronchial pneumonia. At seventy he was leading a life to strain a forty-year-old. Since Revere's death he had lost weight

* Cushing.

but not his grief. Those close to him knew he must ease off or die. But still he maintained his (sometimes deplorable) love for practical jokes. He committed his last, or last recorded, during the illness that killed him. Two revered specialists had come from London in consultation on his case. William knew the routine. A specimen of urine would be called for. In spite of fever and cough he escaped his room, his house, his wife and collected a handful of fine gravel with which, when the time came, he sprinkled his offering. He was a happy child when two gravely worried yet puzzled physicians told him that his kidneys were in shocking condition.

In September, 1919, he caught a cold that again developed into pneumonia—this time with complications. His illness killed him slowly. He watched the course of his disease with an expert's eye, making notes on findings and prognosis. Death, he said, was inevitable. The good diagnostician remained one to the end.

On Christmas Eve he asked to have Milton's 'Ode on the Morning of Christ's Nativity' read to him from his first edition; the poem he had read on so many Christmas Eves to his son Revere. He died five days later on Dec. 29, 1919.

Grace wrote to her brother-in-law, Featherston Osler, on Jan. 1, 1920:

My dear Fen
The New Year has come to me as a day of deep sorrow and rejoicing. Willie has had such a terrible illness and has borne it without a murmur or complaint. I rejoice that he is free. . . .
This has been a wonderful day. Never was there such a demonstration of love and respect as exhibited by the World of Medicine and all scientific and literary people as well as

others. Through his illness Willie has followed with deep interest his own case and left a note to me saying he wanted an autopsy. . . . The immediate cause of death was a rupture of the pleura that had been so strained from . . . weeks of coughing and inflamation. Had this not happened he probably would have struggled on with increased discomfort. The autopsy showed a very serious condition in the lung from the influenza bacillus.

Today we . . . had the funeral. It was at our Cathedral—Christ Church where he was really an adored 'Student'. The Cathedral was packed. . . . Representatives of all learned societies [came] to do him honour. As we entered I could simply see a mass of men's faces, and the bits of colour from the scarlet hoods of the canons and university men. I felt a sensation of immense pride and made up my mind to be thankful he had gone in the full mental strength of his career, loved and respected by the world. The coffin was covered by a purple pall. The University Marshall and Bedell [stood] at the head & foot, in their quaint gowns. The Vice Chancellor in his stall and Bedell with his Mace—Bodley's Librarian near him. . . .

Willie is to be cremated and as we could not go to London until tomorrow morning he is now lying in the Lady Chapel of the Cathedral, . . . under the arched roof Revere always sketched, . . . Burton's Monument at his head. . . . Willie Francis and I have been there this evening and I felt the dear Mother would feel that her Benjamin was lying where she would like him to be.

I want you to know all this at once. Thank you for your cable. I know how you are all grieving.

affectly
Grace

William's ashes, at his own request, went with his books to the Osler Library at McGill. And here the story ends for though Featherston, Edmund, Chattie and Frank still lived, the creative days were over.

Craigleigh 1919–24

To SAY we moved from London, Ontario, to Toronto would not be a lie but it would certainly be no more than a half truth; more accurate to say that after our father's death we moved from London to Craigleigh, a relic of the earlier town and the Principality of our maternal grandfather, Sir Edmund Osler.

The house stood in the middle of thirteen acres bordering a Rosedale ravine. The front gates opened on to South Drive; the tradesmen's entrance faced Elm Avenue as did two neat brick houses, one occupied by Mr. Allen, the head gardener, the other by the family of the deceased coachman. A large house on a corner of the property belonged to an uncle and aunt and completed our community. We had no other neighbours.

Beyond the gates we could not go unless escorted by Lizzie, the old Craigleigh nurse, or by our governess. All very well for those to the manner born but we came from London, Ontario.

The Craigleigh nursery had four barred windows. The two facing south gave us a distant view of street life. We knew our elders lied when they told us how lucky we were, with thirteen acres at our disposal, while the Nanton Avenue children were confined to city sidewalks. But they lied in innocence for they believed that by having too much we had everything.

Every afternoon as the grandfather clock struck five we were prepared for the downstairs world—washed, brushed and buttoned into dresses stiff with starch. Supper in the billiard room (the billiard table had vanished but the name remained) was followed by an hour or two in the company of the grandfather, mother and resident or non-resident aunts and uncles.

The governess of the moment presided over supper. If other grandchildren were staying in the house their nanny ruled opposite. The second parlour-maid waited at table. She travelled through two kitchens, the maids' sitting-room, a large pantry and a long corridor before she reached her destination.

The men's lavatory was oddly situated down a flight of stairs leading from a corner of the billiard room. Our evening meal was punctuated by the comings and goings of grandfather and uncles to this inconveniently placed convenience. In addition to the usual facilities it sported a urinal, a dashing piece of plumbing to our provincial eyes.

For some reason, vague and never defined, supper was a joyless meal. Governess and visiting nannies seldom saw eye to eye; the preserved fruit bit like vinegar. In memory it is linked with the smell of linoleum in the back halls and up the back stairs, a lost Victorian smell produced by daily scrubbings with yellow soap.

After an hour with the family we retired from their adult world but not before we had said our goodnights, a formidable procedure when the room was lined with relations. Each must be addressed, each kissed. The grandfather and one uncle

were bald except for their curling back fringes, the others
baldish. As they usually received our salutations from the
comfort of chairs, we chose their shining domes as targets
for our lips. A man seemed over-decorated if his head produced a normal crop of hair. Kissing was a pursuit that only
the passing of time taught us to appreciate. We marvelled
when we read of its delights, accustomed as we were to
counting heads—how many to give and receive before we
left the room and climbed the stairs to bed.

Every other week Mr. Day came to Craigleigh to cut the
grandfather's fringe and wave the hair of his womenfolk,
to shear the grandsons and singe the long locks of granddaughters. Singeing has gone out of fashion but once it was the
necessary treatment for split ends. The smell, the possibility of
going up in flames like a summer haystack, a feeling of affinity
with witches, gave an almost savage air to this domestic ritual.

We were forbidden the warm kingdom of kitchens and
their comforting smells, but the pantry was another matter.
The parlour-maids ignored us, William made us welcome.
He was referred to as William-the-butler to distinguish him
from the many Williams in the family. Behind the scenes he
called us Missy which we preferred to the stiff Miss Anne
and Miss Betty used by the rest of the staff; a form of address
that jarred until our ears adjusted to the sedate measure of
Craigleigh tunes. Sometimes William took time off to play
with us under the oak trees a long way from the house. He
could swing a child higher than any man we knew. When
he married a daughter of the deceased coachman and settled
in an apartment above the stable-garage the family approved,
thankful he had made no foreign alliance.

Ellen Osler on or about her 100th birthday with two great-grandchildren, Phyllis Osler (now Mrs. Allan Aitken of Montreal) and Phillip Osler, also of Montreal

Most of the servants, indoors and out, had been old re-
tainers before we were born. Only the parlour-maids were
fickle. Cook, kitchen-maid, Mary, the second-floor housemaid, William and Lizzie were part of the brick-and-mortar
of the house.

With only three fully equipped bathrooms, an inadequate
number when Christmas added out-of-town grandchildren,
and twenty or more slept under the Craigleigh roof, we
developed a stoical patience which stood us in good stead in
later war-time queues. The family facilities were situated well
away from the bedrooms, one off the landing where the front
stairs turned, between the ground floor and the second, and
one in the same position on the way to the third floor. Another
for the servants I never saw. Their wing of the house was
verboten and we never penetrated its mysteries. An incomplete
bathroom opened off the best spare bedroom. We admired
the large marble bath and wash-basin but it lacked the essential
toilet. Lizzie explained the reason for the omission. 'It's not
'ealthy to 'ave a waste pipe near a bedroom,' she said. This
also explained the awkward situations of the other bathrooms.
To ease congestion the bedrooms were equipped with old-
fashioned wash-stands, flowered china basins, flowered china
tooth-brush jars and flowered china chamber-pots. Mary and
Lizzie brought hot water in copper jugs to the women of the
house when they went to dress for dinner.

The younger children lived on the third floor. My sister
and I slept in the old day nursery, a long room often shared
with one or two visiting cousins. Lizzie's reign as family
nurse had started before our mother's birth and despite com-
petition from a succession of governesses and nannies she kept

her crown. Her room was papered with photographs of three generations of Oslers. In curly gilt frames they covered walls and bureaus and small spindly tables. Victorian babies, Edwardian babies and the latest batch of Georgian babies, big boys and girls and little girls and boys and dozens of lacey brides kept her company as she sat with her mending in the long evenings.

Lizzie and Queen Victoria merged in our minds and became indistinguishable. The resemblance did not end with the physical. They shared common interests. History would read the same if Lizzie had ruled the Empire for sixty years. Church, Throne and Family were mutual and dominant passions.

No shapes remain on earth like the shape of Lizzie. As nature forgot the combination that produced the pterodactyl, so it forgot the formula for Lizzie. Fat is not the word. It was all in the way it was gathered up in sundry places. Five feet short, a presence stiffened by uncompromising stays, she appeared many-aproned. Black buttoned boots, black cotton stockings and long buff-coloured flannel underwear were the staple items of her wardrobe. Her boots squeaked. She never walked but moved at a bustling dog trot, muttering the while a kindly sort of scolding. Cockney born, her aitches remained flighty all the days of her life. Her voice never descended to the sentimental except when she read to us from her book of Bible stories; then, as she sat on a little rocker, steel-rimmed spectacles tipped low on the bridge of her nose, her eyes would water and her voice fill with a special religious quaver. Our mother was her spotless darling and we counted as nothing compared to 'Miss Mary'.

Her aggressive nature came into its own at bath time.

Countless young had suffered before us from the vigour of
her arm and the stiffness of her brush. Her victims swore she
put cleanliness above godliness until she proved her equal
tenacity in spiritual matters. Observing that both mother and
grandfather neglected our religious instruction she did their
duty for them. The grandfather snorted at her childish Bible
stories. 'Read them the King James version,' he advised. Lizzie
only sniffed and went her way, determined to save our souls
for her particular Jehovah. Christ she thought of as the infant
Jesus, a dear baby whom we suspected she wished to remove
from the stable and give the benefits of her expert ministrations.

Bath time was a favourite hour for male members of the
connection to call on the grandfather and they made a point
of coming up to see the children. We used to wonder when they
would realize we were too old for these indelicate bathroom
visits. Fortunately I had read that French courtesans entertained
from the tub and though vague as to their profession we were
consoled in part for our loss of dignity.

The hairbrush followed the bath and the scrubbing-brush.
Lizzie believed that a "ealthy 'ead of 'air' was only achieved
by prolonged and daily brushing. Then came the rags in which
she rolled our lank locks, leaving us to sleep with dozens of
knobby lumps digging into our skulls. In vain our mother
protested. Lizzie was ashamed of our straight brown hair.
She said we made a poor showing beside our blond and curly-
headed cousins.

When we moved to Craigleigh my brother, sister and I,
aged respectively ten, seven and eight, were uncompromising
Laurier Liberals. Our father had been badly beaten when he

ran on the Labour-Liberal ticket in the 1917 election. Two
years had passed but we had scarcely scraped off the last bit
of mud flung by the enemy when we found ourselves sharing
salt with confessed and unrepentant Tories.

Sir Wilfrid's ghost, like Hamlet's father, burned to be
avenged. To us he was a personal as well as a public hero. He
had stayed in our house. We had sat on his knee and fallen in
love with his beautiful spare face and figure, his voice and his
halo of white hair. We were quite prepared to carry his torch
among the infidels.

At home we had discussed politics more often than the
weather. With the courage of a green soldier I tried the direct
approach. In conversation with the grandfather and an uncle
I mentioned the name Laurier. The uncle, good temper barely
covering his scorn, grunted, 'Nothing but a crook and a French
crook too.' In my best platform style I upheld the honour of
our hero until the wicked Conservatives collapsed with
laughter. I can only liken my sensations to those of the mis-
sionaries when their attempts to clothe the bodies of South
Sea Islanders were greeted with golden chuckles.

My brother knew the virtue of restraint. He kept in touch
with the homeland by subscribing to the *London Advertiser*.
Politics became identified with a lost and simpler life and
were coloured by homesickness. With no further hope of
converting the family I went underground. I expected to find
some loyal souls among the servants, but pickings were poor.
Cook and kitchen-maid inhabited a forbidden region. Lizzie's
devotion to church and the Conservative party went without
question. The parlour-maids seemed strangely uninterested in
party affairs. William-the-butler was too obviously amused.

To my distress I found the only Liberal other than ourselves was Mary, the second-floor housemaid, an ageing battle-axe we had no wish to claim. But there was no denying her. She burned with an ardour equal to our own and we hated her for sharing a holy passion. We took the attitude that though we would use her vote we would forget her between elections.

Next I tried my luck with the men who worked outside and in the potting-shed and greenhouses. Top man here was Mr. Allen. The grandfather called him Allen but to everyone else he was Mr. and a man of authority. He preferred flowers to children and considered us little more than potential thieves and a threat to the sanctity of his vegetable kingdom. A professional horticulturist, he directed the gardeners who worked under him. He and his wife lived in a house on the property. He always wore a hat. No need to ask him his political convictions. He WAS the Conservative party. We dismissed the chauffeur as unworthy of the Liberal camp and did not ask him his political affiliations. We had no wish to find a second undesirable professing devotion to the 'cause'. We suspected him of plotting to assassinate the grandfather. Cook we marked as his accomplice and spent many happy hours in counterplots, dreaming of the day when, laden with proof, we exposed the traitors to a grateful grandfather. At this distance it is hard to remember why we cast the chauffeur in so lurid a role. Perhaps we felt that no man would drive so wildly unless his motive was death. Most of the year he manned the lumbering Pierce Arrow, a seven-passenger open touring-car with a right-hand drive. The foot brake had long since worn out and he brought the car to a halt by removing both hands from the wheel and pulling vigorously on the emergency brake. The family seldom used the closed car. The grandfather thought it stuffy. But any car he considered an invention of the devil and never had an easy moment when he ventured forth, sitting unrelaxed in the back seat, exposed to wind, rain, dust or snow. Indeed, with Coll at the wheel it was a perilous business and somewhat similar to lurching round town on the back of a dinosaur.

At last among the under-gardeners I found a fellow soul. He was the 'Boots' as well as an outdoor man. Every morning between eight and nine he could be found in the catacombs before a regiment of family shoes. Busy with polish and brush he lent a sympathetic ear and between the two of us we licked the Conservative party.

John the coachman was dead, but tales of his eccentricities lived on. Hunting-green livery had clothed his stalwart dignity as he sat high on the coachman's seat, wrapped in a buffalo robe and holding the reins of the two white horses. But the elegance was all above the waist. If for some reason he was forced to descend from his perch the startled observer saw old working-trousers below the immaculate coat. Only in summer when no rug hid his legs did he trouble himself with a uniform below the belt.

The two white horses were not without their own distinction, having fought in the Battle of Mafeking. The grandfather had bought them from the ill-fated Lord Dundonald. They were honoured as veterans and even the noise of the bits between their teeth suggested a noble clank of medals. With a fine carriage and heroes to pull it the family, in an equine sense, was well suited.

Rosedale had been almost country then, and in our time Craigleigh still clung to its productive traditions. Eggs, vegetables, mushrooms, hothouse grapes, apples, strawberries and raspberries came fresh to the table. Even in winter we grew our own tomatoes, celery, lettuce as well as flowers enough to fill a flower shop. But from all the wealth of hothouses in winter and gardens in summer my mother could rarely lay her hands on more than a few frugal blooms. An unwritten law gave Mr. Allen the sole right to sever stem from plant and as the act almost broke his heart the results were naturally skimpy. It was useless to appeal to the grandfather. Mr. Allen, he said, created (with some slight assistance from nature) all these growing things and we were privileged to see them when and under such circumstances as he saw fit. The breakfast flower was different. That was a specimen sent from one connoisseur to another. Every morning Mr. Allen paced through his green world until he found the perfect blossom to grace the grandfather's tray. In winter it might be a pale blue butterfly spray of orchids; in summer, the most tender of his roses; in spring a sprig of lily of the valley from his wild garden. The granddaughters of the house took turns in carrying this offering to the grandfather's room. But whether we were flower-bearer or not we always went in to say good morning and plant a kiss on his bald head. In leaning over the bed we never failed to kick the chamber-pot beneath. Its ringing note inevitably accompanied our questions concerning the state of his health and the passage of the night. On his better days he would answer the first with 'so so' but his nights, as I remember them, were always 'hidjus'.

In his last years the grandfather was restless, caged within the aching bars of his body. He cussed at sore legs, the pains in his head and the sorry plight of man in general and old age in particular. His fidgets drove him up and down the morning-room or up and down the path beside the drive. He often had a small grand-daughter on his arm and she could occasionally persuade him to change his route. Once, on some pretext or other, I steered him out of the gate and across the road, then on and on all the way to Bloor Street, an event so miraculous I felt the birds must stop their singing to watch our debut. It never happened again and never again did I see him surrounded by other people's houses and alien trees.

A sightseeing bus passed the gates every afternoon. The grandfather's face would cloud when a man with a megaphone shouted from the open upper deck, 'This is the residence of Sir Edmund Osler, brother of Sir William Osler, the doctor who advocated euthanasia at sixty.' 'That is all they remember,' he said, 'of a great man.'

The grandfather had not always been the stay-at-home we knew. Until old age and apprehension chained him to his house and garden he had been a constant traveller, crossing the Atlan-tic annually and Canada as often. His trips to Europe had usually been family affairs even when prompted by business. He loved to take his wife and all available children and often a niece or nephew joined the party. In London they stayed at Brown's Hotel, an old-fashioned hostel even then. I first crossed the ocean in the company of a father, mother, brother, sister, two grandfathers, an aunt, William-the-butler become William-the-valet and a nurse; but this was a paltry number compared to the mass migrations of my mother's youth.

Though endlessly good-humoured with us, our elders

suffered from the grandfather's gloom. The house was a house
of mourning despite the bustle of grandchildren. Our father's
death was only one black patch. A few months later William
Osler died in Oxford. Edmund, Featherston, and Charlotte
were all that remained of that lusty family (excepting Frank
whose name we never heard and who we presumed had died
in another century).

The grandfather brooded on his failing health. A night and a
day nurse became permanent fixtures in the house, even when
their patient was up and about and attending his office for a few
hours in the morning. The doctor called daily, more to give
moral support than to prescribe therapeutic treatment. Lizzie
remarked cynically that the M.D. chose the hour of six for his
quite unnecessary visits in order to get a free drink before
dinner.

The grandfather extended his fears to include his children
and grandchildren. He treated our smallest indispositions with
the utmost gravity, and being susceptible to suggestion the
children soon learned to suffer in all the proper places. Sleepless-
ness, headaches and twinges of rheumatism were the minor
ailments that afflicted him, and they proved infectious. Pneumonia killed him in the end but not until it had attacked a
dozen times. Once during a critical bout we were farmed out
with relations, but for the most part we lived through his ill-
nesses with him. We developed the usual childish diseases as
well as the suggested ones and the house was always white
with nurses and black with doctors, a hospital rather than a
family dwelling-place. The sickness in the air and the constant
intimations of death made the dark a Hades to which a
child must descend each night at bedtime. How to get

through to morning without calling for help against a thousand ghosts?

Job and Ecclesiastes were always in our ears but when the grandfather muttered 'vanity, vanity...' he tempered his pessimism with humour. Shakespeare, the Bible and Montaigne were at his bedside and in his blood-stream.

Craigleigh meals were as set in their ways as everything else in the house. Cook showed my mother the menu for the day, but it was only a gesture—she did not expect alternate suggestions. The food was prepared in the English manner—straight—no nonsense with sauces or made-up dishes. Though I can find no Jewish blood to explain it the family considered pork a socially inferior meat and ham only a degree better. To this day I am uneasy when faced with the former and wish it had another name or came from a different animal. Veal was for Frenchmen. Bacon (if crisp) was acceptable and a daily item on the breakfast table.

On rare occasions when my mother went away and no aunts and uncles were available the grandfather would send for me to sit with him while he dined. A silent man, he enjoyed the company of any young animal who neither wished nor expected him to hold up his end of the conversation. I met the necessary qualifications and he could limit his remarks to 'Does your tongue never tire?' or 'You talk the hind leg off a donkey, my dear.'

The room was large and lofty and round and the dining-room table was as large and as round as King Arthur's. William-the-butler stood behind the grandfather's chair and two parlourmaids fluttered in other corners. The meal took time. First and always *consommé* and melba toast, next and almost always fried sole, then a roast or filet mignon, pudding, a savoury followed by fruit, nuts, figs and my favourite ginger. After sherry with the soup the champagne was opened and flowed for the duration of the feast. I participated in the last course, peeling a peach or cracking nuts for the grandfather. As I sat beside him I filled with glory at my position of chosen hostess. It happened only two or three times in my life and never lost in radiance. Perhaps it was on one of these occasions that he told me something of his attitude towards money. He had accumulated a considerable pile when still a young man. He remembered the day he consciously stopped the pile's increase. He explained how money begets money and how, beyond a point, it is as useless to man as sand. Compared with big American fortunes or Canada's contemporary mining millions he was not excessively rich. And Bay Street would certainly think anyone a fool who stopped the snowball rolling when the snow lay deep in all directions. Money he respected but he gave his love to animate things like flowers and children.

Mostly the days passed solemnly enough. 'Your grandfather has a headache' or 'Your grandfather had a bad night' were the pleas used to keep our voices low and our games quiet. But now and then something happened to relax both old and young. The Mustard Plaster Episode was such an affair, a tale reminiscent of Henry II and Thomas à Becket.

A child recovering from bronchitis complained to the grandfather of the terrible strength and frequency of Lizzie's plasters. These had achieved renown over a period of two generations and there was nothing new in the protest. But the grandfather proved unexpectedly sympathetic and made a startling suggestion. 'It's high time Lizzie had a taste of her own medicine,' he said. 'I'll give a dollar to man, woman or child who can get a plaster on Lizzie and keep it there until the skin is a deep pink.'

Our eyes brightened and as soon as manners permitted we retired to the catacombs to discuss strategy.

A cousin (Anne Osler) and I elected ourselves for the job. Obviously it was an enterprise that called for at least two people. One to hold the victim down and one to slap on the plaster. With the plaster on we suspected it might take a battalion to keep it there but we felt the younger children would be more trouble than their holding power was worth. Anne conceived the master plan. She was six months older than I and six times more courageous. The following day, by hook or crook we would obtain a box of Keen's mustard and a small amount of flour—no simple matter to children denied access to the kitchen—and store this precious ammunition in some corner of the catacombs. At the stroke of midnight we would make our way down the long flights of stairs, through the sleeping house and down once more to the total blackness of the cellar. Here we would prepare the plaster to end mustard plasters. After some thought we decided to reverse the usual proportions, using five mustard to one flour. A quick burn was essential to our plan for we could not count on immobilizing Lizzie for long. The dollar reward depended on skin warmed to a deep pink. Whether we really believed the grandfather would insist on a peek before paying up seems unlikely but we were leaving nothing to chance.

Somehow we acquired the necessary ingredients and hid them according to plan. Anne was jubilant, I was bowed by thoughts of the midnight trip. I picked at lunch, gagged on my supper. The moment of truth arrived and I threatened to mutiny unless we changed our base of operations. Anne looked at me with the natural contempt of the strong for the weak, called me a lily-livered spoil-sport, a spoon-fed sissy. I had sunk too low to care. To hell with honour. Anne gave in. Even she cowered at the prospect of the catacombs, alone, at night.

We chose the bathroom as an alternative laboratory. High strategy had fallen to the lowly plan of hiding the poultice under a mattress until the stroke of midnight gave the signal to attack. Anne being larger would jump on the victim and pin her arms back while I must somehow manage to penetrate a long-sleeved flannel nightgown with the dripping plaster. At eight o'clock we started our witches' brew. But we had not counted on the powerful whiffs that soon permeated the house. 'Five mustard to one flour' we muttered as we spread the last ribbons of yellow goo on a hand towel appropriated for the occasion. A loud knock and Lizzie's abrupt demand to 'hopen hup' quickly dispelled our dreams of glory. I avoided Anne's eye as she unlocked the door. At first the chatter and scolding continued on a normal level. As far as Lizzie knew we had only made a mess of the bathroom. She was still unaware of the deeper implications. Puzzled, she held up the plaster. Anne, overcome with the sudden frustration of her plan, wailed like a banshee and told the whole story from the original offer of a dollar from the grandfather.

Downstairs, splendid in evening clothes, the family sat drinking their after-dinner coffee. And it was downstairs for us, Lizzie in the lead holding the mustard plaster aloft like Salome with St. John's head. Her dance was a sputter of fury. 'Hexplain yourself, Sir Hedmund,' she demanded. The grandfather wisely said nothing. He waited for the tongue-lashing that came like a whirlwind from the small but potent woman. She held the floor for five minutes, uninterrupted except by Anne's sobs (Anne wept from thwarted ambition, not repentance). When her say was said the grandfather somehow made his peace and Lizzie retired, muttering still but her rage spent. Our elders laughed till they cried and I joined them for had I not witnessed Greek meet Greek? But Anne was inconsolable. She had lost the chance of a lifetime to do a dastardly deed with full permission from the head of the house, indeed at his suggestion. The grandfather, seeing her distress, gave us each fifty cents for what he called 'a good try'. With Anne it wasn't the money. She belonged to that rare company, the pure of heart, for whom honour is the only profit.

Lizzie appeared to forget the incident until the next child caught a cold. Then, adding an extra dash of mustard to the plaster, she slapped it on, vindictively we thought.

The grandfather loved domestic harmony. Conversation, if necessary at all, should touch on only uncontroversial topics. Politics, religion and sex must on no account enter the arena. They led to argument and argument might degenerate into anger. Fresh from London, Ontario, and still holding the Gibbons' point of view that talk and argument were synonymous, we thought words without heat to warm them no better than cold mutton. Religion was never discussed, but we deduced that the grandfather was an unbeliever. In my mother's childhood prayers had started the day. Family and servants gathered round while the grandfather read the lesson at a muttered gallop, quite unintelligible to his respectful audience. On Sunday parents and children attended St. Simon's Church on

Howard Street. As soon as the service ended and the rector moved to the pulpit, the grandfather with no apparent self-consciousness stood up and walked serenely down the aisle and out of the door. His children took it as a matter of course for they had heard him often enough proclaim his admiration for the verbal beauty of the service, always ending, 'But I *won't* be lectured to by a sucking parson.' The church disappeared with the grandmother and though it would have been considered indelicate to discuss one's unbelief—or for that matter one's belief—it was silently understood. Politics roused the passions and passion was out of place in the drawing-room. Sex they treated much as its half-sister, religion. If it was an act of God it was a dubious one and surely the devil had nudged the Almighty's elbow when he conceived the many and fabulous forms of reproduction. We did not know for certain whether they believed in the high fantasy of the 'facts of life'. We suspected they had lost their faith a second time.

Our first knowledge of the mating of mammals came from Anne. Her father bred prize cattle and the farmyard was our encyclopaedia. We rejoiced that our parents shirked those uninformative little talks, so painful to both generations. Indeed we took pains to shelter them from the grosser aspects of nature. If actions speak louder than words the barnyard was a good school. It demonstrated, and with no perceptible embarrassment on the part of the actors.

For a week or two after the enlightenment we saw the family as so many cows and bulls and then for a while we looked on the cattle in the fields as aunts and uncles. But eventually the world righted itself—a cow was a cow, an aunt an aunt.

The grandfather was neither a reformer nor a crusader.

He accepted the ne'er-do-well with humorous resignation, never making it a condition of his generosity that the recipient change his spots. Perhaps his two brothers, Frank and Edward, who ne'er did well in their lives, increased his sympathy for the droves of down-and-outs and impostors who flocked to him for help. He was known as an easy mark, and half his mail consisted of begging letters. He chuckled rather than scowled when, as frequently happened, he discovered he'd been 'had' by one of these. If their sob stories showed ingenuity he was inclined to pay a second time for the fun they had afforded him.

He took it for granted that he should be the family banker and stretched his generosity to include remote relations of his wife as well as his own clan, offering his help so promptly that the timid were never embarrassed by the need to ask it. He made possible William's postgraduate training, and encouraged him with words and cash to collect the books that now make up the Osler Library at McGill. Pelham Edgar in *Across My Path* tells of his interest in the Royal Ontario Museum. '. . . I took Currelly [curator of the Museum] up to Craigleigh one Sunday afternoon to meet Sir Edmund Osler. He was destined to be one of the Museum's most powerful friends, and without his support its establishment might have been indefinitely delayed.' He backed Currelly and the museum project to the tune of ten thousand dollars a year for five years.

The stage never captured his imagination. Actors he considered so many children making damn fools of themselves. Movies existed but not for him. The Oslers were an unmusical lot and the grandfather was no exception. His feelings amounted

Sir Edmund Osler at Craigleigh about 1920

almost to musicphobia and caused my mother and sister some distress. A Steinway grand, unused since the grandmother's death, tempted my mother to renew her piano lessons and she made several attempts at regular practice. At the first note the grandfather would appear like a genie and ostentatiously shut all possible doors, then sit, head in hands, as far away as a large house permitted from the offending 'noise'. My sister's life revolved round her violin. To male Oslers a fiddle was a butt for jokes, and musicians they eyed as unpleasant sports of nature, a race apart and to be kept apart from normal men and women. Artists in general aroused their distrust. Like politics, sex and religion they stirred man's imagination, and were a threat to the status quo.

Books, if not their authors, held an honourable place in the family. Almost as important as the walls that sheltered us were the volumes that lined these walls. We had a catholic collection at our disposal. The nursery contained innumerable Victorian tales of piety as well as the standard children's classics—Grimm, Hans Andersen, Lewis Carroll, Stevenson and many others. Our mother provided us with contemporary literature and every age had access to the big downstairs library. The grandfather encouraged anyone with an appetite for print. Sometimes he overestimated a child's intelligence and recommended books beyond our comprehension. Pride forced me to read, word for word, everything he suggested, and if I read Thackeray and Jane Austen, innocent of the irony and wit embodied in their pages, I enjoyed the story. We had not learned that Kipling was unfashionable and wallowed in the *Jungle Books*, *Captains Courageous* and *Kim* and all the short stories. India became the land of my waking dreams. A page of *Kim* still brings me the smell of the East, modified by the smell of Craigleigh. Dickens and Scott were required reading for children of that era. I placed them lower on the scale of pleasure than the now forgotten tales of Charles Harrison Ainsworth. His *Tower of London* and many others gave the blood and thunder found today in the comic strips.

Sometimes the grandfather read aloud to us before bed-time: nursery rhymes, folk tales and ballads. His deep bass voice still echoes in Poe's 'Raven' and 'Annabel Lee'. We may have shuddered at the former but it cast a spell and children welcome any magic, white or black. 'Annabel Lee' filled us with pleasurable sadness, bringing the same mood as Arnold's 'Forgotten Merman'.

A small anonymous figure arrived every Saturday to wind and regulate the clocks. I remember him on winter afternoons when the dusk was not yet deep enough for the parlour-maids to pull the curtains and wake the house with light. I never heard him speak or in any way acknowledge the presence of another person in the room. As he went about his occult business I pictured him moving from house to house, all over the world, setting men's clocks with such precision that their mornings and their midnights would strike exactly, not in accord with Greenwich but tuned to some universal meas-urement. In the suffocating silence of the night when the grandfather clock chimed and struck the quarter hours, the half hours and the hours, it seemed as though the silent Satur-day man was the scuttling figure of Time and lived inside the commodious body of that big hall clock.

William-the-butler owned the ground floor, the wine cellar and the souls of the two parlour-maids. He accompanied the grandfather when he travelled, changing in a trice from butler to 'gentleman's gentleman'. To watch him swoop about the dining-room like a great black bird, tail-coat flying, a tray balanced on the palm of his hand, was one of the sights of the house. He played his part with enormous style, never relaxing his mask for a moment. Neither by wink nor smile would our merry friend of the pantry acknowledge his playmates. Our informal life in London had left us sadly deficient in matters of etiquette. Our first meals at Craigleigh were a strain on both host and guests. We tossed remarks to William as naturally as to the grandfather. William met our quips with silence. His wooden expression led us to believe he had not heard. A little deaf, we thought, and shouted. The embarrassed hush and William's discreet disapproval taught us in time.

William had his own method of ensuring that we did not eat food unsuitable for young palates. It was unthinkable that we should not be offered everything and so the forbidden fruits were passed with a kind of legerdemain—here and gone before we could transfer a spoonful to our plates.

Sunday at Craigleigh, though not in our time a day of prayer, preserved a solemn ritual of its own. Nothing was denied us because it was the Sabbath but a heaviness persisted long after the religious significance had been discarded. No one liked Sunday except perhaps William-the-butler who organized the gathering of the clan.

He rounded up the weekly Sunday party. On Friday he telephoned the various families to ask how many would attend. He liked a big turn-out and felt dispirited if only twelve or so accepted his invitation. He cheered up when holidays brought the children back from school and he could seat twenty or thirty round the round table in the round dining-room. The grandfather came downstairs at noon. If he was feeling chipper he wore a morning coat and grey striped trousers. His morning coats were very old and he used to show us the dates written in the waistcoat pockets, eighteen hundred and something or other. He would tell us how Bloor Street had looked when these suits were new, and thus we peered back into history through the almost obliterated figures scratched on a grandfather's waistcoat.

At half past one uncles and aunts and cousins began to arrive. The children stood awkwardly about while their elders decorously exchanged the week's news. William struck the gong at two. The meal itself was an ordeal, the menu fixed: *consommé*, roast beef, Yorkshire pudding, apple pie, meringues and jelly or trifle, with fruit, ginger and nuts at the end. Excitement or apprehension so affected the nerves of one small cousin that he was frequently sick before, after or during these banquets.

Observing the order of precedence, the wife of the eldest son sat on the grandfather's right, on his left the wife of the next son or the eldest grand-daughter. William and his two parlour-maids circled round and round till we were stuffed like so many Christmas geese. The signal that we could 'arise and go now' came when the grandfather dipped his fingers in his finger-bowl and shook a little water at the nearest child. Then a half-hour in the library with everyone yawning from food, ennui and Sunday sadness. Release came, but too late. The day was dead and we wished we could bury it decently in sleep.

Sometimes on a Sunday afternoon Uncle Fen (Judge Osler) called on the grandfather. He too had entertained his children and grandchildren at a similar repast. The brothers would sit together for an hour or so, devoted but almost dumb in each other's presence. Featherston's long white beard and patrician nose combined with the title Judge led me to confuse him with the God in Lizzie's Bible stories. We never became intimate with this senior member of the family and stood in awe of his critical eye. We knew by hearsay that he was a stickler for manners and expected an inhuman decorum from every age. Anything distasteful, physically or mentally, provoked his famous shudder. To blow one's nose in his presence was to commit an indecency; a slip in syntax affected him like a fingernail scratched on a blackboard.

Aunt Grace (Lady Osler) after entertaining four of the six brothers (William, Featherston, Britton and Edmund) at dinner, was asked what they talked about. 'They didn't talk,' she answered, 'but they grunted now and then and seemed happy.'

Uncle Fen had three sons. The eldest, Hal, supplied our lives with glamour. Like his father he wore a beard; not the substantial growth of a patriarch but the well-clipped whiskers of an Edwardian man-about-town. He had no daughters and adopted nieces and young cousins to fill the void. He spent most of the year abroad, hunting big game in Africa or sunning himself at his villa in Cannes. Craigleigh was his first port of call when a few weeks' business brought him to Toronto. He would carry us off to his house or the York Club for grown-up dinners with all the frills. We stared at his African trophies and his modern French pictures and listened to tales of tigers, rhinos and elephants.

His marriage differed from those we saw around us. His beautiful wife lived most of the year in the south of France.

They met on and off and when it suited them. The Family thought them gay, which we considered as fine a thing as to be beautiful, though we knew our elders associated gaiety with frivolity and did not count it a serious virtue. To us they represented the dashing, sophisticated world in contrast to our solid respectable one and we speculated at length on their undomestic lives. Years later my sister lunched at their villa in Cannes. She came back with stories of marble floors, fourteen-carat gold hardware and the Mediterranean breaking on three sides of the property. We were at last convinced that our childish imagining had been in no way an exaggeration.

Prohibition started its dismal term either shortly before or soon after we moved to Craigleigh. The grandfather had laid down a stock of whisky and wine sufficient to last him his lifetime even should he live, as his mother before him, to be a hundred. A rash of robberies increased his ever-present anxiety and he devised an ingenious plan for the protection of his cellar. In one part of the catacombs he stored a year's supply, properly padlocked; in another room he put his lifelong stock. The door of the latter was then cemented over so that no means of entrance was visible. We could see that it was burglar proof, but it looked family proof as well. When we consulted William-the-butler he answered simply, 'Dynamite'. There was some apprehension when the year was up and the dynamite resorted to. We were removed from the house during the operation. All went well. The house stood, and the family could drink without a care for another year. Although I have no further recollection of subsequent blastings I presume it became an annual event like spring cleaning. Not that spring cleaning cut any dirt at Craigleigh. The grandfather couldn't abide it. The maids worked surreptitiously, careful not to be discovered at anything so disrupting as 'turning out a room'. No walls had been redecorated, no furniture recovered for a decade or more. The luxury in which we lived was worn and shabby and, like the family, neither fashionable nor unfashionable. The Oslers were a law unto themselves and never really merged with any social clique.

In our day few outsiders came to Craigleigh, for thus did we refer to those not related by blood or marriage, much as the Greeks referred to all non-Greeks as barbarians. Apart from Sir Augustus Nanton, Mrs. H. D. Warren, Beatty of the Canadian Pacific Railway, and a few other close friends I only remember Mrs. Pankhurst and Dr. Harvey Cushing, two quite dissimilar personalities.

Mrs. Pankhurst sat in the morning-room, as straight as her views, and talked to the grandfather of battles won and battles still to be fought. He listened to her with respectful amusement, unswayed by her oratory but impressed by her spirit. With women's suffrage achieved she had moved on to the Society for the Prevention of Venereal Disease, a plague, according to her statistics, as common as dandelions in June. She roped our mother in as captain for her Toronto campaign and thus the widow took her first step back to the world under the banner of the SPVD. She wrote letters to prosperous friends appealing for funds. Several business men answered with notes of protest. They objected to receiving envelopes with the name of the Society printed in large type for all to see. Whether their squeamishness stemmed from a delicate wish to preserve the eyes of their womenfolk from outrage or because they feared graver misunderstandings she never learned.

Harvey Cushing, the brain surgeon, stayed some days at Craigleigh collecting material for his *Life of Sir William Osler*. The grandfather expected everyone to dote on the interests of his old age, flowers and children. Cushing was bored with both and we were kept out of sight as much as possible. For this reason we suspected the grandfather shared our distrust of the famous surgeon. We mistook his name for Cushion and soon changed it to Pincushion as more suitable to what we imagined must be a prickly nature. Not to like children indeed! Who had ever heard of such a thing?

The Duke of Connaught and his entourage had stayed at Craigleigh long ago and we heard stories and looked at pictures taken during their visit. The grandfather had turned the house over to his royal guests and had moved in next door with a married daughter. The grandfather and the Duke entertained at a joint garden party. They failed to see eye to eye on certain vital points connected with the affair. The situation of the marquee was one of these. Connaught chose the wide sweep of velvet lawn between the house and the gates as the obvious site. The grandfather refused, polite but adamant, on the grounds that he wasn't going to have his best grass ruined for a mere garden party. As property owner he won, and the party was held in a less conspicuous part of the garden on less valuable grass.

Of past distinguished visitors Winston Churchill headed the list. He stayed at Craigleigh when lecturing in Toronto shortly after the Boer War. He did not shine as a house guest. The pillows did not suit; neither did this and neither did that. When told the family never dressed for Sunday supper Winston replied 'I do,' and did. The grandfather considered youth an in-

sufficient excuse for bad manners and even in later years when
Winston had reached the rank of cabinet minister he referred
to him as 'that young pup'.

If the grandfather referred to his childhood it was usually
to grumble that we, his grandchildren, were soft and spoiled,
an accusation too obvious to be ignored. We suffered the
double stress of guilt and resentment; guilt because we
were not, as our forebears, sturdy and self-reliant, resentment because the opportunity to acquire these virtues was
denied us.

In this environment we listened to tales of great-grandfather and great-grandmother and the early days in Bond
Head. We shivered politely at descriptions of their first winter
with only a shed for shelter. Great-grandmother had made
shoes for the boys when snow blocked the road to Newmarket,
cutting off supplies, or so the myth ran. Great-grandfather had
ridden forty miles a day, through blizzards and over corduroy
cart tracks, preaching in barns and sleeping in flea-ridden beds.
Good stories, yes, but the events they described seemed as far
away in time as tales of the early Britons.

.   .   .

Chattie died in 1925 at the age of seventy-eight; Featherston
and Edmund in 1924. Featherston achieved a decent eighty-
six years, the grandfather seventy-nine. During the latter's last
illness my brother and sister and I stayed on family acres at
Lake Simcoe. Only our brother went to Toronto for the
funeral. The customary prominent citizens made up the list
of honorary pall-bearers but the real ones were William-the-
butler, Mr. Allen and his five under-gardeners and the chauffeur
Coll. A few months later the Craigleigh house was pulled

down, the property facing Elm Avenue sold and the north lawns and ravine given to the city for a park.

Only Frank remained. Though each was unaware of the existence of the other, we were both in London in 1933. When news reached me that he whom I had thought dead was dying I called on Aunt Belle and she led me to a nearby nursing home where lay the mythical uncle.

Modern hospitals with their merciless sterility seem fresh and lively compared to London nursing homes: large Victorian houses with sickness creeping from folds of plush, from roses fading on threadbare carpets, from air, settled a hundred years ago and now too old to move.

He lay in a big brass bed. First he looked like William, then like Edmund. His head belonged to an elder statesman, a bishop, a retired general. I looked everywhere for Frank. I found, instead, Ellen's six sons gathered together in this last survivor. Time had already diminished the gap between the strong and the weak and death was about to close it.

APPENDICES

I

SAMUEL DREW was born near St. Austell, Cornwall, in 1765. His father made a poor living streaming for tin, with a little farming on the side. The seven-year-old Samuel was put to work in the fields, his parents receiving twopence a day for his labour. At ten he was apprenticed to a shoemaker but ran away and joined a band of smugglers. The life suited him well enough till the night he met 'a Being with fiery eyes'. It trotted past him, 'disappearing through the gate in a supernatural manner'. Samuel was not one to ignore signs and portents and quickly returned to his last. The death of a brother and the funeral service preached by Adam Clarke, one of Wesley's later preachers, completed his conversion. He joined the Wesleyan Society, educated himself through borrowed books and wrote poetry, using his bellows as a desk. Later he became a local preacher until an accusation of heresy forced him from the pulpit.

He wrote a number of books, among them *Anecdotes of Methodism, Essay on the Identity and Resurrection of the Body*, and finally, *Essay on the Immateriality and Immortality of the Soul*. The last-named brought him a modest fame (four editions appeared in England and two in America) and earned him the title Cornish Metaphysician.

From 1819 until his death in 1833 he edited the *Imperial Magazine* and superintended the business of the Caxton Press, first in Liverpool and later in London. The *Dictionary of National Biography* condemns his books but gives an excellent character reference, proclaiming Samuel an honest, independent man, devoted to his wife and family.

II

THE peace with France was not a year old when Edward and his father sailed from Falmouth to London in May, 1816.

For several days they were windbound at Dartmouth which Edward described as 'the worst town I ever saw. . . . Everyone seems to be poor. If our Falmouth grumblers were here, they would learn contentment. I believe there is more business in our shop than in any six in Dartmouth. In Broadstreet the signpost of the Commercial Inn reaches above two thirds across the street. In one street *only* and that a very short one, is there room for two carts to pass abreast. In all the others two dogs *might* walk abreast . . . and to avoid an ass and paniers you must take shelter in a passage. . . .'

Their ship seems to have had no special accommodation for passengers and small comforts were of their own making. Thus Edward described his method of settling in for the night. '. . . [I] make my bed by placing planks across the cabin lockers. . . . On these I lay a mattress, blanket quilt & great watchcoat. I then cut out a good supper, take off my coat and shoes and turn in. . . . I have no trouble dressing in the morning. . . .'

Five days later the wind changed and they were off.

Edward (3) Osler to his mother, London, May 29th, 1816:

'A ream of paper would not suffice for a description of all I have seen since I left Dartmouth. We sailed on Saturday morning with a fine wind from the westward and were soon out of sight of land.

'In the afternoon we came in sight of the Bill of Portland and when we had passed it had a most beautiful view of "England's chalky Clifts" shooting up like a long row of white spires. Never before did I see anything half so fine. I stood at the extremity of the quarter deck, every other part of the vessel being wet with the sea that broke over us. . . .

'At 4 on Monday morning we were half way through the downs and from this time [on] I only went below for my meals (which I dispatched as fast as possible) till we anchored in the evening. . . .

'We had a bird's-eye view of Margate, a beautiful town full of elegant houses. There I first saw a steam vessel. We hove to soon after to wait the flood tide to sail over the flats. . . . A brig drawing less water than the Enterprise, attempting them too soon, grounded. . . .

'We then ran up to the Nore where a beautiful new fifty gun frigate was lying ready for sea. . . . The wind was easterly & so fresh that we could go about four miles an hour against the tide.

'Before we got to the Thames, the steam boat that we [had] left at anchor off Margate passed us.

'There are many shoals on this part of the river . . . [and] we saw two recent wrecks. The banks on each side, as level as a bowling green, were clothed with the gayest verdure & ornamented with the finest trees. Cottages, farms and Seats were scattered round. To crown all the river, gliding along, on which a whole fleet of vessels were sailing . . . a scene which I *then* thought could not be surpassed.

'In the afternoon we passed Gravesend. . . . Opposite . . . is Tilbury Fort, but how different is its condition from that time when Queen Elizabeth reviewed and harangued her army before it, when the Armada was on its voyage to England. Now the long grass fills the embrasures and the black mouths of the cannon are scarcely seen through it. . . .

'Further up, on the north side of the river, is Purfleet. It derives its name from an expression of Queen Anne, who, when the Dutch fleet was sailing up the Thames . . . where the British ships were anchored, so infinitely inferior to the Dutch as to preclude all possibility of success in battle, stood on a hill . . . and exclaimed . . . "O my poor fleet". . . .

'Next morning we weighed and went up the river with the tide. We passed Woolwich at noon. There are enormous heaps of cannon balls and vast quantities of artillery, it being the grand depot of those stores. There are also convict ships, a dockyard with two 74s building one nearly ready to launch, another not yet planked. . . . After attentively observing those immense floating castles I observed an 18 gun sloop of war and a 10 gun schooner by her side, both dismantled. They appeared so small among the line of battle ships that I fancied I could sit in the middle [of one] and row her along myself. [Our] schooner looked like a plaything—a boat made with a penknife. . . .

'We reached Blackwell, The East India Company's dock and here were . . . thirty or forty East Indiamen. The only thing which defaces this beautiful place is the hideous spectacle of six men hanging in chains. . . .

'Greenwich was the next object of our attention. . . . [Its] hospital is so superior to St. James that it is a saying of foreigners that the English build a palace for their invalids and hovels for their kings. . . .

'We now began to see the skyline of London. The shipping lay tolerably thick. Manufactures, docks with ship building and repairing fill both sides of the river. When we came among the grand fleet it was indeed astonishing. The vessels lie in tiers on each rise, six or eight in a tier, side by side, leaving the middle of the river free for vessels going or coming. In the West India Dock & Canal there are more ships than were ever in Falmouth harbour together. In the whole river there are from four to six thousand vessels . . . they reach to London bridge. It is indeed a forest of masts. . . .'

In 1816, when Edward arrived in London to study surgery, medicine had groped its way out of the dark ages and was beginning to merit the title science. Between 1720 and 1745 many of London's great hospitals were founded, among them Guy's where Edward received his training. The barber-surgeon was dying out, due in part to the famous Hunter brothers who had left the wilds of Scotland for London in the latter part of the eighteenth century. But a hospital still resembled a slaughter-house. Pasteur and Lister were yet to come. Whisky or gin, the only anaesthetics, could not guarantee oblivion to the patient on the operating-table.

Edward Osler (3) to James Cornish, a young Falmouth physician, London, June 14, 1816:

'After a passage agreeable enough, we arrived at this infernal place on Tuesday fortnight. I took an antipathy to it the first moment I saw it. I have yet met with nothing that can induce me to change my opinion.

'The day after my arrival I went to the vessel to get out my luggage. The waterman wanted 2/- for bringing it on shore. I paid him 1/6, more than double his proper charge. . . . A hackney coachman who conveyed me a mile & a quarter charged 3/. This was a little too bad. I took his number and summoned him & [he] was fined 10/. . . .

'A week ago I entered perpetual at Brookes. He shewed my father and myself his museum. Father fancied himself in Hades (such is the power of imagination) and thought himself almost poisoned by the smell.

'On the second day of my attendance I entered the dissecting room. . . . The first object which met my view was the body of an old man stretched on a shutter in the court, the brains taken out and the scalp hanging about his ears, while his straggling white locks were matted together by his blood. A hungry wolf was snarling at it, and straining . . . as far as his chain would allow him. A tub full of human flesh was standing near it, some pieces of which I gave the eagles who devoured it with avidity.

'On entering the room the stink was most abominable. About twenty chaps were at work, carving limbs and bodies in all the stages of putrefaction and of all colors; black, green, yellow, blue, white. The pupils carved them apparently with as much pleasure as they would carve their dinner. One was pouring Ol Teabinth on his subject and amused himself with striking with his scalpel at the maggots as they issued from their retreats. Here, were five or six [students] who had served but a

three years apprenticeship most vehemently exclaiming against
that regulation in the Apothecary's bill which obliges everyone
to serve for five years. . . .'

In the same letter Edward lists the current rhymes in ridicule
of royalty.

'. . . The shops are now full of squibs on the Prince of Saxe-
Cobourg and his wife. "Wooing & Cooing", "The Royal
Courtship", "The Royal Marriage", "Epithalium extraordi-
nary", "The Royal Runaway or Charlotte & Coacher",
"The Royal Honeymoon" & "Miss Lump & the Grenadier",
all are exhibited for sale, all written of course by Peter Pindar
Esq., P. Pindar the elder, the real Peter Pindar etc., etc. A
caricature exhibits them fighting for the breeches, he backed
by the P.R. [prince regent] & she by the queen.

'I am becoming tolerably resigned but I still don't like
London. . . . In dry weather the dirt suffocates me . . . , in wet
weather I am covered with mud from coaches & waggons. . . .
It requires but a very little rain to make the streets ankle deep.
. . . I am smothered by the smoke, deafened, jostled and
impeded by the mob, sick of being run against by sweeps.

'I should be . . . happy to share your work with you and be
out of this earthly Tartarus. . . .'

Edward Osler to James Cornish:

London, July 8, 1816.

'. . . We had a woman brought in three weeks ago which
was drowned in Regents canal. She is the fattest carcase I ever
saw; so much so that none of the pupils would take her.
The thigh is larger in circumference than my body . . . ,
the fat is four inches deep in some places. Indeed she is a ball
of grease & is now lying in the dissecting room untouched

except that one hip, shoulder & heart & skull cap are taken off. She stinks most abominably and when the sun shines hot the yellow globules of melted fat run from her upon the floor like fresh butter, and in the evening it congeals there like little saffron buns. . . .

'The week before last I nearly went into the sink in the cellar under the dissecting room. I stepped on the trap door covering it and one foot went down but fortunately the other was on terra firma. . . . I brought myself up by a desperate jump. I was dressed to go out to dinner !

'On Saturday I was at Westminster Hall & heard a very interesting trial in the Court of Common Pleas before Sir V. Gibbs. Being aware that impudence is the sine qua non in London I pushed in among the sergeants & took & kept my seat during a three hour trial. . . . I dislike London as much as ever. It is without hyperbole. . . .

'. . . There are indeed some exceptions to this general charge of knavery . . . men who are an honour to the human form, . . . whose virtues shine like glow worms in the dark forest. . . .'

He found it 'practicable to visit the wards of the hospitals daily. . . . Mr. Travers castrated an Irishman this forenoon at St. Thomas', who roared most lustily. He was to have performed the operation for hydrocile on a poor devil of a taylor but he, being frightened I suppose at the terrible outcries of the Irishman, would not get upon the table. Mr. Travers endeavoured to persuade him . . . but in vain. He accompanied his refusals with gesticulations which gave such an effect to his pale, trembling, vacant, sartorial physiognomy that the whole theatre was kept in a roar of laughter.

'Another patient was brought in and underwent the same

operation without flinching, as might be expected. The taylor stood by & observed it, trembling in every joint and when it was over slunk downstairs to his ward, amidst the laughter of the pupils, the hootings of the patients, who collected at the doors of the wards to see him pass. . . .

'The child on whom Mr. Travers performed the operation of lythotomy three weeks since, is dead, as might have been predicted. There are now three infants in one ward with caries of the os femus. . . .'

Beside the barbarity of the hospital and its inmates, place the Elgin marbles. For here they are, cheek by jowl in these letters. Their juxtaposition has a certain fitness, can almost be made a symbol of the two extremes of regency London.

Edward to James Cornish:

March 28, 1817.

'. . . I have not forgotten your commission respecting the catalogue of the Elgin marbles. I went to the British Museum a few days after they were opened for public view and candidly confess I was disappointed. They are very numerous, principally bas-reliefs but in a dreadful state of delapidation. There is not, I believe, a single figure which is perfect. I could not find one nose among them all though I really searched purposely for one. Numbers have lost heads, arms, legs, indeed they are mutilated in every way you can conceive. This is not the worst. Exposed for so many centuries to the weather, they have not merely lost their polish but are quite fretted out. They seem as if they had been acted on by muriatic acid for a few hours. Still, if we examine them they are exquisitely fine. The attitudes are most noble, the figures finely grouped, the draperies easy and elegant. Centaurs form a very large proportion of the bas-reliefs and it would not be possible to express the manner in which they are executed. The horses are done uncommonly well. In short, to give my opinion of them, they will never delight the multitude but men of taste and science will like them better every time they see them. . . .'

Then, in the same letter, a quick transition:

'. . . A month since, a dresser in examining the arm of a man who died of inflamation of the vein following bleeding, cut his finger. The Auxillary glands were enlarged the following day and he is since dead. We have lost four students this season . . . a fifth is not expected to recover.

'I am now dissecting part of a female subject. Wonderful to relate, though 28 years of age her hymen [is] perfect. A handsome woman too. I gave it to Brookes at his request to place among the rarities of his museum. . . .'

With many pages of rhetoric Edward upheld the faith of his fathers to the sceptical James Cornish. The letter ends, '. . . With regard to your defense of atheists I would only observe that a good atheist appears to me much the same sort of phrase as a gentle shark.

'. . . I have begun seriously to reflect on the importance of preparing for a future state. . . . I shall not enter here into a defense of my principles. . . . If you can controvert them I shall not shrink from defense. Ridicule is a despicable weapon. . . . It is like trying to pierce a diamond with a straw. . . .

'If you can show that religion is degrading in its principles, low in its object & mean in its pursuit—that it is derogatory to the dignity of man—if in short you will undertake a talk which would puzzle the most ingenious big-wig at the bar and prove that evil is better than good and misery preferable to happiness, I am open to conviction. . . .'

Shortly before his return to Falmouth Edward wrote to his father (Feb. 26, 1818):

'. . . I shall feel some regret at leaving London. . . . Wherever I may finally pitch my tent I can never hope to experience more kindness than I have received from . . . my friends in town. To Literary Society I must in a great degree bid goodbye and perhaps few have enjoyed that more than myself. Almost invariably I have gone home with Mr. Travers (surgeon at Guy's Hospital) and Mr. Allen after their lectures and have learnt as much from their conversation as from the lectures themselves. . . . When Mr. Travers Jr. has any of his literary friends with him (and he has a tolerable large circle of them) I am generally invited to make one of the party.

'Under the loss of this kind of Society I must console myself with the resolution that instead of being a second I will be a principal, so that a few years hence instead of being invited to a party that I may be honored with the company of a distinguished author, my friends will invite their acquaintance . . . that they may say they have been in company with me. . . .

'There is a bill now going through the House to regulate the practice of surgeons. . . . Its main object is to prevent any persons practicing in future as surgeons except Members of the College [and includes] clauses calculated to increase the respectability [of the profession]. . . .'

From Swansea, Wales, the practising surgeon wrote in 1819:

'. . . As to what are called the Pleasures of Company, the Society of Swansea is far too little intellectual to afford me the smallest temptation to join them. . . . I need not say that a card table has no attraction for me, so I sit at home, content to live for a few years in obscurity while I put forth all my strength in those pursuits which I hope will one day raise me to Honor & Fortune.

'As I calculate with a tolerable degree of certainty on being an old bachelor & certainly must "sigh & live single" for a few years at least, I shall have no incumbrance to drag on with me. . . .'

Six months later he announced his forthcoming marriage.

July 15, 1820.

My dear Father,

. . . Know that I, yes I, Edward Osler, the cynic, hermit, solitaire, misanthrope, after all my vows of celibacy, have been obliged, like another Benedict, to say, "When I said I would die a bachelor I did not think I should live to be married".

As to the lady whose name I suppose will be no news, you will consider of course that she is a Paragon, as you never can imagine that I would be satisfied with anything less than the very best girl that does, did, or ever will live; or at least, which is the same thing, than one whom I suppose so. . . .

But to be serious on a subject on which none but fools trifle; if happiness is to be found in the society of a female who is amiable, affectionate, elegant, accomplished, domestic and pious, then happiness will be mine, for after a . . . close examination of her character and conduct I will confidently assert that I have never met . . . her equal.

. . . Our opinions, tastes, views and principles appear to be perfectly in unison. . . . You know I am not one very liable to be carried away by mere feeling. Few think more . . . closely then myself & cooly, and from the firmest conviction do I say that I do not believe the world could produce a superior female, or one better calculated for me. . . .

Her fortune joined to my income will be a genteel & comfortable competency & make her in a considerable degree independent of my life. . . .

His father had apparently compared his son's romance to those of the younger Samuel, for Edward replied:

'. . . I can assure you that you are wasting [your jokes] on one who is proof to bantering. . . .

'I think . . . you might have spared the comparison of my description of Miss Powell with the pictures of a certain brother who can find time in three . . . months to become acquainted, fall in love, court, quarrel, separate & court another, every succeeding sweetheart being of course better than all her predecessors. . . .

'Had you only my opinion of Jennette by which to form yours you might fairly have supposed that my picture was highly coloured; but when a young female is idolized and venerated by all her relations, and has had to reject proposals from almost every young man who has known her, she must be allowed to possess no ordinary merit.

'. . . To sustain heavy duties, to be exposed to powerful temptations . . . is not the lot of many; but when Providence exposes a young person to all these and at the same time gives strength enough to meet them . . . the character comes forth with a dignity and lustre peculiarly its own. It is too little to say that its gold is purified and its dross destroyed. . . . It realizes the fables of the alchemists and has its dross itself changed into the noblest and purest gold. And thus it has been with her, who is now my ornament, pride and happiness. . . .

'I think you will be gratified by a short sketch of . . . the principal circumstance in the life of your future daughter.

[She] is one of a family consisting of six children. The eldest, William [is] now Commander of a ship in the Turkey trade. . . . Jennette, at the age of fourteen, went to London on a visit to her mother's brother, who, with his wife, became so fond of her that they kept her with them for the greater part of seven years. . . .

'When she was eighteen a young gentleman who visited her uncle's [house] proposed himself to her and met with a decided refusal. Her uncle and aunt, surprised at her decision as the offer was not merely advantageous but splendid, tried every means of persuasion to induce her to accept him and at last wrote to her father, requesting him to . . . use his authority. Mr. Powell consequently went to London but on her stating to him that though the offer was far superior to what she had a right to expect, yet she never would marry any man whom she did not esteem and respect above every other, whatever might be his property or accomplishments. He refused to interfere and took her back to Swansea with him. . . .

'A superior mind . . . enabled her to see through the deception of worldly pleasures and . . . a sense of religion, which gives a sting and bitterness to every fashionable folly, preserved her from contamination. . . .'

This letter, which almost reaches the proportions of a book, concludes, '. . . I have managed the business . . . very well. Reports, which became . . . general I treated with contempt till I found that she occupied a larger share of my thoughts than was consistent with my prejudices against marriage. On this, I took a calm and comprehensive view of my situation, circumstances and prospects, with regard to the prudence of marriage in itself, and of her character, temper, principles,

accomplishments and manners. . . . I was convinced that to
secure her for a partner would promote my happiness &
interests. I . . . came to the resolution of addressing her and
when our behaviour towards each other left nothing to be
explained on either side, I proposed myself to her and was of
course accepted without hesitation. A few minutes conversation
with her parents arranged the whole. . . . I have now a life of
happiness before me. The Infirmary is at once an excellent
professional school and an admirable introduction to a superior
practice. . . . The world has not the power to injure us and we
have no sorrows to fear but such as come from the hand which
never gives an affliction without a blessing. . . .'

Index